Sydney Edward Williams

A Concise Treatise on the Law Relating to Legal Representatives

Real and Personal

Sydney Edward Williams

A Concise Treatise on the Law Relating to Legal Representatives
Real and Personal

ISBN/EAN: 9783337232726

Printed in Europe, USA, Canada, Australia, Japan

Cover: Foto ©Suzi / pixelio.de

More available books at **www.hansebooks.com**

A

CONCISE TREATISE

ON

THE LAW

RELATING TO

LEGAL REPRESENTATIVES:

REAL AND PERSONAL.

BY

SYDNEY E. WILLIAMS,

AUTHOR OF "THE LAW AND PRACTICE RELATING TO PETITIONS,"
"FORENSIC FACTS AND FALLACIES," ETC

LONDON:

STEVENS AND SONS, LIMITED,

119 & 120, CHANCERY LANE,

Law Publishers.

1899.

PREFACE.

The object of this little work is to give, in as short a form as possible, a summary of the law of legal representatives as modified by the Land Transfer Act, 1897. In aiming at conciseness something of comprehensiveness has of course had to be sacrificed, but it is hoped that little or nothing of real importance has been omitted. Branches of the subject, such as probate practice and death duties, have necessarily received but very inadequate notice in the present treatise. For the sake of brevity the time-honoured custom of prefixing "in the goods of" to probate cases has been departed from; and for a like reason only one case has generally been cited as an authority, but such case will generally be found to include others bearing on the same subject. The author desires to express his deep obligation to the classical work on Executors by the late Mr. Justice Williams.

TEMPLE,
    June, 1899.

CONTENTS.

CHAPTER I.

OF THE OFFICE OF EXECUTOR.

	PAGE
Who may be executor.	1
The appointment of executors	4
How the appointment may be qualified	6
When the office may be transmitted	7
Executors *de son tort*	9
Refusal or acceptance of office	13
Probate jurisdiction	16
What may be done before probate	17

CHAPTER II.

OF THE OFFICE OF ADMINISTRATOR.

What may be done before administration	20
General administration	21
Administration *cum testamento annexo*	25
Administration *de bonis non*	27
Administration *durante minore ætate*	28
Administration *pendente lite*	30
Administration *durante absentiâ*	32
Administration *durante dementiâ*	34
Other limited administrations	35
The bond	36

CHAPTER III.

THE EFFECT OF PROBATE AND LETTERS OF ADMINISTRATION.

Revocation and its effect	40

CHAPTER IV.

OF THE ESTATE OF REPRESENTATIVES GENERALLY.

	PAGE
The quantity of the estate	42
The quality of the estate	48
The estate of several representatives	49
The estate of the executor of an executor, of an administrator *de bonis non*, &c.	50

CHAPTER V.

PERSONAL ESTATE IN POSSESSION.

Chattels real	53
Chattels real of wife	56
Chattels personal in possession	57
Animate	57
Inanimate	59
Heirlooms	60
Fixtures	61
Paraphernalia	62
Donations *mortis causâ*	62

CHAPTER VI.

CHOSES IN ACTION.

Generally	64
Particular instances	67
Husband and wife	69
Where action accrues after death	69
Executory and contingent interests	71
Of the continuing of actions	72

CHAPTER VII.

REAL ESTATE.

What real estate vests	73
Probate of	75
Administration of	77
Powers of representatives over	78
Assent to devise	79
Appropriation	81

CHAPTER VIII.

THE POWERS OF LEGAL REPRESENTATIVES.

	PAGE
Generally	83
Of one of several representatives	91
Of executor of executor, administrator *de bonis non*, &c.	95

CHAPTER IX.

THE PAYMENT OF DEATH DUTIES.

Estate duty	97
Settlement estate duty	100
Legacy and succession duties	101

CHAPTER X.

THE PAYMENT OF DEBTS.

Funeral and other debts having priority	104
Debts of record	108
Specialty and simple contract debts	111
Preference by executor	113
Retainer	115
Set-off against legacies	120
Extinguishment of executor's debt	122

CHAPTER XI.

THE PAYMENT OF LEGACIES.

Legacy to executor	126
Abatement of	130
Assent to	132
Time for payment	136
Appropriation	138
To whom paid	139
Interest	142
Refunding	143
Payment of residue	144

CHAPTER XII.

OF DISTRIBUTION UNDER THE STATUTE	147

CHAPTER XIII.

Assets 150

CHAPTER XIV.

The Liability of Representatives for the Acts of Deceased.

On contract 155
On tort 156

CHAPTER XV.

The Liability of Representatives for their own Acts.

On contract 170
Devastavit 175
Account 186

CHAPTER XVI.

The Remedies for Representatives . . 192

CHAPTER XVII.

The Remedies against Representatives . 204

APPENDIX.

The Land Transfer Act, 1897, Part I. . 231

TABLE OF CASES.

	PAGE
Abbis *v.* Winter, 3 Swans. 579, n.	110
Abbott *v.* Abbott, 2 Phillim. 578	36
——— *v.* Parfitt, L. R. 6 Q. B. 346	70, 193, 202
Abdullah *v.* Rickards, 4 Times R. 622	91
Aberdein, *Re*, (1896) W. N. 154	107
Ackland *v.* Pring, 2 M. & Gr. 937 ; 10 L. J. C. P. 231	54
Adams *v.* Barry, 2 Coll. 290	224
Adcock *v.* Adams, (1896) 2 Ch. 345 ; 65 L. J. Ch. 760 ; 75 L. T. 136 ; 44 W. R. 644	119
Aird, *Re*, 1 Hagg. Eccl. 336	5
Akerman, *Re*, (1891) 3 Ch. 212 ; 61 L. J. Ch. 34 ; 65 L. T. 194 ; 40 W. R. 12	121, 193
Akers *v.* Dupuy, 1 Hagg. 473	27
Alexander's Case, 15 Sol. J. 788	164
Alexander *v.* Mullins, 2 R. & M. 568	205
Allan *v.* Gott, L. R. 7 Ch. 439	153
Allen, *Re*, Adcock *v.* Adams	119
——— *v.* Humphrys, 8 P. D. 16 ; 52 L. J. P. D. A. 24 ; 48 L. T. 125	22
Almes *v.* Almes, 2 Hagg. App. 155	28
Alsager *v.* Rowley, 6 Ves. 748	222
Alston, *Re*, (1892) P. 142 ; 61 L. J. P. 92 ; 66 L. T. 591	22
Alton *v.* M. R. Co., 19 C. B. N. S. 213	66
Ambler *v.* Lindsay, 3 C. D. 198 ; 35 L. T. 93 ; 24 W. R. 982	206
Ames, *Re*, 25 C. D. 72	189
Andrew *v.* Cooper, 45 C. D. 444 ; 59 L. J. Ch. 815 ; 39 W. R. 219	143
——— *v.* Wrigley, 4 Bro. C. C. 125	88
Andros *v.* Andros, 24 C. D. 637 ; 52 L. J. Ch. 793 ; 49 L. T. 163 ; 32 W. R. 30	149
Angermann *v.* Ford, 29 Beav. 349	129
Angerstein *v.* Martin, 1 T. & R. 239	136
Ann, *Re*, (1894) 1 Ch. 549 ; 63 L. J. Ch. 334 ; 70 L. T. 273	152

TABLE OF CASES.

	PAGE
Austier, Re, 54 L. J. Ch. 1104	211
Applebee, Re, Leveson v. Beales	122
Appleton, Re, Barber v. Tebbit	127
Ardern, Re, (1898) P. 147 ; 67 L. J. P. 70 ; 78 L. T. 536	21, 75
Armstrong v. Burnet, 20 Beav. 432	168
Ashbee v. Pidduck, 1 M. & W. 564	159
Ashby v. Ashby, 7 B. & C. 444	170
Ashley, Re, 15 P. D. 120 ; 59 L. J. P. 72	24
Ashwell, Re, Johns. 112	225
Askew v. Askew, (1891) P. 174 ; 60 L. J. P. 52 ; 64 L. T. 145	36
Astbury v. Astbury, (1898) 2 Ch. 111 ; 67 L. J. Ch. 471 ; 78 L. T. 494 ; 46 W. R. 536	197
—— v. Beasley, (1869) W. N. 96	182
Atkins v. Humphrey, 2 C. B. 654	170
—— v. Shephard, 43 C. D. 131 ; 59 L. J. Ch. 83 ; 62 L. T. 337 ; 38 W. R. 133	159
Att.-Gen. v. Alford, 2 D. M. & G. 851 ; 24 L. T. 265 ; 3 W. R. 200	188
—— v. Chapman, 3 Beav. 255 ; 10 L. J. Ch. 90	212
—— v. Fletcher, 5 L. J. Ch. 75	94
—— v. Köhler, 9 H. L. C. 654 ; 5 L. T. 35 ; 9 W. R. 933	142, 187
—— v. New York, &c., (1899) A. C. 62 ; 68 L. J. Q. B. 135 ; 79 L. T. 568	13, 14
—— v. Potter, 5 Beav. 164 ; 14 L. J. Ch. 16	135
Aubin v. Daly, 4 B. & Ald. 59	67
Austin v. Beddoe, (1893) W. N. 78 ; 41 W. R. 619	133
Anther v. Anther, 13 Sim. 440	130
Ayres, Re, 8 P. D. 168 ; 31 W. R. 660	36
Bacon, Re, Camp v. Coe	145, 146
—— v. Simpson, 3 M. & W. 87	43
Badenach, Re, 3 S. & T. 465 ; 33 L. J. P. & M. 179 ; 11 L. T. 275	14
Bafield v. Collard, Sty. 6	67
Bailey v. Bailey, 12 C. D. 268 ; 48 L. J. Ch. 628 ; 41 L. T. 157 ; 27 W. R. 909	130
—— v. Gould, 4 Y. & C. Ex. 221	166, 179
Baillie v. Baillie, L. R. 5 Eq. 175	197
Baily, Re, 1 P. & D. 628 ; 20 L. T. 278 ; 17 W. R. 401	6
Bain v. Brand, 1 App. Cas. 762	61
—— v. Sadler, 12 Eq. 570 ; 40 L. J. Ch. 791 ; 19 W. R. 1077	117
Bainbrigge v. Blair, 8 Beav. 588 ; 9 Jur. 765	189
Baird's Case, 5 Ch. 725 ; 23 L. T. 424 ; 18 W. R. 1094	162
Baker, Re, Collins v. Rhodes	125, 185
—— Re, Nichols v. Baker	115, 221

TABLE OF CASES.

xiii

	PAGE
Baker v. Farmer, L. R. 7 Ch. 537	131, 134
—— v. Martin, 8 Sim. 25	129
Ballard v. Marsden, 14 C. D. 374 ; 49 L. J. Ch. 614 ; 42 L. T. 763 ; 28 W. R. 914	80, 121
Banks, Re, 45 W. R. 206	105
Barber, Re, 34 C. D. 77	189
—— Re, Burgess v. Vinnicome	189
—— v. Mackrell, 12 C. D. 538	191, 210
—— v. Tebbit, 29 C. D. 893 ; 54 L. J. Ch. 954 ; 52 L. T. 906	127
—— v. Walker, 15 W. R. 728	221
Barclay v. Owen, 60 L. T. 220	81
Baring, Re, (1893) 1 Ch. 61	167
Barker, Re, Buxton v. Campbell	134, 196
—— v. Birch, 1 De G. & S. 376	222
—— v. Ivimey, (1897) 1 Ch. 536 ; 66 L. J. Ch. 282 ; 76 L. T. 116 ; 45 W. R. 495	182
—— v. Talcot, 1 Vern. 473	51
Barnard v. Pumfrett, 5 M. & C. 63 ; 10 L. J. Ch. 124	211
Barnesley v. Powell, 1 Ves. Sen. 119	39
Barnett, Re, (1898) P. 145 ; 67 L. J. P. 85 ; 78 L. T. 391	25, 76
Barr v. Barr, (1876) W. N. 44	32
Barrett, Re, Whitaker v. Barrett, 43 C. D. 70 ; 59 L. J. Ch. 218 ; 38 W. R. 59	89, 114
Barry v. Rush, 1 T. R. 691	172
Barton v. Hassard, 3 Dr. & W. 461	187
—— v. L. & N. W. R., 24 Q. B. D. 77 ; 59 L. J. Q. B. 33 ; 62 L. T. 164	93, 162
—— v. N. S. R., 38 C. D. 458 ; 57 L. J. Ch. 800 ; 36 W. R. 754	93
Basham, Re, Hannay v. Basham, 23 C. D. 195 ; 52 L. J. Ch. 408	228
Baskett, Re, 78 L. T. 843	3
Batthyany v. Walford, 36 C. D. 269 ; 56 L. J. Ch. 881 ; 57 L. T. 206	156
Baud v. Fardell, 7 De G. M. & G. 628	181
Baxter v. Gray, 3 M. & Gr. 771	169
Bayley v. Bayley, 11 Beav. 256	198
Bayne, Re, 1 S. & T. 132	8
Beatty, Re, L. R. 1r. 29 C. D. 290	125
Beck v. Rebow, 1 P. W. 94	61
Beckett v. Ramsdale, 31 C. D. 177 ; 55 L. J. Ch. 241 ; 54 L. T. 222	160, 217
Bedell v. Constable, Vaugh. 182	7
Beeman, Re, (1896) 1 Ch. 48 ; 65 L. J. Ch. 190 ; 73 L. T. 555 ; 44 W. R. 247	120
Beer, Re, 2 Rob. 349	8

xiv   TABLE OF CASES.

	PAGE
Bellew v. Bellew, 4 S. & T. 58	31
Bennett v. Lytton, 2 J. & H. 155	199
——— v. Rebbeck, 63 L. J. Ch. 596	86
Bentinck v. Bentinck, (1897) 1 Ch. 673; 66 L. J. Ch. 359; 76 L. T. 284	106
Beresford v. Browning, 20 Eq. 564; 1 C. D. 34; 45 L. J. Ch. 36	160
Berry v. Gibbons, 8 Ch. 747; 42 L. J. Ch. 231; 28 L. T. 5; 21 W. R. 255	78, 85
——— v. Usher, 11 Ves. 87	122
Beswick v. Orpen, 16 C. D. 202; 50 L. J. Ch. 25; 43 L. T. 728	121, 194
Bethell v. Abraham, 17 Eq. 24; 43 L. J. Ch. 180	178
——— v. Bethell, 34 C. D. 561; 56 L. J. Ch. 334; 56 L. T. 92	197
Betty, Re, (1899) 1 Ch. 821	167, 168
Bignell v. Harpur, 4 Exch. 773	170
Bill v. Kinaston, 2 Atk. 82	137
Billing v. Brogden, 38 C. D. 546; 59 L. T. 650; 37 W. R. 84	91
Billinghurst v. Spearman, 1 Salk. 297	54
Binns, Re, (1896) 2 Ch. 584; 65 L. J. Ch. 83; 75 L. T. 99	121
Birch, Re, 27 C. D. 622; 54 L. J. Ch. 119; 51 L. T. 777; 33 W. R. 72	124
Blackborough v. Davis, 1 Salk. 38; 1 P. W. 41	117
Blackett v. Blackett, 24 L. T. 276; 19 W. R. 559	206
Blackford, Re, 27 C. D. 676	225
Blackmore v. White, (1899) 1 Q. B. 293	156
Blackwell, Re, 2 P. D. 72	4
Blake, Re, 29 C. D. 913	199
——— v. Blake, 2 S. & L. 26	208
Blasson v. Blasson, 2 De G. J. & S. 665	148
Blenkinsop v. Foster, 3 Y. & C. 207	209
Blogg v. Johnson, 2 Ch. 225; 16 L. T. 306; 15 W. R. 626	187
Blount, Re, 27 W. R. 865	219
Bluett v. Jessop, Jac. 240	227
Blundell, 40 C. D. 370	184
Board, Re, (1895) 1 Ch. 499	78, 153
Boatwright v. Boatwright, 17 Eq. 71; 43 L. J. Ch. 12; 29 L. T. 603	196
Boddicott v. Dalzeel, 2 Lee, 296	5
Boddy v. Dawes, 1 Keen, 362	143
Bodger v. Arch, 10 Exch. 333; 24 L. J. Ex. 19	43
Bolton v. Powell, 2 D. M. & G. 1	37
Bonney v. Ridgard, 1 Cox, 145	87
Bootle v. Blundell, 1 Mer. 220	153
Bosworth, Re, 58 L. J. Ch. 432	199, 210
Bothamley v. Sherson, 20 Eq. 304	168

TABLE OF CASES.

	PAGE
Bothomly *v.* Fairfax, 1 P. W. 334	111
Bourne *v.* Bourne, 2 Ha. 35	56
Bowden *v.* Layland, 26 C. D. 783 ; 54 L. J. Ch. 640	17, 176, 214
Bowen, *Re*, 20 C. D. 538	211
—— *v.* Phillips, (1897) 1 Ch. 174 ; 66 L. J. Ch. 165 ; 75 L. T. 628 ; 45 W. R. 286	2
Bowes, *Re*, 37 C. D. 128 ; 57 L. J. Ch. 455 ; 58 L. T. 309 ; 36 W. R. 303	165
Bowker *v.* Evans, 15 Q. B. D. 565	72
Bowles *v.* Hyatt, 38 C. D. 609 ; 57 L. J. Ch. 777 ; 59 L. T. 297	214
Boxall *v.* Boxall, 27 C. D. 220 ; 53 L. J. Ch. 838 ; 32 W. R. 896	41
Boyd *v.* Brooks, 34 Beav. 7 ; 34 L. J. Ch. 605	119
Boyse, *Re*, 15 C. D. 591 ; 49 L. J. Ch. 689 ; 29 W. R. 169	109, 198
Bracken, *Re*, 43 C. D. 1 ; 59 L. J. Ch. 18 ; 61 L. T. 531 ; 38 W. R. 48	125
Bradley *v.* Heath, 3 Sim. 543	171
Bradshaw *v.* Lancashire, &c., 10 C. P. 189 ; 44 L. J. C. P. 148	66
Braithwaite, *Re*, 21 C. D. 121	138
Brassington *v.* Ault, 2 Bing. 197	18
Bray *v.* Tofield, 18 C. D. 551 ; 50 L. J. Ch. 811 ; 45 L. T. 464 ; 30 W. R. 55	219
Brewster *v.* Prior, 55 L. T. 271 ; 35 W. R. 251	213
Brice *v.* Stokes, 11 Ves. 319	185
—— *v.* Wilson, 3 N. & M. 518	173
Bridge, *Re*, 56 L. J. Ch. 779	218
Brier *v.* Evison, 26 C. D. 238 ; 51 L. T. 133 ; 33 W. R. 20	182, 184
Briesemann, *Re*, (1894) P. 260 ; 63 L. J. P. 159	3
Briggs *v.* Wilson, 5 D. M. & G. 12	197
Brindley *v.* Partridge, 13 C. D. 654 ; 28 W. R. 711	179, 181
British Guardian, &c., *Re*, 14 C. D. 335 ; 49 L. J. Ch. 446	164
Brogden, *Re*. *See* Billing *v.* Brogden	91
Broker *v.* Charter, Cro. Eliz. 92	135
Bromage *v.* Lloyd, 1 Exch. 32	90
Brooke *v.* Brooke, (1894) 2 Ch. 600 ; 64 L. J. Ch. 21 ; 71 L. T. 398	174, 202
—— *v.* Haymes, 6 Eq. 25	14, 15, 144
Broughton *v.* Broughton, 5 De G. M. & G. 160	189
Brown, *In the goods of*, 2 P. D. 110	5
—— *Re*, 80 L. T. 360	35
—— *v.* De Tastet, Jac. 284	202
—— *v.* Douthwaite, 1 Madd. 446	222
—— *v.* Gordon, 16 Beav. 302 ; 22 L. J. Ch. 65	195
Bruère *v.* Pemberton, 12 Ves. 386	187
Bryant, *Re*, (1896) P. 159 ; 65 L. J. Ch. 96	23
Brydges *v.* Wotton, 1 V. & B. 134	129

	PAGE
Bubb v. Yelverton, 13 Eq. 131 ; 40 L. J. Ch. 38	127
Buchan's Case, 4 App. Cas. 549	162
Buck v. Robson, 10 Eq. 629	161
Buckley v. Barber, 6 Ex. 164 ; 20 L. J. Ex. 114	13
Budgett v. Budgett, (1895) 1 Ch. 202	200
Bullock v. Downes, 9 H. L. C. 1	224
—— v. Wheatley, 1 Coll. 130	179, 181
Bulmer's Case, 33 Beav. 435	163
Bulmer v. Bulmer, 25 C. D. 409	65
Bulwer v. Bulwer, 2 B. & A. 470	59
Burdick v. Garrick, 5 Ch. 233 ; 39 L. J. Ch. 369 ; 18 W. R. 387	42, 188
Burdon v. Morgan, 2 P. & D. 371	35
Burge v. Brutton, 2 Ha. 373	118
Burgess v. Burgess, 1 Coll. 367	128
—— v. Vinnicome, 31 C. D. 665 ; 55 L. J. Ch. 373	189
Burke v. Jones, 2 V. & B. 275	223
Burrage, Re, 62 L. T. N. S. 752	215
Burrows v. Walls, 5 D. M. & G. 233	185
Burton v. Roberts, 29 L. J. Eq. 484	198
Butler, Ex parte, 1 Atk. 213 ; Ambl. 74	46
—— Re, (1898) P. 9 ; 67 L. J. P. 15 ; 46 W. R. 445	35
Buxton v. Buxton, 1 M. & Cr. 80	179, 181
—— v. Campbell, (1892) 2 Ch. 491 ; 62 L. J. Ch. 76	134, 196
Byrchall v. Bradford, 6 Madd. 240	137
CABBURN, Re, 46 L. T. 848	227
Cadbury v. Smith, 9 Eq. 37	212
Calver v. Laxton, 31 C. D. 440 ; 55 L. J. Ch. 350 ; 53 L. T. 856	115, 116
Camp v. Coe, 31 C. D. 460	145, 146
Campbell, Ex parte, 16 C. D. 981	219
—— v. Re, 2 Hag. 555	35
—— v. Campbell, 2 Y. & C. 607	190
—— v. —— 16 C. D. 189 ; 43 L. T. 727	116
—— v. Radnor, 1 Bro. C. C. 271	213
Caney v. Bond, 6 Beav. 486	178
Carlyon, Re, 56 L. J. Ch. 219	218
Carr v. Ingleby, 1 De G. & S. 362	131
Carton v. Maclaren, 5 H. L. C. 441 ; 24 L. J. Ch. 620 ; 3 W. R. 597	106, 197
Cartwright's Case, 1 Freem. 258	28
Cartwright, Re, 1 P. D. 422	37
Cary v. Hills, 15 Eq. 79 ; 42 L. J. Ch. 100 ; 28 L. T. 6	11
Cassidy, Re, 4 Hagg. 360	33

TABLE OF CASES.

	PAGE
Catherwood v. Chabaud, 1 B. & C. 150	51, 96
Cave v. Roberts, 8 Sim. 214	148
Chamberlain, Re, 1 P. D. 316; 36 L. J. P. & M. 52	41
—— v. Williamson, 2 M. & S. 408	66
Chambers v. Howell, 11 Beav. 6	88
—— v. Kingham, 10 C. D. 743; 48 L. J. Ch. 169	48
—— v. Minchin, 7 Ves. 198	184
Chapman, Re, 72 L. T. 66	200
—— Re, Cocks v. Chapman	138, 144
—— v. Dalton, Plowden, 236	70
—— v. Day, 48 L. T. 907	72
—— v. Mason, 40 L. T. 678	198, 220
Chappell, Re, (1894) P. 98; 63 L. J. P. 98; 70 L. T. 245	3
Chapple, Re, Newton v. Chapman	189
Charles v. Jones, 33 C. D. 80	228
Charlton v. Durham, 4 Ch. 433; 38 L. J. Ch. 183; 20 L. T. 467	87, 91
Chauncey v. Graydon, 2 Atk. 616	71
Cherry v. Boultbee, 4 M. & Cr. 442	121
Cheshire, &c., Re, 32 C. D. 301	162
Childs v. Monins, 2 B. & B. 460	171
Christian v. Adamson, (1869) W. N. 208	213
—— v. Devereux, 12 Sim. 264	129
Christison v. Bolam, 36 C. D. 223; 57 L. J. Ch. 221; 57 L. T. 250	193
Christmas v. Jones, (1897) 2 Ch. 190; 66 L. J. Ch. 439; 45 W. R. 598	121, 193
Churchill, Re, 39 C. D. 174; 58 L. J. Ch. 136; 59 L. T. 597; 36 W. R. 805	119
Clark v. Clark, 9 App. Cas. 733; 53 L. J. P. C. 99; 51 L. T. 750	88, 186
—— v. Hougham, 2 B. & C. 149	70
Clarke v. Ormonde, Jac. 108	60
Clegg v. Rowland, 3 Eq. 368; 36 L. J. Ch. 137	125, 223
Cliff v. Rowland, 3 Eq. 368	203
Clough v. Bond, 3 M. & Cr. 496; 8 L. J. Ch. 51	182
—— v. Dixon, 10 Sim. 564	221
Coales, Re, 78 L. J. 820	14
Cobbett v. Clutton, 2 C. & P. 471	83
Cobham v. Dalton, 10 Ch. 655	214
Cockburn v. Raphael, 2 S. & S. 453	190
Cockerell v. Barber, 2 Russ. 585	128, 190
Cockle v. Treacy, (1896) 2 Ir. R. 267	229
Cockroft, Re, 24 C. D. 94	167
—— v. Black, 2 W. P. 298	117
Cocks v. Chapman, (1896) 2 Ch. 763; 65 L. J. Ch. 892; 75 L. T. 196; 45 W. R. 67	117, 178
Coghill v. Freelove, 3 Mod. 326	164

L.R.

TABLE OF CASES.

	PAGE
Cole v. Miles, 10 Ha. 179	92
—— v. Wade, 16 Ves. 45	95
Colegrave v. Dias, 2 B. & C. 76	61
Coles v. Davis, 76 L. T. 771	138
Collier, Re, 2 S. & T. 444	33
Collins v. Rhodes, 20 C. D. 230 ; 51 L. J. Ch. 315 ; 45 L. T. 658 ; 30 W. R. 858	125
Collinson v. Lister, 20 Beav. 356	87, 174
Collis v. Robins, 1 D. & S. 131	200
Colman, Ex parte, 2 Dea. & C. 584	214
Colston v. Morris, 6 Madd. 89	137
Colvin v. Fraser, 2 Hagg. 613	31
Combe's Case, 9 Co. 75 b.	90
Compton, Re, Norton v. Compton	115, 118
—— v. Bloxham, 2 Coll. 201	39, 127
Concha v. Concha, 11 App. Cas. 541 ; 56 L. J. Ch. 257 ; 55 L. T. 522	39
—— v. Murietta, 40 C. D. 543 ; 60 L. T. 798	164
Conduitt v. Soane, 1 Coll. 285	137
Connop v. Hayward, 1 Y. & C. 33	211
Consett v. Bell, 1 Y. & C. 569	222
Cook v. Culverhouse, (1896) 2 Ch. 251 ; 65 L. J. Ch. 484 ; 74 L. T. 347	53, 134
—— v. Martyn, 2 Atk. 3	212
Cooke, Re, (1895) P. 68 ; 64 L. J. P. 35 ; 72 L. T. 121 ; 43 W. R. 428	3
—— Re, 4 C. D. 454	95
—— v. Stevens, (1897) 1 Ch. 422 ; 66 L. J. Ch. 155 ; 76 L. T. 18 ; 45 W. R. 284	14, 210
Coombs v. Coombs, 1 P. & D.	288
Cooper v. Jarman, 3 Eq. 98 ; 36 L. J. Ch. 85 ; 15 W. R. 142	156
—— v. Thornton, 3 Bro. C. C. 96	139
Coote v. Whittington, 16 Eq. 534 ; 42 L. J. Ch. 846 ; 29 L. T. 206 ; 21 W. R. 837	11
Cope, Re, 15 P. D. 107 ; 59 L. J. P. 94	36
—— v. Cope, 16 C. D. 49	29
Coppard v. Allen, 2 D. J. S. 173	222
Coppin v. Coppin, 2 P. W. 296	143
Cordeux v. Trasler, 34 L. J. P. & M. 127	23
Cormack, Re, (1891) P. 151 ; 60 L. J. P. 96 ; 63 L. T. 70	36
Corner v. Shew, 3 M. & W. 350 ; 7 L. J. Ex. 105	170, 173
Corporation, &c. v. Swainson, 1 Ves. Sen. 75	212
Corsellis, Re, Lawton v. Elwes	189
Costeker v. Horrox, 3 Y. & C. 530	208
Coulthart v. Clementson, 5 Q. B. D. 42	168

	PAGE
Courtenay v. Williams, 3 Ha. 539	193
Coward v. Gregory, 2 C. P. 153 ; 36 L. J. C. P. 1 ; 15 L. T. 279 ; 15 W. R. 170	156
Cowper v. Fletcher, 34 L. J. Q. B. 187	95
Cradock v. Piper, 1 Mac. & G. 664 ; 19 L. J. Ch. 107	189
Crallan v. Oulton, 3 Beav. 1	224
Crampton v. Walker, 31 L. R. Ir. 437	122
Crawford v. Forshaw, (1891) 2 Ch. 261 ; 60 L. J. Ch. 683 ; 65 L. T. 32 ; 39 W. R. 484.	16, 94
—— v. Whittal, Dougl. 4, n.	70
Cringan, Re, 1 Hagg. 548	5
Crofton v. Crofton, 15 C. D. 591 ; 49 L. J. Ch. 689 ; 29 W. R. 169	109, 198
Croly v. Weld, 3 D. M. & G. 993	131
Crosse v. Cocke, 3 Keb. 116	118
Crosskill v. Bower, 32 Beav. 86	187
Crowder v. Stewart, 16 C. D. 368 ; 50 L. J. Ch. 136 ; 29 W. R. 331	118
Crowle v. Russell, 4 C. P. D. 186 ; 48 L. J. Q. B. 76 ; 39 L. T. 320 ; 27 W. R. 84	198
Cruickshank v. Duffin, 13 Eq. 555 ; 41 L. J. Ch. 317 ; 26 L. T. 121 ; 20 W. R. 354	86
Cubbidge v. Boatwright, 1 Russ. 549	51
Culverhouse, Re, Cook v. Culverhouse	53, 100, 134
Cunningham v. Foot, 3 App. Cas. 974	224, 225
Curtis v. Blow, 2 B. & A. 426	212
—— v. Vernon, 3 T. R. 587 ; 2 H. Bl. 18	12, 43
Curtius v. Caledonian, &c., 19 C. D. 534	206
Cutbush v. Cutbush, 1 Beav. 184 ; 8 L. J. Ch. 175	174
Da Cunha, Re, 1 Hagg. 237	29
Dagley v. Tolferry, 1 P. W. 285	139
Darke, Re, 1 S. & T. 516	1
—— v. Martyn, 1 Beav. 525	182
Darthez v. Winter, 2 S. & S. 536	205
Dartnall, Re, (1895) 1 Ch. 474 ; 64 L. J. Ch. 341 ; 72 L. T. 404 ; 43 W. R. 644	199
Davenport v. Stafford, 14 Beav. 319 ; 14 L. J. Ch. 414	187
David v. Frowd, 1 M. & K. 100	126, 223
Davidson v. Illidge, 27 C. D. 478 ; 53 L. J. Ch. 991 ; 51 L. T. 523 ; 33 W. R. 18	117
Davies, Re, 38 C. D. 210	218
—— v. Brecknell, L. R. 2 P. & D. 177	17
—— v. Hodgson, 25 Beav. 177 ; 27 L. J. Ch. 449	185
—— v. Nicolson, 2 De G. & J. 693 ; 27 L. J. Ch. 719	23, 126

TABLE OF CASES.

	PAGE
Davies v. Parry, (1899) 1 Ch. 602 ; 68 L. J. Ch. 346	116
———— v. Ridge, 3 Esp. 101	213
———— v. Williams, 34 C. D. 558 ; 56 L. J. Ch. 123 ; 55 L. T. 633	79, 196
Davis, Re, 4 S. & T. 213	24
———— Re, Evans v. Moore	196, 225
———— v. Spurling, 1 R. & M. 66	183
Dawson v. Kearton, 3 Sm. & G. 186 ; 25 L. J. Ch. 166 . . .	112
Day, Re, 67 L. J. Ch. 619	156
Dean, Re, 21 C. D. 518	41
———— v. Allen, 1 Beav. 1	124
De Chatelain v. Pontigny, 1 S. & T. 34	31
De Cordova v. De Cordova, 4 App. Cas. 692 ; 41 L. T. 43 ; 28 W. R. 105	91, 186
De Penny v. Christie, (1891) 2 Ch. 63 ; 63 L. J. Ch. 518 ; 39 W. R. 517	106
De Rosaz, Re, 2 P. D. 66 ; 46 L. J. P, & M. 6	3, 6
Dendy, Re, 3 De G. F. & J. 350	127
Denton v. Davy, 1 Moo. P. C. 40	190
Devitt v. Kearney, L. R. Ir. 13 C. D. 45	86
Dick v. Fraser, (1897) 2 Ch. 181 ; 66 L. J. Ch. 630 ; 45 W. R. 628	92
Dickinson, Re, (1891) P. 292 ; 60 L. J. P. 94 ; 64 L. T. 808 .	22
———— Re, (1884) W. N. 199	199
Dicks v. Hare, 44 C. D. 236 ; 59 L. J. Ch. 375 ; 62 L. T. 819 .	218
Digby v. Boycott, 4 Ha. 444	136
Dimes v. Scott, 4 Russ. 195	180
Dimsdale v. Dudding, 1 Y. & C. 265	211
Dingle v. Coppen, 79 L. T. 693	121
Dix v. Barford, 19 Beav. 409	134
———— v. Reed, 1 S. & S. 237	127
Dixon v. Dixon, 9 C. D. 587	185
Dobbs v. Brain, (1892) 2 Q. B. 207 ; 61 L. J. Q. B. 749 ; 67 L. T, 371	37
Dodds v. Tuke, 25 C. D. 617 ; 53 L. J. Ch. 598 ; 32 W. R. 424 .	229
Dodgson, Re, 1 S. & T. 259	35
Dodson v. Sammell, 1 Dr. & Sm. 575	124
Doe v. Guy, 3 East, 120	134, 205
———— v. Sturgess, 7 Taunt. 233	135
Dollond v. Johnson, 2 Sm. & G. 301	110
Donald v. Bather, 16 Beav. 26	221
Donovan, Re, 78 L. T. 567	22
Dornford v. Dornford, 12 Ves. 130	178
Doughty v. Townson, 43 C. D. 1 ; 59 L. J. Ch. 18 ; 61 L. T. 531 ; 38 W. R. 48	125
Douglas v. Forrest, 4 Bing. 704	196
Dove v. Everard, 1 R. & M. 231	15
Dowdeswell v. Dowdeswell, 9 C. D. 294	221

TABLE OF CASES.   xxi

	PAGE
Dowse v. Gorton, (1891) 1 A. C. 190; 63 L. J. Ch. 745; 64 L. T. 809; 40 W. R. 17	174, 201
Dowsett v. Culver, (1892) 1 Ch. 210; 61 L. J. Ch. 153; 66 L. T. 360	138
Doyle v. Blake, 2 S. & L. 231	13, 184
Drage v. Hartopp, 28 C. D. 414	192
Drewry v. Thacker, 3 Sw. 543	211
Drohan v. Drohan, 1 B. & B. 185	89
Drue v. Baylie, 1 Freem. 402	51, 84
Dudley v. Warde, Ambl. 113	62
Duff's Case, 32 C. D. 301	163
Duncan, Re, (1899) 1 Ch. 387; 68 L. J. Ch. 253	64, 158
—— v. Lawson, 41 C. D. 394; 58 L. J. Ch. 502; 60 L. T. 732; 37 W. R. 524	149
—— v. Watts, 16 Beav. 204	126
Dupleix v. De Roven, 2 Vern. 540	109
Eames v. Hacon, 18 C. D. 347; 50 L. J. Ch. 740; 29 W. R. 877	150
Earl, Re, 1 P. & D. 450; 36 L. J. P. & M. 127; 16 L. T. 799	3
Easton v. Landor, 67 L. T. 833	200
Eaton v. Daines, (1894) W. N. 32; 70 L. T. 761	4, 207
Eaves v. Hickson, 30 Beav. 136	142
Ecc. Com. v. N. E. Rly., 4 C. D. 860	226
Edmonds, Ex parte, 30 W. R. 432	107
Edwards v. Edwards, 10 Ha. App. 63	209
Eland v. Medland, 41 C. D. 476; 58 L. J. Ch. 572; 60 L. T. 851; 37 W. R. 753	181
Elliott v. Dearsley, 16 C. D. 322	156
—— v. Elliott, 9 M. & W. 28; 11 L. J. Ex. 3	133
—— v. Kemp, 7 M. & W. 313; 10 L. J. Ex. 321	44
Elworthy v. Sandford, 3 H. & C. 330	12
Emmet v. Emmet, 17 C. D. 142; 50 L. J. Ch. 341; 44 L. T. 173	188
Etheridge v. Womersley, 29 C. D. 557; 33 W. R. 935	198
Eton Coll. v. Beauchamp, 1 Ch. Cas. 121	74
European Ass. v. Radcliffe, 7 C. D. 733; 26 W. R. 417	114
Evans, Re, 15 P. D. 215; 60 L. J. P. 18; 63 L. T. 254	30
—— v. Evans, 34 C. D. 597; 56 L. T. 768; 35 W. R. 586	202
—— v. Jackson, 8 Sim. 217; 6 L. J. Ch. 8	89
—— v. Moore, (1891) 3 Ch. 119; 65 L. T. 128; 39 W. R. 524	196, 225
Everson v. Matthew, 3 W. R. 159	198
Ewer v. Corbet, 1 P. W. 148	86
Ewing, Re, 1 Hagg. 381	29
—— v. Orr-Ewing, 9 App. Cas. 34; 53 L. J. Ch. 435; 50 L. T. 401; 32 W. R. 573	149, 150

TABLE OF CASES.

	PAGE
FAIRCLOUGH *v.* Marshall, 4 Ex. D. 37	192
Farhall *v.* Farhall, 7 Ch. 123 ; 41 L. J. Ch. 147 ; 25 L. T. 685 ; 20 W. R. 157	170, 215
Farman, *Re*, 57 L. J. Ch. 637	217
Farr *v.* Newman, 4 T. R. 621	45
Farrow *v.* Wilson, 4 C. P. 744 ; 38 L. J. C. P. 326	64
Fawcett, *Re*, 14 P. D. 152 ; 58 L. J. P. 87 ; 61 L. T. 303	31
Fawkes *v.* Gray, 18 Ves. 131	137
Fearns *v.* Young, 10 Ves. 184	201
Fell, *Re*, 2 S. & T. 126	24
Fells, *Re*, 4 C. D. 509 ; 46 L. J. B. 23 ; 36 L. T. 38 ; 25 W. R. 382	175
Ferguson *v.* Gibson, 14 Eq. 379 ; 41 L. J. Ch. 640	119
——— *v.* Mahon, 11 A. & E. 179	109
Fernie, *Re*, 6 No. of Cas. 657	2
Ferns *v.* Carr, 28 C. D. 409 ; 54 L. J. Ch. 478 ; 52 L. T. 348 ; 33 W. R. 604	68
Fernside *v.* Flint, 22 C. D. 579	225
Field *v.* Peckett, 29 Beav. 576	177
——— *v.* White, 29 C. D. 358 ; 54 L. J. Ch. 950 ; 52 L. T. 825 ; 33 W. R. 604	120, 177
Fielder *v.* Hanger, 3 Hagg. 769	21
Finlay *v.* Chirney, 20 Q. B. D. 494 ; 57 L. J. Q. B. 247 ; 58 L. T. 664	66
Fisher *v.* Dixon, 12 Cl. & F. 312	61
Flemings *v.* Jarrat, 1 Esp. 336	10
Fletcher *v.* Rodgers, 27 W. R. 96	197
Flockton *v.* Bunning, 8 Ch. 323	186, 210
Flood *v.* Paterson, 29 Beav. 295 ; 30 L. J. Ch. 486	204
Fludyer, *Re*, (1898) 2 Ch. 562 ; 67 L. J. Ch. 620 ; 79 L. T. 298 ; 47 W. R. 5	115
Forbes *v.* Ross, 2 Cox, 43	180
Ford *v.* Tynte, 2 J. & H. 150	58
Fordham *v.* Wallis, 10 Ha. 217 ; 22 L. J. Ch. 548	197
Forrest *v.* Prescott, 10 Eq. 545	152
Fosbroke *v.* Balguy, 1 M. & K. 226 ; 2 L. J. Ch. 135	187
Foster, *Re*, 2 P. & D. 304	6
——— *v.* Bates, 12 M. & W. 226 ; 13 L. J. Ex. 88	43
——— *v.* Foster, 2 Bro. C. C. 616	212
Fotherby *v.* Pate, 3 Atk. 604	30
Fowler, *Re*, 16 C. D. 723	166
——— *v.* James, (1896) 1 Ch. 48 ; 65 L. J. Ch. 190 ; 73 L. T. 555 ; 44 W. R. 247	120
Fox *v.* Buckley, 3 C. D. 508 ; 25 W. R. 170	130
——— *v.* Fisher, 3 B. & A. 135	45

	PAGE
Fox v. Garrett, 28 Beav. 16 ; 29 L. J. Ch. 423	119
Foy, Re, 78 L. T. 49	24
Franks v. Cooper, 4 Ves. 763	117
Fraser v. S. C. Co., 1 A. & E. 354	69
—— v. Murdock, 6 App. Cas. 855	139
Freeman v. Fairlie, 1 Mer. 24	208, 210, 212
Frewen v. Relfe, 2 Bro. C. C. 220	145
Friend, Re, 78 L. T. 222	143
Fry v. Fry, 27 Beav. 144 ; 28 L. J. Ch. 591	163, 178
—— v. Tapson, 28 C. D. 268 ; 54 L. J. Ch. 224 ; 51 L. T. 326 ; 33 W. R. 113	182
Fryer, Re, 3 K. & J. 317	210
Fuge v. Fuge, 27 L. R. Ir. 59	146
Fulwood's Case, 4 Co. 65 a	68
GADD, Re, 23 C. D. 134	215
Gardiner, Re, 9 P. D. 66 ; 53 L. J. P. 31 ; 32 W. R. 756	29
Garland, Ex parte, 10 Ves. 110	174, 202
Garner v. Moore, 3 Dr. 277 ; 24 L. J. Ch. 687 ; 3 W. R. 497	89, 179
Garrard v. Garrard, 2 P. & D. 238 ; 19 W. R. 569	13, 15
Garrett v. Noble, 6 Sim. 504 ; 3 L. J. Ch. 159	174
Garthshore v. Chalie, 10 Ves. 13	136
Gaskell v. Marshall, 5 C. & P. 31	46
Gasquoine v. Gasquoine, (1894) 1 Ch. 470 ; 63 L. J. Ch. 377 ; 70 L. T. 196	184
Gaynor, Re, 1 P. & D. 723 ; 38 L. J. P. 79	27
Geary v. Beaumont, 3 Mer. 431	214
Gibson, Re, 1 P. & D. 105 ; 35 L. J. P. 114	15
Gilbert, Re, (1898) 1 Q. B. 282 ; 67 L. J. Q. B. 229 ; 77 L. T. 775 ; 46 W. R. 351	47, 115
Giles, Re, 34 W. R. 712	203
—— Re, Jones v. Pennefather	116, 119
—— v. Dyson, 1 Stark. 32	146
Gill, Re, 3 P. & D. 113	15
Gillespie v. Alexander, 3 Russ. 130	126
Gittins v. Steele, 1 Sw. 199	144
Gjers, Re, (1899) W. N. 77	167
Gladstone, Re, (1888) W. N. 185	218
Glass v. Oxenham, 2 Atk. 121	221
Glendow v. Atkin, 2 Cr. & J. 548 ; 1 L. J. Ex. 228	95
Goodman, Re, 17 C. D. 266 ; 50 L. J. Ch. 425 ; 44 L. T. 527 ; 29 W. R. 586	148
Goodwin, Ex parte, 1 Atk. 100	241

TABLE OF CASES.

	PAGE
Goold, Re, 4 S. & T. 20 ; 34 L. J. P. 105	36
Gordon v. Trail, 8 Pr. 416	191
Gough v. Gough, (1891) 2 Q. B. 665	59
Grant, Re, 1 P. D. 435	33
—— v. Grant, 1 P. & D. 654 ; 38 L. J. P. 55	31
Granville v. M'Neille, 7 Ha. 156 ; 18 L. J. Ch. 164	16
Gray v. Siggers, 15 C. D. 74 ; 29 W. R. 13 ; 19 L..J. Ch. 819	181
Grayburn v. Clarkson, 3 Ch. 605 ; 37 L. J. Ch. 550 ; 18 L. T. 495	159, 179
Graysbrook v. Fox, 1 Plowd. 279	40
Greaves, Re, 18 C. D. 551 ; 50 L. J. Ch. 817 ; 45 L. T. 464	196, 222, 226
Green, Ex parte, 1 Jac. & W. 253	140
Gregory v. Williams, 3 Mer. 590	171
Gregson, Re, Christison v. Bolam	193
Greig v. Somerville, 1 R. & M. 338	126
Gray v. Stamford, (1892) 3 Ch. 98 ; 61 L. J. Ch. 622 ; 41 W. R. 60	149
Griffin, Re, 79 L. T. 422	217
Griffiths, Re, 26 C. D. 465	229
—— v. Hamilton, 12 Ves. 298	38
—— v. Lewis, 26 C. D. 465	229
—— v. Pruen, 11 Sim. 202	129
Grove v. Price, 26 Beav. 103	178
Groves v. Levi, 9 Ha. App. 47	206, 221
Guidon v. Badcock, 6 Beav. 159 ; 12 L. J. Ch. 62	213
Gurney, Re, Clifford v. Gurney, (1896) 2 Ch. 863	109
Gwyer v. Peterson, 26 Beav. 83	220
HALDENBY v. Spofforth, 9 Beav. 195	229
Hall, Re, 33 W. R. 508	215
—— v. Andrews, 29 W. R. 799	87
—— v. Austin, 2 Coll. 570	222
—— v. Elliott, Peake, N. P. C. 119	10
—— v. Hallett, 1 Cox, 134	88, 186
—— v. Huffam, 2 Lev. 228	160
Hallett, Re, 13 C. D. 696	47
—— v. Hallett, 13 C. D. 232	193
Halliwell, Re, 10 P. D. 198 ; 54 L. J. P. 32 ; 33 W. R. 371	36
Haly v. Barry, 3 Ch. 452 ; 18 L. T. 490 ; 16 W. R. 654	198
Hammond, Re, 6 P. D. 104 ; 50 L. J. P. 70 ; 44 L. T. 649 ; 29 W. R. 807	33
Hampson, Re, 35 L. J. P. 1	33
Hanbury v. Spooner, 5 Beav. 630 ; 12 L. J. Ch. 434	127

	PAGE
Hankey, *Re*, (1899) 1 Ch. 541 ; 68 L. J. Ch. 242 ; 80 L. T. 47	115
Hankin *v.* Turner. *See Re* Ivory	38
Hannay *v.* Basham, 23 C. D. 195 ; 52 L. J. Ch. 408 ; 48 L. T. 476 ; 31 W. R. 743	228
Hanson *v.* Stubbs, 8 C. D. 155 ; 47 L. J. Ch. 671 ; 26 W. R. 736	109
Harbin *v.* Darby, 28 Beav. 325 ; 29 L. J. Ch. 622	189, 191
Harcourt *v.* White, 28 Beav. 809	224
Hardy, *Re*, 17 C. D. 798	131
Hare, *Re*, 6 Bing. 163	72
Harford *v.* Browning, 1 Cox, 302	129
Hargreaves, *Re*, Dicks *v.* Hare	218
——— *v.* Mitchell, 6 Madd. 326	224
Harkness and Allsopp, *Re*, (1896) 2 Ch. 358 ; 65 L. J. Ch. 726 ; 74 L. T. 652 ; 44 W. R. 683	78, 96
Harman *v.* Harman, 2 Show. 492	105
Harper, *Re*, (1899) P. 59	26
Harrald, *Re*, 52 L. J. Ch. 436	217
Harris, *Re*, 2 P. & D. 83	7
——— *v.* Saunders, 4 B. & C. 411	109
Harrison, *Re*, 30 C. D. 390	39
——— *Re*, 34 C. D. 214	167
——— *Re*, Latimer *v.* Harrison, 32 C. D. 395	116, 119
——— *v.* Harrison, 2 H. & M. 237 ; 33 L. J. Ch. 647	146
——— *v.* Rowley, 4 Ves. 212	128
Harriss *v.* Fawcett, 15 Eq. 311	168
Hartley, *Re*, (1899) P. 40 ; 68 L. J. P. 16 ; 47 W. R. 287	25, 75
Harvey *v.* Harvey, 2 Stra. 1141	61
Hastings, *Re*, 4 P. D. 73	24
——— *Re*, Shirreff *v.* Hastings, 6 C. D. 610	111
Hatchard *v.* Mege, 18 Q. B. D. 771 ; 56 L. J. Q. B. 397 ; 56 L. T. 662	65
Hathornthwaite *v.* Russell, 2 Atk. 127	207
Havers *v.* Havers, Barnard. 23	29
Hawkins, *Re*, 33 Beav. 570 ; 34 L. J. Ch. 80	127
Hay, *Re*, 1 P. & D. 51 ; 35 L. J. P. 3 ; 13 L. T. 335 ; 14 W. R. 147	22
——— *v.* Bowen, 5 Beav. 616	199
Haymes *v.* Matthews, 1 S. & T. 460	23
Haynes, *Re*, 3 Curt. 75	1
Hearn *v.* Wells, 1 Coll. 333	47
Heath *v.* Chilton, 12 M. & W. 632	50
Hedges *v.* Hedges, Prec. Ch. 269	62
Heighington *v.* Grant, 5 M. & Cr. 258	188
Henderson, *Re*, 2 Times R. 322	206
——— *v.* M'Iver, 3 Madd. 275	190

TABLE OF CASES.

	PAGE
Henderson-Roe v. Hitchen, 42 C. D. 302; 58 L. J. Ch. 860; 61 L. T. 363; 37 W. R. 705	140
Henry v. Lewis, 22 C. D. 397	197
Herbert v. Pigott, 2 C. & M. 384	91
Herlakenden's Case, 4 Co. 63	58
Hertford v. Lichi, 9 Beav. 11	222
Hewes v. Hewes, 4 Sim. 1	211
Hewett v. Foster, 6 Beav. 259	183
Heywood, Re, (1897) 2 Ch. 593; 67 L. J. Ch. 25; 77 L. T. 423; 46 W. R. 72	107, 113
Hibernian Bank v. Lander, (1898) 1 Ir. R. 262	200, 229
Hickling v. Boyer, 3 Mac. & G. 635	168
Hill's Case, 20 Eq. 585; 44 L. J. Ch. 423; 32 L. T. 747; 23 W. R. 646	163
Hill v. Curtis, 1 Eq. 90; 35 L. J. Ch. 133	11
—— v. Gomme, 1 Beav. 540	176
—— v. Simpson, 7 Ves. 152	87
Hillersden v. Grove, 21 Beav. 518	146
Hilliard v. Fulford, 4 C. D. 389; 46 L. J. Ch. 43	144
Hinings v. Hinings, 2 H. & M. 32	141
Hirst v. Smith, 7 T. R. 182	50
—— v. Tolson, 2 Mac. & G. 134; 19 L. J. Ch. 441	168
Hitchen v. Birks, 10 Eq. 471; 18 W. R. 1015	32
Hodgkinson, Re, (1895) 2 Ch. 190	227
Hodgson, Re, Beckett v. Ramsdale	160, 217
—— v. Fox, 9 C. D. 673; 48 L. J. Ch. 52; 27 W. R. 38	121
Holden v. Kynaston, 2 Beav. 204	222
Holland v. Prior, 1 M. & K. 237	222
Hollingsworth v. Grasett, 15 Sim. 52	128
Hollis v. Smith, 10 East, 293	69
Holme v. Hammond, L. R. 7 Ex. 218; 20 W. R. 747	175
Hood, Re, (1896) 1 Ch. 270	202
Hooper v. Summersett, Wightw. 16	10
Hope v. Hope, (1892) 2 Ch. 336; 61 L. J. Ch. 441; 66 L. T. 522; 40 W. R. 522	57
Hopkinson v. Roe, 1 Beav. 180	190
Horrell v. Witts, 1 P. & D. 103; 35 L. J. P. 55; 14 L. T. 258	31
Horsley v. Chaloner, 2 Ves. Sen. 85	212
Hoskin, Re, 6 C. D. 281; 46 L. J. Ch. 817; 35 L. T. 935; 25 W. R. 779	151
Houghton v. Franklin, 1 S. & S. 390	137
Houseman v. Houseman, 1 C. D. 535; 34 L. T. 633; 24 W. R. 592	41
Hovey v. Blakeman, 4 Ves. 596	184
How v. Winterton, (1892) 2 Ch. 626; 65 L. J. Ch. 832; 75 L. T. 40; 45 W. R. 103	196

TABLE OF CASES.

	PAGE
Howard v. Baillie, 2 H. Bl. 618	173
Howe v. Dartmouth, 7 Ves. 137	181
Hubback, Re, 29 C. D. 934	118
Hughes v. Coles, 27 C. D. 231	225
—— v. Empson, 22 Beav. 181	179, 181
—— v. Wynne, 1 T. & R. 307	223
Hulkes, Re, Powell v. Hulkes, 33 C. D. 552	142, 185, 188
Hull v. Christian, 17 Eq. 546; 22 W. R. 611	129
Humberston v. Humberston, 1 P. W. 332	128
Hume v. Lopes, (1892) A. C. 112; 61 L. J. Ch. 423; 66 L. T. 425; 40 W. R. 593	180
Humphrey v. Moore, 2 Atk. 108	200
Hunt, Re, (1896) P. 288; 66 L. J. P. 8; 45 W. R. 236	2, 36
—— v. Wenham, (1892) 3 Ch. 59; 61 L. J. Ch. 565; 67 L. T. 648; 40 W. R. 636	114, 117
Hunter v. Young, 4 Ex. D. 256; 41 L. T. 142; 27 W. R. 657	125, 203, 223
Hursell v. Bird, 65 L. T. 709	10
Hutton v. Rossiter, 24 L. J. Ch. 106	212
Hyam v. Helm, 24 C. D. 531	197
Hyatt, Re, Bowles v. Hyatt, 38 C. D. 609	214
Hyslop v. Chamberlain, (1894) 3 Ch. 522; 64 L. J. Ch. 168	122
IHLER, Re, 3 P. & D. 50; 42 L. J. P. 18; 28 L. T. 479; 21 W. R. 550	23
Illidge, Re, Davidson v. Illidge	117
Ingle v. Partridge, 34 Beav. 411	209
—— v. Richards, 28 Beav. 366	226
Ingleby, Re, 13 L. R. Ir. 326	95
Irby v. Irby, 24 Beav. 525	114
Irvin v. Ironmonger, 2 R. & M. 531	137
Irving, Re, 1 P. & D. 658; 35 L. J. P. 83; 20 L. T. 684	37
Isted v. Stanley, Dyer, 372	19
Ivory, Re, Hankin v. Turner	38
JACKSON v. Paulet, 2 Rob. 344	6
—— v. Turquand, L. R. 4 H. L. 305	163
—— v. Whitehead, 3 Phillim. 577	15
Jacomb v. Harwood, 2 Ves. Sen. 265	91
James, Ex parte, 8 Ves. 346	187
—— Ex parte, 9 Ch. 609	45
—— v. Buena, &c., (1896) 1 Ch. 456; 65 L. J. Ch. 284; 74 L. T. 1; 44 W. R. 372	162
—— v. Dean, 11 Ves. 393	54
Jay v. Johnstone, (1893) 1 Q. B. 189	224

TABLE OF CASES.

	PAGE
Jenks v. Clifden, (1897) 1 Ch. 694; 66 L. J. Ch. 338; 76 L. T. 382; 45 W. R. 424	65
Jenney v. Andrews, 6 Madd. 264	73
Jennison v. Lexington, 1 P. W. 555	68
Jervis v. Wolferstan, 18 Eq. 18; 43 L. J. Ch. 809; 30 L. T. 452	123, 143
Jesse v. Bennett, 6 De G. M. & G. 609	206
Job v. Job, 6 C. D. 562; 26 W. R. 206	151, 179
Jobson v. Palmer, (1893) 1 Ch. 71	182
John v. Bradbury, 1 P. & D. 245	29
—— v. John, (1898) 2 Ch. 573; 67 L. J. Ch. 616; 79 L. T. 362; 47 W. R. 52	75
Johnson, Re, 1 Ch. 325	207
—— Re, Shearman v. Robinson	174
—— Re, Sly v. Blake	196, 224
—— v. Mills, 1 Ves. Sen. 282	138
Johnston v. Aston, 1 S. & S. 73	208
Jolliffe, Ex parte, 8 Beav. 168; 14 L. J. Ch. 134	38
Jones, Re, 2 S. & T. 155	4
—— Re, Calver v. Laxton	115
—— Re, Christmas v. Jones	121
—— v. Evans, 2 C. D. 420; 24 W. R. 778	116
—— v. Jukes, 2 Ves. Sen. 518	114
—— v. Lewis, 2 Ves. Sen. 240	179
—— v. Morrell, 2 Sim. 252	187
—— v. Pennefather, (1896) 1 Ch. 956; 65 L. J. Ch. 419; 74 L. T. 21; 44 W. R. 283	116, 119
—— v. Simes, 43 C. D. 607; 59 L. J. Ch. 351; 62 L. T. 447	195
—— v. Stöhwasser, 16 C. D. 177; 50 L. J. Ch. 624; 44 L. T. 333; 29 W. R. 497	87
—— v. Strafford, 3 P. W. 88	29
Joseph, Re, 1 R. & M. 496	172
Joy v. Campbell, 1 S. & L. 339	189
Jubber v. Jubber, 9 Sim. 503	129
Kay, Re, (1897) 2 Ch. 518; 66 L. J. Ch. 759; 46 W. R. 74	125
Keene v. Dee, 1 Al. & N. 496	43
Kellow v. Westcombe, 1 Freem. 122	10
Kelly v. Kelly, 8 Ir. Eq. 403	167
Kemp v. Westbrook, 1 Ves. 278	71
Kenny v. Ryan, (1897) 1 Ir. R. 513	11
Kent v. Pickering, 2 Keen, 1; 6 L. J. Ch. 375	120
Kidd v. Kidd, (1894) W. N. 73; 70 L. T. 648; 42 W. R. 571	174

	PAGE
Kinderley v. Jarvis, 22 Beav. 23	46
King, Re, 8 P. D. 162 ; 31 W. R. 843	27
—— v. Jones, 4 M. & S. 188	66
—— v. St. Dunstan, 4 B. & C. 686	61
Kingston, Ex parte, 6 Ch. 632	182
Kirby's Case, 15 Sol. J. 922	164
Kirkman v. Booth, 11 Beav. 273 ; 18 L. J. Ch. 75	174, 190
Kitchen v. Ibbetson, 17 Eq. 46	45
Kloebe, Re, 28 C. D. 175 ; 54 L. J. Ch. 297 ; 52 L. T. 19 ; 33 W. R. 391	106, 150
Knapman v. Wreford, 18 C. D. 300 ; 50 L. J. Ch. 629 ; 45 L. T. 102	121, 194
Knatchbull v. Fearnhead, 3 M. & Cr. 126	199
Knight, Re, 26 C. D. 82	228
—— v. Roberts, 76 L. T. 479	178
Knolle's Case, Dyer, 5	68
Knox, Re, (1895) 2 Ch. 483	200
LABOUCHERE v. Tupper, 11 Moo. P. C. 198 ; 5 W. R. 797	201
Laing, Re, (1899) 1 Ch. 232	179
Lambaco v. Cassavilli, 11 Eq. 439	220
Lambardi v. Older, 17 Beav. 542	193
Lambert, Re, Stanton v. Lambert	147
Laming v. Gee, 10 C. D. 715 ; 48 L. J. Ch. 196 ; 40 L. T. 33 ; 27 W. R. 227	191, 210
Land Credit, Re, (1872) W. N. 210	203
Land v. Land, 43 L. J. Ch. 311	174
Langford, Re, 1 P. & D. 458 ; 37 L. J. P. 20	6
—— v. Mahoney, 4 Dr. & W. 107	50
Langley, Re, (1899) W. N. 23 ; 68 L. J. Ch. 361	116
Latch v. Latch, 10 Ch. 464 ; 44 L. J. Ch. 445 ; 23 W. R. 686	198, 205
Latimer v. Harrison, 32 C. D. 395 ; 55 L. J. Ch. 687 ; 34 W. R. 736	116
Laundy v. Williams, 2 P. W. 478	136
Laury v. Aldred, 2 Brownl. & G. 183	12
Laver v. Botham, (1895) 1 Q. B. 59 ; 64 L. J. Q. B. 110 ; 71 L. T. 570	107, 120
Lawton v. Lawton, 3 Atk. 13	62
Lazonby v. Rawson, 4 D. M. & G. 556	212
Leach, Re, 80 L. T. 170	36
Leask, Re, (1891) W. N. 159	204, 218
Lee, Re, (1898) 2 Ir. R. 81	29
—— v. Binns, (1897) 2 Ch. 584 ; 65 L. J. Ch. 83 ; 75 L. T. 99	21
—— v. Brown, 4 Ves. 362	141

TABLE OF CASES.

	PAGE
Lee *v.* Wilson, (1892) 1 Ch. 86 ; 61 L. J. Ch. 38 ; 40 W. R. 204	186
Leeke, *Ex parte*, 2 Bro. 597	214
Leggott *v.* G. N. Ry., 1 Q. B. D. 599 ; 42 L. J. Q. B. 557	66
Leman, *Re*, (1898) P. 215	22
Leng, *Re*, Tarn *v.* Emmerson	118
Lepine, *Re*, Dowsett *v.* Culver	138
Leven *v.* Melville, 15 P. D. 22 ; 59 L. J. P. 35	5
Leveson *v.* Beales, (1891) 3 Ch. 422 ; 60 L. J. Ch. 793 ; 65 L. T. 406	122
Lewis *v.* Lewis, 13 Beav. 82	101
——— *v.* Matthews, 8 Eq. 277 ; 38 L. J. Ch. 510	128
——— *v.* Nobbs, 8 C. D. 591 ; 47 L. J. Ch. 662 ; 26 W. R. 631	183
——— *v.* Trask, 21 C. D. 864	228
Lighton, *Re*, 1 Hagg. 235	6
Lincoln *v.* Windsor, 9 Ha. 158	189
——— *v.* Wright, 4 Beav. 427	184
Liverpool, &c. *v.* Walker, 4 De G. & J. 24	160
Livesey *v.* Livesey, 3 Russ. 287	144
Lloyd *v.* Mason, 4 Ha. 132	106
Lloyd's *v.* Harper, 16 C. D. 219 ; 50 L. J. Ch. 140 ; 43 L. T. 408	168
Loane *v.* Casey, 2 W. Bl. 965	120
Lonergan *v.* Hoban, (1896) 1 Ir. R. 401	84
Long *v.* Symes, 3 Hagg. 774	15
Lord-Adv. *v.* Fleming, (1897) A. C. 145	99
Lord *v.* Purchase, 17 Beav. 171	209
Lorimer, *Re*, 2 S. & T. 473 ; 31 L. J. P. 189	8, 13
Love, *Re*, 29 C. D. 348	228
——— *v.* Honeybourne, 4 D. & R. 814	172
Lovett, *Re*, Ambler *v.* Lindsay	206
Low, *Re*, (1894) 1 Ch. 147	110
——— *v.* Bouverie, (1891) 3 Ch. 82 ; 60 L. J. Ch. 594 ; 65 L. T. 533 ; 40 W. R. 50	186
Lowe, *Re*, 60 L. T. 599	134
——— *Re*, 3 S. & T. 478 ; 33 L. J. P. & M. 155	6
——— *v.* Peskell, 16 C. B. 500	122
Lowis *v.* Rumney, 4 Eq. 451	177
Lowry, *Re*, 3 P. & D. 157 ; 43 L. J. P. 34 ; 22 W. R. 352 ; 30 L. T. 695	5
——— *v.* Fulton, 9 Sim. 115	221
Lucey *v.* Walrond, 3 Bing. 841 ; 6 L. J. C. P. 290	173
Luke *v.* Tonkin, 21 C. D. 757 ; 46 L. T. 684 ; 30 W. R. 874	191
Lunham *v.* Blundell, 4 Jur. N. S. 3	182
Lynch *v.* Bellew, 3 Phillim. 424	7

TABLE OF CASES.

	PAGE
Lyon v. Baker, 5 De G. & S. 622	189
Lysaght v. Edwards, 2 C. D. 499	167
Lyttelton v. Cross, 3 B. & C. 322	113
M'Ewan v. Crombie, 25 C. D. 175	228
M'Ferran v. M'Ferran, (1871) 1 Ir. R. 66	218
M'Leod v. Drummond, 17 Ves. 168	46, 87
M'Mullen v. O'Reilly, 15 Ir. Ch. R. 251	86
M'Myn, Re, Lightbown v. M'Myn	104
M'Neillie v. Acton, 4 D. M. & G. 744 ; 23 L. J. Ch. 11 ; 22 L. T. 111	86, 202
M'Rea, Re, 32 C. D. 613	219
Macdonald, Re, Dick v. Fraser	92
Mackenzie v. Taylor, 7 Beav. 467	180
Maclean v. Dawson, 27 Beav. 369	204
Macpherson v. Macpherson, 1 H. L. C. 243	183
Maddison v. Andrew, 1 Ves. Sen. 59	71
Maggi, Re, 20 C. D. 545 ; 51 L. J. Ch. 560 ; 46 L. T. 432 ; 30 W. R. 729	108
Mander v. Harris, 27 C. D. 169 ; 54 L. J. Ch. 143 ; 51 L. T. 380 ; 32 W. R. 941	2
Mann, Re, (1891) P. 293 ; 60 L. J. P. 95 ; 40 W. R. 144	35
Manning, Re, 30 C. D. 480	215
——— v. Purcell, 5 D. M. & G. 55	39
Mansel, Re, 33 W. R. 727	215
Mara v. Browne, (1896) 1 Ch. 199	182
Markwell's Case, 21 W. R. 135	125, 163
Marsden, Re, Bowden v. Layland	17, 176, 205
——— v. Kent, 5 C. D. 598 ; 46 L. J. Ch. 497 ; 37 L. T. 48 ; 25 W. R. 522	179
Marshall, Re, 1 Curt. 297	34
Masonic, &c., Re, 32 C. D. 373 ; 55 L. J. Ch. 666 ; 34 W. R. 739	198
——— v. Sharpe, (1892) 1 Ch. 154 ; 61 L. J. Ch. 193 ; 65 L. T. 806 ; 40 W. R. 241	164, 223
Master, &c. v. Pearson, 66 L. J. P. C. 25	161
Masters v. Barnes, 2 Y. & C. 616	222
Matson, Re, (1897) 2 Ch. 507	73
Matthews v. Bagshaw, 14 Beav. 123	190
Matthison v. Clarke, 3 Dr. 3 ; 24 L. J. Ch. 202	190
May, Re, Crawford v. May, 45 C. D. 499 ; 60 L. J. Ch. 34 ; 63 L. T. 375 ; 38 W. R. 765	108, 115, 118
——— v. Newton, 34 C. D. 345	223
Mayer, Re, 3 P. & D. 39 ; 42 L. J. P. 57 ; 29 L. T. 247	24

TABLE OF CASES.

	PAGE
Mayer v. Murray, 8 C. D. 424	119
Mayhew, Re, 5 C. D. 596 ; 46 L. J. Ch. 552 ; 37 L. T. 48 ; 25 W. R. 521	220
Mayor of B. v. Murray, 7 D. M. & G. 497	188
Mead v. Orrery, 3 Atk. 237	87, 132
Medland, Re, Eland v. Medland	181
Mendes v. Guedella, 2 J. & H. 259	183
Mersey, &c. v. Naylor, 9 Q. B. D. 648	108
Messenger v. Andrews, 4 Russ. 478	129
Metcalfe, Re, 1 Add. 343	35
—— Re, 13 C. D. 236	126
Meyrick v. Anderson, 14 Q. B. 719	11
Midgley v. Crowther, (1895) 2 Ch. 56 ; 64 L. J. Ch. 537 ; 72 L. T. 762 ; 43 W. R. 571	181
—— v. Midgley, (1893) 3 Ch. 282 ; 62 L. J. Ch. 905 ; 69 L. T. 241 ; 41 W. R. 659	114, 117
Mid. Rly. Co. v. Silvester, (1895) 1 Ch. 572 ; 64 L. J. Ch. 390	168
Miles v. Durnford, 2 D. M. & G. 641	95
Miller v. Douglas, 56 L. J. Ch. 91 ; 56 L. T. 583 ; 35 W. R. 122	93
Mills v. Roberts, 1 R. & M. 555	143
Milnes v. Sherwin, 33 W. R. 927	79
Mohamidu v. Pitchey, (1894) A. C. 437 ; 63 L. J. P. C. 90 ; 71 L. T. 99	14, 38, 205
Molony v. Brooke, 45 C. D. 569 ; 59 L. J. Ch. 810 ; 63 L. T. 521 ; 39 W. R. 139	178, 207
Monk, Re, 35 C. D. 588 ; 56 L. J. Ch. 809 ; 56 L. T. 856 ; 35 W. R. 691	113
Monsell v. Armstrong, 14 Eq. 423 ; 41 L. J. Ch. 415	30
Moody, Ex parte, 2 Rose, 413	214
Moore, Re, (1891) P. 299 ; 60 L. J. P. 98	22
—— Re, (1892) P. 145 ; 61 L. J. P. 119	24
—— v. Morris, 13 Eq. 140	206
—— v. Petchell, 22 Beav. 172	224
Morant, Re, 3 P. & D. 151 ; 43 L. J. P. 16	15
Mordaunt v. Clarke, 1 P. & D. 592 ; 38 L. J. P. 45 ; 19 L. T. 610	13
More's Case, Cro. Eliz. 26	89
Morewood v. Currey, 28 W. R. 213	212
Morgan, Re, 18 C. D. 93 ; 50 L. J. Ch. 834 ; 45 L. T. 183 ; 30 W. R. 223	46, 85, 167
—— v. Abergavenny, 8 C. B. 768	58
—— v. Richardson, (1896) 1 Ch. 512 ; 65 L. J. Ch. 512 ; 74 L. T. 12	138
—— v. Thomas, 8 Exch. 302 ; 22 L. J. Ex. 131	21
Morison v. Morison, 4 M. & Cr. 216	190

	PAGE
Morris v. Morris, 10 Ch. 68 ; 44 L. J. Ch. 178 ; 31 L. T. 491 ; 23 W. R. 120	120
Mortimer v. Paull, 2 P. & D. 85 ; 39 L. J. P. 47 ; 18 W. R. 901	31
Mortlock v. Leathes, 3 Mer. 491	208, 212
Moseley v. Rendall, L. R. 6 Q. B. 338 ; 40 L. J. Q. B. 111	193
Moses v. Levi, 3 Y. & C. 359	183
Mountford v. Gibson, 4 East, 446	9, 12
Moyle v. Moyle, 2 R. & M. 710	182, 184
Muggeridge, Re, 10 Eq. 443 ; 39 L. J. Ch. 620 ; 18 W. R. 963	161
Munns v. Burn, 35 C. D. 266 ; 35 W. R. 790	196
Murguia, Re, 9 P. D. 236 ; 53 L. J. P. 47 ; 32 W. R. 799	8
Murray v. E. J. Co., 5 B. & Al. 204	42
——— v. Sanger, (1873) W. N. 79	128
Nares, Re, 13 P. D. 35	22
Nation v. Tozer, 1 C. M. & R. 174 ; 3 L. J. Ex. 234	93
Neeves v. Burrage, 14 Q. B. 504 ; 19 L. J. Q. B. 68	89
Neil, Re, (1882) W. N. 46	214
——— Re, 62 L. T. 649	218
Nelson v. Searle, 4 M. & W. 795	171
New Z., &c. v. Peacock, (1894) 1 Q. B. 622 ; 63 L. J. Q. B. 227 ; 70 L. T. 110	162
Newman v. Barton, 2 Vern. 205	143
Newton, Re, 3 Curt. 428	35
——— v. Chapman, 27 C. D. 584 ; 51 L. T. 748 ; 33 W. R. 236	189
——— v. Met. Ry. Co., 1 Dr. & S. 583	18
——— v. Sherry, 1 C. P. D. 246 ; 45 L. J. C. P. 257 ; 34 L. T. 251	125
Nicholls v. Judson, 3 Atk. 301	205
Nichols v. Baker, 44 C. D. 262 ; 59 L. J. Ch. 661 ; 62 L. T. 817 ; 38 W. R. 417	115, 221
Nicholson, Re, (1895) W. N. 106	188
Nickels, Re, (1898) 1 Ch. 630 ; 67 L. J. Ch. 406 ; 78 L. T. 379 ; 46 W. R. 422	138
Nield v. Smith, 14 Ves. 491	168
Nightingale v. Lawson, 1 Cox, 23	201
Nokes v. Seppings, 2 Phill. 19	208
Norburn v. Norburn, (1894) 1 Q. B. 448 ; 63 L. J. Q. B. 341 ; 70 L. T. 411	110, 159
Norrington, Re, Brindley v. Partridge	179, 181
Northard v. Proctor, 1 C. D. 4	206
Northey v. Cock, 1 Add. 329	31
Norton v. Compton, 30 C. D. 15 ; 54 L. J. Ch. 904	115
——— v. Dashwood, (1896) 2 Ch. 497	61

	PAGE
Norton v. Turvill, 2 P. W. 145	211
Nunn v. Barlow, 1 S. & S. 588	116
Nussey, Re, 78 L. T. 169	4
Nutter v. Holland, (1894) 3 Ch. 408	209
Oakey, Re, (1896) P. 7 ; 65 L. J. P. 38 ; 44 W. R. 432	36
—— v. Dalton, 35 C. D. 700 ; 57 L. T. 18 ; 35 W. R. 709	65, 195
Oceanic, &c. v. Sutherberry, 16 C. D. 243 ; 50 L. J. Ch. 308 ; 43 L. T. 743	78, 88
Oliphant, Re, 1 S. & T. 525	5
Oriental Bank, Re, 28 C. D. 643	108
Orleans, Re, 1 S. & T. 255	29
Orpen, Re, Beswick v. Orpen	121, 194
Orr v. Kaines, 2 Ves. Sen. 194	143
—— v. Newton, 2 Cox, 274	15, 185
Ottley v. Gilby, 8 Beav. 602 ; 14 L. J. Ch. 177	186
Overington v. Ward, 34 Beav. 175	207
Owen, Re, Poe v. Shortt, L. R. Ir. 23 C. D. 328	119
—— Re, 66 L. T. 718	229
—— v. Delamere, 15 Eq. 139 ; 42 L. J. Ch. 232 ; 27 L. T. 647 ; 21 W. R. 218	215
—— v. Richmond, (1895) W. N. 29	188
Oxenham v. Clapp, 2 B. & Ad. 309	12
Padget v. Priest, 2 T. R. 97	11
Page v. Page, 2 P. W. 488	145
Palmer v. Reiffenstein, 1 M. & G. 94	72
Paradice v. Shepherd, 1 Dick. 136	198
Parker v. Ringham, 33 Beav. 535	109
Parker's Trusts, Re, (1894) 1 Ch. 707 ; 63 L. J. Ch. 316 ; 70 L. T. 165	39, 75
Parkin, Re, (1892) 3 Ch. 510	168
Parsons v. Parsons, 8 Eq. 260 ; 17 W. R. 1005	67, 137
—— v. Saffery, 9 Pr. 578	146
Partington v. Att.-Gen., L. R. 4 H. L. 109	21
Patten v. Patten, 1 Al. & N. 493	43
—— v. Reid, 6 L. J. Q. B. 281	166
Paull v. Simpson, 9 Q. B. 365 ; 15 L. J. Q. B. 382	10
Paxton, Re, 14 P. D. 40 ; 58 L. J. P. 55 ; 60 L. T. 513	36
Payne v. Evans, 18 Eq. 356	186
—— v. Little, 22 Beav. 69	200, 213
—— v. Mortimer, 4 De G. & J. 447 ; 28 L. J. Ch. 716	112
—— v. Tanner, 55 L. J. Ch. 611 ; 34 W. R. 314	213

TABLE OF CASES.

	PAGE
Peacock v. Colling, 54 L. J. Ch. 743	228
Peake v. Ledger, 8 Ha. 213	198
Pearce v. Radclyffe, 50 L. J. Ch. 317 ; 44 L. T. 96 ; 29 W. R. 420	186
Pearson v. Henry, 5 T. R. 6	172
—— v. Parrott, 1 Ves. Sen. 236	71
—— v. Pearson, 1 S. & L. 11	142
Peck v. Gurney, L. R. 6 H. L. 377 ; 43 L. J. Ch. 19 ; 22 W. R. 29	164
Peel, *Re*, 2 P. & D. 46 ; 39 L. J. P. 36 ; 22 L. T. 417	4
Pemberton v. Barnes, (1899) 1 Ch. 544	75
Penny v. Penny, 11 C. D. 440	104
—— v. Watts, 2 Phill. 149 ; 16 L. J. Ch. 146	204
Peppercorn v. Wayman, 5 De G. & S. 230	94
Perry v. Phillips, 10 Ves. 34	111
Philanthropic Soc. v. Hobson, 2 M. & K. 357	211
Phillips, *Re*, 2 Add. 335	35
—— v. Beal, 32 Beav. 26	114, 177
—— v. Hartley, 8 C. & P. 121	20
—— v. Homfray, 24 C. D. 439 ; 52 L. J. Ch. 833 ; 49 L. T. 5 ; 32 W. R. 6	157
—— v. Jones, 28 Sol. J. 360	207
—— v. Phillips, 32 Beav. 26	195
—— v. ——, 2 Freem. 11	178
Pickering v. Stamford, 2 Ves. 583	191
Piety v. Stace, 4 Ves. 622	187
Piggott v. Green, 6 Sim. 74	127
Pinède, *Re*, 12 C. D. 667	73
Pinney v. Hunt, 6 C. D. 100 ; 26 W. R. 69	38
Pollard v. Doyle, 1 Dr. & S. 319	189
Ponsonby, *Re*, (1895) P. 287 ; 64 L. J. P. 119 ; 44 W. R. 240	3
Portlock v. Gardner, 1 Ha. 604	224
Pottinger, *Ex parte*, 8 C. D. 621 ; 47 L. J. Bk. 43	112
Pountney, *Re*, 4 Hagg. 290	22
Powell v. Evans, 5 Ves. 843	179, 181
—— v. Graham, 7 Taunt. 580 ; 1 Moo. 305	156, 170
—— v. Hulkes, 33 C. D. 552 ; 55 L. J. Ch. 846 ; 34 W. R. 733	142, 185, 188
—— v. Rees, 7 A. & E. 426	158
Powers, *Re*, 30 C. D. 291	218
Powis, *Re*, 34 L. J. P. & M. 55	36
Preston v. Melville, 8 Cl. & F. 1	24
Price, *Re*, 11 C. D. 163	122
Prince, *Re*, (1898) 2 Ch. 225 ; 67 L. J. Ch. 531 ; 78 L. T. 790	105
—— v. Hine, 26 Beav. 634	140

xxxvi TABLE OF CASES.

	PAGE
Prior v. Horniblow, 2 Y. & C. 200	224
Prosser v. Mossop, 29 W. R. 439	136
Prothero, Re, 3 P. & D. 209	158
Pulling v. G. E. Ry., 9 Q. B. D. 110 ; 51 L. J. Q. B. 453 ; 3 W. R. 798	65
Punchard, Re, 2 P. & D. 369 ; 41 L. J. P. 25	5
Pym v. G. N. Ry., 4 Best & S. 406	65
QUEALE, Re, L. R. Ir. 17 C. D. 361	87
Queen's Proc. v. Williams, 2 S. & T. 353	31
Quick v. Ludborrow, 3 Bulstr. 30	156
——— v. Quick, 33 L. J. P. & M. 177	29
——— v. Staines, 1 B. & P. 293	46
RADCLIFFE, Re, European Ass. v. Radcliffe	114
Ramsay v. Simpson, (1899) 1 Ir. R. 69	229
Ramskill v. Edwards, 31 C. D. 100 ; 55 L. J. Ch. 81 ; 53 L. T. 949	164
Ratcliff, (1898) 2 Ch. 352 ; 67 L. J. Ch. 562 ; 78 L. T. 834	207
Ratcliffe, Re (1899) P. 110 ; 80 L. T. 170	35
Rawlings v. Lambert, 1 J. & H. 458	207
Rawlinson v. Scholes, 79 L. T. 350	217
——— v. Shaw, 3 T. R. 557	16, 94
Ray v. Ray, Coop. 264	46
Raymond v. Fitch, 2 C. M. & R. 588 ; 5 L. J. Ex. 45	66
Rayner v. Kohler, 14 Eq. 262 ; 24 L. J. Ch. 697 ; 27 L. T. 506 ; 20 W. R. 859	11
Rebbeck, Re, Bennett v. Rebbeck	86
Reech v. Kennegal, 1 Ves. Sen. 123	171
Reed v. Devaynes, 2 Cox, 285 ; 3 Bro. C. C. 95	127
——— v. Harris, 7 Sim. 639	209
Rees v. Rees, 60 L. T. 260	121, 193
Reeve, Re, 4 C. D. 841 ; 46 L. J. Ch. 412 ; 36 L. T. 906 ; 25 W. R. 628	128
Reg. v. Price, 12 Q. B. D. 247	104, 173
——— v. Winterbottom, 2 C. & K. 37	91
Reid, Re, (1896) P. 129 ; 65 L. J. P. 60 ; 74 L. T. 462	8, 15
——— v. Tenterden, 4 Tyr. 118	55
Reitz, Re, 3 Hagg. 766	24
Rendall v. Andreæ, 61 L. J. Q. B. 630	165
Rennell v. Lincoln, 7 B. & C. 147 ; 1 Cl. & F. 527	53
Rex v. Bettesworth, 2 Str. 956	28
——— v. Horsley, 8 East, 405	43
——— v. Wade, 5 Pr. 627	104
Reynolds v. Wright, 2 De G. F. & J. 59	55

TABLE OF CASES. xxxvii

	PAGE
Rhoades, *Re*, (1899) 1 Q. B. 905	115
Rhodes *v.* Barret, 12 Eq. 479	220
——— *v.* Smethurst, 6 M. & W. 357	196
Richards, *Re*, 8 Eq. 119	142
——— *v.* Browne, 3 Bing. 493 ; 6 L. J. C. P. 95	135
——— *v.* Perkins, 3 Y. & C. 299	207
Richardson, *Re*, 14 C. D. 611	219
——— *Re*, Morgan *v.* Richardson	138
——— *v.* Bank of England, 4 M. & C. 174	208
Richmond *v.* White, 12 C. D. 361 ; 48 L. J. Ch. 798 ; 41 L. T. 570	116
Ricketts *v.* Lewis, 20 C. D. 745 ; 51 L. J. Ch. 837 ; 30 W. R. 609	84, 167
——— *v.* Weaver, 12 M. & W. 718 ; 13 L. J. Ex. 195	66
Riddell *v.* Sutton, 5 Bing. 200	172
Roberts, *Re*, (1898) P. 149 ; 67 L. J. P. 71 ; 78 L. T. 390	35, 76
——— *Re*, Knight *v.* Roberts	178
——— *v.* Peacock, 4 Ves. 150	132
——— *v.* Roberts, 1 Bro. 487	211
——— *v.* Walker, 1 R. & M. 572	153
Robinson, *Re*, L. R. Ir. 3 C. D. 429	30
——— *v.* Gee, 1 Ves. 254	112
——— *v.* Harkin, (1896) 2 Ch. 415 ; 65 L. J. Ch. 773 ; 74 L. T. 777 ; 44 W. R. 702	95
——— *v.* Killey, 30 Beav. 520	140
——— *v.* Pett, 3 P. W. 249	189
——— *v.* Robinson, 1 D. M. & G. 247 ; 21 L. J. Ch. 111	181
——— *v.* Tickell, 8 Ves. 142	139
Robson *v.* Flight, 4 D. J. & S. 608	95
Rock *v.* Callen, 6 Ha. 531	225
——— *v.* Leighton, 1 Salk. 310	213
Roe *v.* Birch, 27 C. D. 622 ; 54 L. J. Ch. 119 ; 51 L. T. 777 ; 33 W. R. 72	124
Rogers *v.* Ingham, 3 C. D. 351 ; 35 L. T. 677 ; 25 W. R. 338	142
——— *v.* Soutten, 2 K. 598 ; 7 L. J. Ch. 118	211
Rose *v.* Bartlett, Cro. Car. 293	7
——— *v.* Bowler, 1 H. Bl. 108	170
——— *v.* Poulton, 2 B. & Ad. 822	50
Ross, *Re*, 2 P. D. 275 ; 25 W. R. 808	36
Rosser, *Re*, 3 S. & T. 490	15
Rothwell *v.* Rothwell, 2 S. & S. 218	208, 212
Rowley *v.* Adams, 2 H. L. C. 725	179
——— *v.* ———, 4 M. & C. 534 ; 9 L. J. Ch. 34	164
Rownson, *Re*, Field *v.* White	120, 177

TABLE OF CASES.

	PAGE
Rowsell, 17 Eq. 20 ; 43 L. J. Ch. 97 ; 29 L. T. 446 ; 22 W. R. 67	221
Roy v. Gibbon, 4 Ha. 65	208, 209
Royle, Re, 43 C. D. 18	218
—— Re, 5 C. D. 540	219
Ruddy, Re, 2 P. & D. 330 ; 41 L. J. P. 63	33
Russell, Re, 1 P. & D. 634	16
—— Re, (1892) P. 380 ; 62 L. J. P. 91 ; 68 L. T. 260 ; 41 W. R. 303	4
—— v. Clowes, 2 Coll. 648	145
—— v. Plaice, 18 Beav. 21	86
—— v. Simpson, 18 L. J. Ch. 55	140
Russell's Case, 15 Sol. J. 790	163
Ryan, Re, 17 L. R. Ir. 42	88
Sabin v. Heape, 27 Beav. 553	85
Salt, Re, (1895) 2 Ch. 203	154
—— v. Locker, (1898) 2 Ch. 643	100
Salter v. Salter, (1896) P. 291 ; 65 L. J. P. 117 ; 75 L. T. 7 ; 45 W. R. 7	30
Saltmarsh v. Barrett, 3 De G. F. & J. 279	146
Samson, Re, 3 P. & D. 48 ; 42 L. J. P. 59 ; 28 L. T. 478 ; 21 W. R. 268	2
Sander v. Heathfield, 19 Eq. 21 ; 44 L. J. Ch. 117	117
Sanderson v. Stoddart, 32 Beav. 155	104
Savage v. Lane, 6 Ha. 33	213
Sawyer v. Birchmore, 1 Keen, 391	223
Sayer v. Sayer, Prec. Ch. 393	131
Scard v. Jackson, 24 W. R. 159	90
Scarsdale v. Curzon, 1 J. & H. 40	60
Score v. Ford, 7 Beav. 333	209
Scott, Re, (1895) P. 342 ; 65 L. J. P. 15 ; 73 L. T. 317	37
—— v. Jones, 4 Cl. & F. 382	224
—— v. Tyler, 2 Bro. C. C. 433	86
—— v. Wheeler, 12 Beav. 366	208
Scottish, &c. v. Beatty, L. R. Ir. 29 C. D. 290	125
Seagram v. Knight, 2 Ch. 633 ; 36 L. J. Ch. 918	196
—— v. Tuck, 18 C. D. 296 ; 50 L. J. Ch. 572 ; 44 L. T. 800	111
Seaman v. Everard, 2 Lev. 40	178
Second East Dulwich, &c., 68 L. J. Ch. 179 ; 79 L. T. 726	184
Seers v. Hind, 1 Ves. 294	89
Senhouse v. Mawson, 52 L. T. 745	221
Severs v. Severs, 1 Sm. & G. 400	212
Sewell v. Ransford, 27 L. T. 816 ; 21 W. R. 244	30
Shadbolt v. Woodfall, 2 Coll. 30	124

TABLE OF CASES.   xxxix

	PAGE
Shafto v. Powel, 3 Lev. 355	110
Shallcross v. Wright, 12 Beav. 558 ; 19 L. J. Ch. 443	169, 177
Sharland v. Mildon, 5 Ha. 469	11
Sharp v. Lush, 10 C. D. 468 ; 27 W. R. 728	105, 173
Sharpe, Re, Masonic, &c. v. Sharpe	164, 223
Shaw, Ex parte, 1 Gl. & J. 127	214
Shearman v. Robinson, 15 C. D. 548 ; 49 L. J. Ch. 745 ; 43 L. T. 372	174
Shephard, Re, Atkins v. Shephard	159
Sheppard, Re, (1897) 2 Ch. 67	74
Shewen v. Vanderhorst, 1 R. & M. 347 ; 1 L. J. Ch. 107	114, 177
Shirreff v. Hastings, 6 C. D. 610 ; 25 W. R. 842	111
Shoosmith, Re, (1894) P. 3 ; 63 L. J. P. 64 ; 70 L. T. 809	22
Shorey, Re, 79 L. T. 349 ; 47 W. R. 188	215
Simmons, Ex parte, 16 Q. B. D. 308	45
——— v. Gutteridge, 13 Ves. 264	122
Simpson v. Gutteridge, 1 Madd. 609	92
——— v. Morley, 2 K. & J. 71	84
Sims v. Doughty, 5 Ves. 243	93, 121
Sinclair, Re, 66 L. J. Ch. 514	131
Skeffington v. Budd, 9 Cl. & F. 219	51
Slade's Case, 4 Co. 95	69
Slaney v. Watney, 2 Eq. 418 ; 35 L. J. Ch. 783	127
Slanning v. Style, 3 P. W. 336	137
Slater v. Alvey, 2 P. & D. 154	17
Slaughter v. May, 1 Salk. 42	34
Sleet, Re, (1894) 2 Q. B. 797	20
Sloman v. Bank of England, 14 Sim. 475	142
Sly v. Blake, 29 C. D. 964 ; 52 L. T. 682 ; 33 W. R. 502	196, 224
Smethurst v. Tomlin, 2 S. & T. 143	2
Smith, Re, Henderson-Roe v. Hitchen	140
——— v. Armitage, 24 C. D. 727 ; 52 L. J. Ch. 711 ; 49 L. T. 235	210
——— v. Dale, 18 C. D. 561 ; 50 L. J. Ch. 352 ; 44 L. T. 460 ; 29 W. R. 330	228
——— v. Everett, 27 Beav. 446 ; 29 L. J. Ch. 236	91
——— v. Langford, 2 Beav. 362	190
——— v. Smith, Yelv. 130	94
Sneesby v. Thorne, 7 D. M. & G. 399	92
Somerset, Re, 1 P. & D. 350	35
Speight v. Gaunt, 9 App. Cas. 1 ; 53 L. J. Ch. 419 ; 50 L. T. 330 ; 32 W. R. 435	182, 184
Spence's Case, 17 Beav. 203	162
Spicer v. James, 2 M. & K. 387	118
Spurway v. Glynn, 9 Ves. 483	142

TABLE OF CASES.

	PAGE
Spyer v. Hyatt, 20 Beav. 621	75
St. John v. Bawdripp, Noy. 43	155
Stacey v. Elph, 1 M. & K. 195	15
Stacpoole, Re, 2 S. & T. 316	36
—— v. Howell, 13 Ves. 417	127
Stafford v. Buckley, 2 Ves. Sen. 171	67
Stahlschmidt v. Lett, 1 Sm. & G. 415	115, 120
Staines v. Morris, 1 V. & B. 8	165
Stainton, Re, 2 P. & E. 212 ; 40 L. J. P. 25 ; 24 L. T. 320 ; 19 W. R. 567	23
—— v. Carron Co., 18 Beav. 146	3, 222
Stammers v. Elliott, 3 Ch. 195 ; 37 L. J. Ch. 353 ; 18 L. T. 1 ; 16 W. R. 489	121
Stanton v. Lambert, 39 C. D. 626 ; 57 L. J. Ch. 927 ; 59 L. T. 429	147
Stark, Re, 1 P. & D. 76 ; 35 L. J. P. 42 ; 14 W. R. 349	36
Steer v. Steer, 2 Dr. & S. 311	206
Stephens v. Hotham, 1 K. & J. 571	167
—— v. Venables, 31 Beav. 124	141
Stephenson, Re, 1 P. & D. 287 ; 36 L. J. P. 20	22
Sterndale v. Hankinson, 1 Sim. 393	226
Stevens, Re, (1898) P. 126	13
—— Re, Cooke v. Stevens	14, 210
—— v. Phelips, 10 Ch. 417 ; 23 W. R. 716	169
Stevenson v. Liverpool, L. R. 10 Q. B. 81 ; 31 L. T. 673 ; 23 W. R. 246	133
Stickney v. Sewell, 1 M. & Cr. 8	180
Stiles, Re, (1898) P. 12	16
Storer v. Prestage, 3 Madd. 168	137
Storry v. Walsh, 18 Beav. 559	87
Stott v. Lord, 31 L. J. Ch. 391 ; 5 L. T. 817 ; 10 W. R. 284	91, 92
Strange v. Harris, 3 Bro. C. C. 365	208
Stratton v. Linton, 31 L. J. P. & M. 48	23
Strickland v. Symons, 26 C. D. 245 ; 53 L. J. Ch. 582 ; 32 W. R. 889	202, 215
Stroughill v. Anstey, 1 D. M. & G. 635	87
Styles v. Guy, 1 Mac. & G. 422	178, 184
Surman v. Wharton, (1891) 1 Q. B. 491	21, 57
Sutton v. Sutton, 22 C. D. 511	225
Swindell v. Bulkeley, 18 Q. B. D. 250 ; 56 L. J. Q. B. 613	196
Swinfen v. Swinfen, 29 Beav. 211	182
Swire, Re, 21 C. D. 647	220
Sykes v. Sykes, 5 C. P. 113 ; 39 L. J. C. P. 179 ; 18 W. R. 551	11
Symons, Re, Luke v. Tonkin	191

TABLE OF CASES. xli

	PAGE
TALBOT v. Frere, 9 C. D. 568 ; 27 W. R. 148	118
—— v. Marshfield, 3 Ch. 622 ; 37 L. J. Ch. 52 ; 19 L. T. 223	186
Tanqueray-Willaume, Re, 20 C. D. 465	88
Tarn v. Commercial, &c., 12 Q. B. D. 294 ; 50 L. T. 365	19
—— v. Emmerson, (1895) 1 Ch. 652 ; 64 L. J. Ch. 468 ; 43 W. R. 406	118
Tasker v. Tasker, (1895) P. 1	62
Tayler v. Hawkins, 8 Ves. 209	87
Taylor v. Johnson, 2 P. W. 504	143
—— v. Martindale, 12 Sim. 158	137
—— v. Roe, (1894) 1 Ch. 413	110
—— v. Shum, 1 B. & P. 21	164
—— v. Tabrum, 6 Sim. 281	178
—— v. Taylor, 10 Eq. 477 ; 39 L. J. Ch. 676	123, 163
—— v. ——, 20 Eq. 155 ; 44 L. J. Ch. 718	120, 193
—— v. ——, 6 P. D. 29 ; 40 L. J. P. & M. 45	32
—— v. Wade, (1894) 1 Ch. 671 ; 63 L. J. Ch. 424 ; 70 L. T. 556	121
Taynton v. Hannay, 3 B. & P. 26	33
Tebbs v. Carpenter, 4 Madd. 290	178
Teece, Re, (1896) P. 6 ; 65 L. J. P. 41 ; 73 L. T. 631 ; 44 W. R. 400	23
Tempest v. Camoys, 21 C. D. 571	215
Terrell v. Matthews, 1 Mac. & G. 433	183
Tharpe v. Stallwood, 5 M. & Gr. 760	43
Thomas, Re, 1 Phill. 159	45
—— Re, 34 C. D. 166	167
—— v. Montgomery, 1 R. & M. 729	136, 138
Thompson, Re, (1896) 1 Ir. R. 356	30
—— v. Cooper, 1 Coll. 81	118
—— v. Dunn, 5 Ch. 573	215
—— v. Harding, 2 E. & B. 630	12
—— v. Stanhope, Ambl. 734	195
—— v. Waithman, 3 Dr. 628	195
Thorley, Re, Thorley v. Massam, (1891) 2 Ch. 613 ; 60 L. J. Ch. 537 ; 64 L. T. 515	126
Thorne v. Kerr, 2 K. & J. 54	214
—— v. Thorne, (1893) 3 Ch. 196 ; 63 L. J. Ch. 38 ; 69 L. T. 378...86, 133	
Threlfall v. Wilson, 8 P. D. 18	96
Tichborne v. Tichborne, 1 P. & D. 730 ; 38 L. J. P. & M. 55	30
—— v. ——, 2 P. & D. 41 ; 39 L. J. P. & M. 22 ; 22 L. T. 22	32
Toleman, Re, Westwood v. Booker	221
Tomlin v. Beck, 1 T. & R. 438	10
Tomlinson, Re, 6 P. D. 209 ; 50 L. J. P. 74 ; 30 W. R. 61	76

	PAGE
Tomlinson v. Gill, Ambl. 330	171
Toplis v. Hurrell, 19 Beav. 423	183
Torre v. Browne, 5 H. L. C. 555	142
Tottenham, Re, (1896) 1 Ch. 628	219
Townend v. Townend, 1 Giff. 201	212
Townsend v. Townsend, 23 C. D. 100	220
Townson v. Tickell, 3 B. & Al. 40	136
Trafford v. Blanc, 36 C. D. 600 ; 57 L. J. Ch. 135 ; 57 L. T. 674 ; 36 W. R. 163	149
Trail v. Bull, 1 Coll. 352	135
Trattle v. King, T. Jones, 170	44
Tredwell, Re, 65 L. T. 742	138
Trethewy v. Helyar, 4 C. D. 53	144
Trott v. Buchanan, 28 C. D. 446 ; 54 L. J. Ch. 678 ; 52 L. T. 248 ; 33 W. R. 339	152, 153
Trufort, Re, Trafford v. Blanc	149
Turner, Re, 12 P. D. 18 ; 56 L. J. Ch. P. 41 ; 57 L. T. 372 ; 35 W. R. 384	24
—— Re, Barker v. Ivimey	182
—— v. Buck, 18 Eq. 301	142
—— v. Cox, 6 Moo. P. & C. 317	106
—— v. Hardey, 9 M. & W. 770	92
—— v. Watson, (1896) 1 Ch. 925 ; 65 L. J. Ch. 553 ; 74 L. T. 453	121
Turwin v. Gibson, 3 Atk. 720	106
Twigg v. Black, (1892) 1 Ch. 579 ; 61 L. J. Ch. 444 ; 66 L. T. 604 ; 40 W. R. 297	148
Twycross v. Grant, 4 C. P. D. 40 ; 46 L. J. C. P. 636	64
Tyler v. Bell, 2 M. & Cr. 89	204
—— v. Jones, 2 B. & C. 144	72
Tyson v. Chambers, 9 M. & W. 460	44
Underwood v. Stevens, 1 Mer. 712	184
Utterson v. Mair, 2 Ves. 95	2
Van Bunan v. Piffard, 13 W. R. 425	220
Van Gelder v. Sowerby, 44 C. D. 374	192
Van Gheluive v. Nerinckx, 21 C. D. 189 ; 51 L. J. Ch. 929 ; 47 L. T. 46	110
Vane and Rigden, 5 Ch. 663 ; 39 L. J. Ch. 797 ; 18 W. R. 1092	86
Veiga, Re, 3 S. & T. 13 ; 32 L. J. P. & M. 9	15
Velho v. Leite, 3 S. & T. 456	7
Venn and Furze, Re, (1894) 2 Ch. 101 ; 63 L. J. Ch. 303 ; 70 L. T. 312 ; 42 W. R. 440	78, 88

TABLE OF CASES.

	PAGE
Veret *v.* Duprez, 6 Eq. 329 ; 18 L. T. 501 ; 16 W. R. 750	32
Vibart *v.* Coles, 24 Q. B. D. 364 ; 59 L. J. Q. B. 152	114
Vickers *v.* Bell, 4 De G. J. & S. 274 ; 4 Jur. (N. S.) 376	15
Vincent, *Re*, 26 W. R. 94	219
Vowles, *Re*, 32 C. D. 273 ; 55 L. J. Ch. 661 ; 34 W. R. 639	228
Vulliamy *v.* Noble, 3 Mer. 614	160
Vyse *v.* Foster, L. R. 7 H. L. 318 ; 44 L. J. Ch. 37 ; 31 L. T. 177 ; 23 W. R. 355	186

Walker, *Re*, 59 L. J. Ch. 386	180
—— *v.* Symonds, 3 Sw. 58	185
—— *v.* Walker, 20 W. R. 162	179
—— *v.* Wetherell, 6 Ves. 474	140
Wall *v.* Bushby, 1 Bro. 484	211
Walsh *v.* Gladstone, 1 Phil. 294	39
—— *v.* Walsh, 1 Dr. 64	139
Walters *v.* Walters, 18 C. D. 182 ; 29 W. R. 888 ; 44 L. T. 769	116
Wankford *v.* Wankford, 1 Salk. 301	18
Warren, *Re*, 32 W. R. 916	91
Watson, *Re*, 19 Q. B. D. 234 ; 56 L. J. Q. B. 619 ; 57 L. T. 215	43, 173
—— *Re*, (1893) 1 Q. B. 21	110
—— *Re*, Turner *v.* Watson	121
—— *v.* Toone, 6 Madd. 153	88
Weall, *Re*, 42 C. D. 674	184
Webb, *Re*, 13 P. D. 71 ; 57 L. J. P. 36 ; 58 L. T. 683 ; 36 W. R. 847	29
—— *v.* Kirby, 7 D. M. & G. 376	34
—— *v.* Needham, 1 Add. 494	23
Webber *v.* Webber, 1 S. & S. 311	138
Webster *v.* Webster, 10 Ves. 93	225
Wedderburn *v.* Wedderburn, 4 M. & Cr. 41 ; 8 L. J. Ch. 177	186
Weeks *v.* Gore, 3 P. W. 184	118
Welchman *v.* Sturgis, 18 Q. B. 552 ; 18 L. J. Q. B. 211	43
Wells, *Re*, Molony *v.* Brooke	178, 207
Wenham, *Re*, Hunt *v.* Wenham	114, 177
Werderman *v.* Société, &c., 19 C. D. 246	192
West *v.* Wilby, 3 Phillim. 375	29
Westwood *v.* Booker, (1897) 1 Ch. 866 ; 66 L. J. Ch. 452 ; 76 L. T. 381 ; 45 W. R. 548	221
Whale *v.* Booth, 4 T. R. 625	87
Wheelwright, *Re*, 3 P. D. 71 ; 47 L. J. P. & M. 87 ; 39 L. T. 127	16
Wheldale *v.* Wheldale, 16 Ves. 376	214
Whincup *v.* Hughes, 6 C. P. 78 ; 40 L. J. C. P. 104	169
Whistler, *Re*, 35 C. D. 561 ; 56 L. J. Ch. 827 ; 57 L. T. 79 ; 35 W. R. 662	224

	PAGE
Whitaker, *Re*, 42 C. D. 119 ; 58 L. J. Ch. 487 ; 61 L. T. 102; 37 W. R. 673	112
———— *v.* Barrett, 43 C. D. 70 ; 59 L. J. Ch. 218 ; 38 W. R. 59	89, 114, 177
White, *Re*, (1898) 1 Ch. 297	127, 189
———— *v.* Barton, 18 Beav. 192	208
———— *v.* Cordwell, 20 Eq. 644 : 44 L. J. Ch. 746 ; 23 W. R. 826...	121, 193
Whitehead *v.* Taylor, 10 A. & E. 210 ; 2 P. & D. 367	42
Whiteley, *Re*, 33 C. D. 347	228
Whittaker *v.* Kershaw, 45 C. D. 320 ; 60 L. J. Ch. 9 ; 63 L. T. 203 ; 39 W. R. 23	123, 144
Whittle *v.* Henning, 2 Beav. 396	212
Widdowson *r.* Duck, 2 Mer. 494	180
Wieland *v.* Bird, (1894) P. 262 ; 33 L. J. P. 162 ; 71 L. T. 267	31
Wightwick *v.* Lord, 6 H. L. C. 217 ; 26 L. J. Ch. 825 ; 5 W. R. 713	180
Wigley *v.* Ashton, 3 B. & Al. 101	179
Wilcocks, *Re*, 67 L. T. 528	36
Wilde, *Re*, 13 P. D. 1 ; 57 L. J. P. 7 ; 57 L. T. 815	27
Wildes *v.* Davies, 1 Sm. & G. 475	128
Wilkes *v.* Sannion, 7 C. D. 188	201
Wilkins *v.* Fry, 1 Mer. 266	165
Wilkinson, *Re*, (1892) P. 227 ; 61 L. J. P. 134 ; 67 L. T. 238	5
———— *v.* Wilkinson, 2 S. & S. 237	190
Willey, *Re*, (1890) W. N. 1	3
Williams, *Re*, 40 W. R. 636	217
———— *Re*, Davies *v.* Williams	79, 196
———— *v.* Arkle, L. R. 7 H. L. 615 ; 45 L. J. Ch. 590 ; 33 L. T. 187	146
———— *v.* Breedon, 1 Bos. & P. 330	65
———— *v.* Heales, 9 C. P. 177 ; 43 L. J. C. P. 80 ; 22 W. R. 317	10
———— *v.* Innes, 1 Camp. 364	151
———— *v.* Lee, 3 Atk. 223	205
———— *v.* Wilkins, 2 Phillim. 100	23
———— *v.* Williams, 15 Eq. 270 ; 42 L. J. Ch. 158 ; 21 W. R. 160	110
———— *v.* ————, 20 C. D. 659 ; 51 L. J. Ch. 385 ; 46 L. T. 275...104, 173	
Willis *v.* Kibble, 1 Beav. 559	190
Wilmot *v.* Jenkins, 1 Beav. 401	131
Wilson *v.* Coxwell, 23 C. D. 764 ; 52 L. J. Ch. 975	115
———— *v.* Dunsany, 18 Beav. 293	111
———— *v.* Moore, 1 M. & K. 337	85
———— *v.* Rhodes, 8 C. D. 777	133
———— *v.* Tucker, 3 Stark. 154	155
Winchester, B. of *v.* Knight, 1 P. W. 406	158
Wingrove *v.* Thompson, 11 C. D. 419 ; 27 W. R. 910	206

TABLE OF CASES. xlv

	PAGE
Wise v. Metcalfe, 10 B. & C. 299 ; 5 M. & R. 235	159
Wollaston v. Wollaston, 7 C. D. 58 ; 47 L. J. Ch. 117 ; 37 L. T. 631	218
Wolverhampton v. Marston, 7 H. & N. 148	84
Womersley, Re, Etheridge v. Womersley	198
Wood, Re, (1896) 2 Ch. 596	146
——— v. Gaynon, Ambl. 395	61
——— v. Penoyre, 13 Ves. 333	84
——— v. Weightman, 13 Eq. 436 ; 26 L. T. 385 ; 20 W. R. 459	125
——— v. Wood, 21 W. R. 135	203
Woodgate v. Field, 2 Ha. 211 ; 11 L. J. Ch. 321	211, 219, 222
Woodhouse v. Woodhouse, 8 Eq. 514 ; 38 L. J. Ch. 481	223
Woolley v. Clark, 5 B. & Al. 744	42
Wormald v. Muzeen, 17 C. D. 167	131
Worthington v. Barlow, 7 T. R. 453	172
Wright, Re, 79 L. T. 473	2, 3
Wrigley v. Sykes, 21 Beav. 337	85
Wroughton v. Colquhoun, 1 De G. & S. 357	131
Wrout v. Dawes, 25 Beav. 369	193
Yaites v. Gough, Yelv. 33	51
Yare v. Harrison, 2 Cox, 377	208
Yeatman v. Yeatman, 7 C. D. 210 ; 47 L. J. Ch. 6 ; 38 L. T. 374	222, 223
York, Re, 36 C. D. 233	221
Young, Re, 1 P. & D. 186 ; 35 L. J. P. & M. 126 ; 14 L. T. 634 ; 14 W. R. 821	37
——— v. Walter, 9 Ves. 365	212
Youngs, Re, 30 C. D. 431	210

TABLE OF STATUTES.

	PAGE
43 Eliz. c. 8	119
22 & 23 Car. 2, c. 10	148
29 Car. 2, c. 3	171
3 & 4 Wm. & M. c. 42	158
4 & 5 Wm. & M. c. 24	156
17 Geo. 2, c. 38, s. 3	107
36 Geo. 3, c. 52	130
38 Geo. 3, c. 87	29, 32
55 Geo. 3, c. 184	14, 107
57 Geo. 3, c. 29, s. 51	108
1 Wm. 4, c. 40	145
3 & 4 Wm. 4, c. 27 (Limitations)	44, 79, 195
c. 42 (Limitations)	65, 83, 113, 158
c. 104	117
1 Vict. c. 26 (Wills Act, 1837), ss. 3, 6	55, 71, 151
9 & 10 Vict. c. 93 (Lord Campbell's Act)	65
17 & 18 Vict. c. 113 (Locke King's Act)	152
19 & 20 Vict. c. 97 (Mercantile Law Amendment Act)	172, 195
20 & 21 Vict. c. 77 (Court of Probate Act, 1857)	3, 15, 17, 30, 31, 33, 38, 40
c. 85 (Matrimonial Causes Act)	22
21 & 22 Vict. c. 95 (Court of Probate Act, 1858)	13, 17, 33, 44
22 & 23 Vict. c. 35 (Lord St. Leonards' Act)	72, 124, 125
23 & 24 Vict. c. 38 (Law of Property Act, 1860)	110, 196
25 & 26 Vict. c. 89 (Companies Act, 1862)	67, 161
26 & 27 Vict. c. 57	107
c. 87, s. 14	107
27 & 28 Vict. c. 95	66
30 & 31 Vict. c. 23 (Re-insurance)	90
c. 69 (Locke King's Amendment Act)	152
32 & 33 Vict. c. 46 (Hinde Palmer's Act)	111, 114, 115
33 & 34 Vict. c. 14 (Naturalization Act, 1870)	2
c. 23 (Felony Act, 1870)	141

TABLE OF STATUTES.

	PAGE
33 & 34 Vict. c. 35 (Apportionment Act, 1870)	68
c. 71 (National Debt Act), s. 23	67, 93, 132
34 & 35 Vict. c. 43 (Ecclesiastical Dilapidations Act)	113, 158
36 & 37 Vict. c. 52 (Intestates' Widows and Children Act, 1873)	17
c. 66 (Judicature Act, 1873), s. 25	48, 68, 198
37 & 38 Vict. c. 57 (Real Property Limitation Act, 1874)	196, 224
38 & 39 Vict. c. 27 (Intestates' Widows and Children Act, 1875)	17
c. 77 (Judicature Act, 1875), s. 10	108, 112, 115
40 & 41 Vict c. 34 (Locke King's Amendment Act, 1877)	152
43 & 44 Vict. c. 42 (Employers' Liability Act, 1880)	66
44 Vict. c. 12, s. 40	14
44 & 45 Vict. c. 41 (Conveyancing Act, 1881)	48, 55, 89, 95, 140, 142
45 & 46 Vict. c. 38 (Settled Land Act, 1882)	157
c. 61 (Bills of Exchange Act, 1882)	89
c. 75 (Married Women's Property Act)	21, 52, 56, 69, 141, 185
46 & 47 Vict. c. 52 (Bankruptcy Act, 1883)	45, 69, 104
c. 57 (Patents Act, 1883)	67
c. 61 (Agricultural Holdings Act, 1883)	59
51 & 52 Vict. c. 59 (Trustee Act, 1888)	223
c. 62 (Preferential Payments in Bankruptcy Act)	107, 111
53 Vict. c. 5 (Lunacy Act, 1890)	3, 34
53 & 54 Vict. c. 29 (Intestates' Estates Act, 1890)	147
c. 39 (Partnership Act, 1890)	160, 161
c. 63 (Companies Act, 1890)	164
56 & 57 Vict. c. 53 (Trustee Act, 1893)	80, 90, 95, 142, 166, 180, 182, 183, 185, 209
57 & 58 Vict. c. 30 (Finance Act, 1894)	97
59 & 60 Vict. c. 25 (Friendly Societies Act, 1896)	107
c. 28 (Finance Act, 1896)	98
c. 35 (Judicial Trustees Act, 1896)	159, 175, 207
60 & 61 Vict. c. 37 (Workmen's Compensation Act)	66
c. 65 (Land Transfer Act, 1897)	*passim*

THE LAW

RELATING TO

LEGAL REPRESENTATIVES.

CHAPTER I.

OF THE OFFICE OF EXECUTOR.

Who may be Executor.

GENERALLY speaking, all persons capable of making wills, and some others besides, are capable of being made executors.

From the earliest time it has been a rule that every person may be an executor, saving such as are expressly forbidden. Swinb. pt. 5, s. 1.

It seems to be admitted that the king may be an executor; in which case he appoints persons to execute the will. Godolp. ii. 1 (2); Wms. 183. _{The king.}

It seems to be now settled that a corporation aggregate may be named as executor; and on their being so named they may appoint persons to receive administration with the will annexed, who are sworn like other administrators. *Re Darke*, 1 Sw. & T. 516. _{Corporations.}

There seems to be no doubt that a corporation sole can be an executor. Went. 39; *Re Haynes*, 3 Curt. 75.

Where a limited company were appointed executors the Court granted administration with the will annexed to the general manager as their nominee. *Re Hunt*, (1896) P. 288; 66 L. J. P. 8. _{Company.}

Where a firm was appointed, it was held that the _{Firm.}

appointment was not of the firm, but of the persons composing it individually, and that each of the members was entitled to prove. *Re Fernie*, 6 Notes of Cas. 657.

Alien. Under the Naturalization Act, 1870, an alien is now capable of being an executor or administrator. See sect. 2.

Infant. An infant may be appointed executor how young so ever he be. Went. p. 390.

But if he is sole executor, he is, by 38 Geo. 3, c. 87, s. 6, disqualified from acting during minority, and administration *cum testamento annexo* will be granted to the guardian or other person until he is of age. *Post*, p. 28.

But if he is one of several, and one is of full age, no administration ought to be granted, for he who is of full age may execute the will. Wms. 185.

It has been said that if it be a woman infant who is made executrix, and her husband be of age and assent, the husband shall have the execution of the will. Went. 392.

Feme covert. A married woman may be an executrix or administratrix, and can act independently of her husband in all respects as if she were a *feme sole*. M. W. P. Act, 1882, ss. 24, 18.

Felon. It seems that an outlaw or felon may act as executor. Wms. 186; *Smethurst v. Tomlin*, 2 Sw. & T. 143; but see *Re Mander*, 6 Q. B. 867. And by the Trustee Act, 1893, s. 48, trust estates of an executor are not affected by his becoming a convict; and the Court cannot appoint another executor in his place (sect. 25 (3); *Re Willey*, W. N. 1890, 1), except under the Jud. Trustees Act.

The Court will in some cases pass over an executor, but not by reason of his bad character only. *Re Samson*, 3 P. & D. 48; *Re Wright*, 79 L. T. 473; *Bowen v. Phillips*, *infra*.

Pauper. The Court cannot refuse to grant probate to a person on account of his poverty or insolvency.

Bankrupt. But the Chancery Division will restrain an insolvent or bankrupt executor from acting and appoint a receiver; and if it is necessary to bring actions to recover the effects, it will compel him to allow his name to be used (*Uterson* v.

Mair, 2 Ves. Jun. 95); but it cannot appoint another executor in his place. *Re Willey, supra*.

But where there is a co-executor willing to continue to act, the Court will not require the appointment of a receiver. *Bowen* v. *Phillips*, (1897) 1 Ch. 174; 66 L. J. Ch. 165.

If, however, a person known by the testator to be a bankrupt is appointed, such person cannot, on the ground of insolvency alone, be controlled by the appointment of a receiver. *Stainton* v. *Carron*, 18 Beav. 146.

Idiots and lunatics are incapable of being executors or administrators. Godolph. ii. 6 (2). Lunatic.

Therefore if an executor become insane the Court will grant administration to another. *Post*, p. 34.

And where a single administrator becomes insane and a person is appointed under sect. 116 of the Lunacy Act, 1890, with only specified powers, the Court will make a grant to another of the next of kin for the use of such administrator, impounding the original grant. *Re Cooke*, (1895) P. 68.

A grant may be made *durante corporis aut animi vitio*.

Therefore where a person appointed executor was too ill to be served with a citation to accept or refuse probate, administration with the will annexed was granted to a residuary legatee for life for the use and benefit of the executor till his recovery. *Re Ponsonby*, (1895) P. 287.

Foreigners residing abroad may be executors and may take probate limited to the English assets. *Re Briesemann*, 72 L. T. 268; and see *Re Earl*, L. R. 1 P. & D. 450. Foreigner.

But by Court of Probate Act, 1857, s. 73, an executor may be passed over if resident abroad and if it is convenient to grant administration with the will annexed to some other person. *Re Wright*, 79 L. T. 473.

Where it is shown that a testator has misdescribed the name and residence of an executor, probate may be granted to the executor in his real name and as of his real residence. *Re Baskett*, 78 L. T. 843; and see *Re Chappell*, (1894) P. 98; *Re De Rosaz*, 2 P. D. 66. Uncertain person.

But the ambiguity must be real. *Re Peel*, 2 P. & D. 46. And the appointment may be void for uncertainty. *Re Blackwell*, 2 P. D. 72.

The Appointment of Executors.

An executor can derive his office from a testamentary appointment only. *Re Willey*, W. N. 1890, 1.

His appointment may be either express or implied; and in the latter case he is usually called executor according to the tenor.

Executor according to the tenor.

For although no one is nominated in the will by the word executor, yet if by any word or circumlocution the testator recommend or commit to one or more the charge and office or the rights which appertain to an executor, it amounts to constituting him or them to be executors. Went. 20.

Thus if he declares that A. B. shall have his goods after his death to pay his debts or otherwise dispose of; or commits all his goods to the administration of A. B.; or makes A. B. lord of all his goods; or leaves the residue of all his goods to A. B., it will amount to the appointment of such persons as executors according to the tenor. Wms. 189.

So where a testator appointed persons to carry out his will and for the due execution of his will, they were held to be executors according to the tenor and entitled to probate. *Re Russell*, (1892) P. 380.

And a reference in a marginal note to certain persons as executors, whose express appointment as executors has been cancelled, but who are left trustees of the will, may have the effect of appointing them executors, and not only according to the tenor. *Re Nussey*, 78 L. T. 169.

But a mere trustee is not entitled to probate as executor according to the tenor. *Re Jones*, 2 S. & T. 155; and see *Eaton v. Daines*, (1894) W. N. 32; 70 L. T. 761.

So where property is given to trustees for particular purposes, or persons without any general power to receive and pay what is due to and from the estate, which is the office of an executor, such trustees are not entitled to probate as executors according to the tenor. *Boddicott* v. *Dalzeel*, 2 Lee, 294; *Re Leven*, 15 P. D. 22.

But where the testator expressed a wish that his trustees should pay his debts, they were held executors according to the tenor. *Re Wilkinson*, (1892) P. 227.

Nor is a universal legatee so entitled, though he may take out administration with the will annexed. *Re Oliphant*, 1 S. & T. 525.

In short, unless the Court can gather from the will that the person named is required to pay debts and generally administer the estate, it will not grant probate to him as executor according to the tenor. *Re Punchard*, L. R. 2 P. & D. 369; *Re Lowry*, L. R. 3 P. & D. 157; *Re Brown*, 2 P. D. 110.

There is no objection either in principle or practice to admit an executor according to the tenor to probate jointly with an executor expressly nominated. *Re Brown, supra.*

An executor may also be appointed by necessary implication, as where the testator says, "I will that A. B. be my executor if C. D. will not," in which case C. D. may be admitted, if he please, into the executorship.   *By implication.*

There is a great distinction between an executor and a coadjutor or overseer, the latter having no power to administer, but only to counsel and advise. As to what words amount only to the appointment of a coadjutor, see Wentw. 2.

And an executor expressly appointed for a limited purpose in a will may be appointed general executor by a codicil by implication merely. *Re Aird*, 1 Hagg. 336.

Instances occur of granting probate to persons nominated by those authorised by the testator so to nominate. Thus where legatees were authorised to appoint two persons to execute the testamentary bequests, probate was granted to the nominees as executors. *Re Cringan*, 1 Hagg. 548.   *Testator may delegate.*

THE OFFICE OF EXECUTOR.

Substituted executors.

A testator may appoint several executors in several degrees, as where he makes A. his executor, but if he will not, then he makes B., and if he will not, then he makes C. his executor; in which case A. is said to be instituted executor in the first degree, B. is said to be substituted in the second degree, and so on. *Re Langford*, L. R. 1 P. & D. 458.

But if an instituted executor once accepts the office, and afterwards dies intestate, the substitutes are all excluded (Swinb. pt. 4, s. 19 (10)), unless the testator otherwise expressly provides. *Re Lighton*, 1 Hagg. 235; *Re Foster*, L. R. 2 P. & D. 304.

Power of survivor to appoint another.

Where there are two or more executors, power may be given to the survivor to appoint another. *Re Deichman*, 3 Curt. 123; *Jackson* v. *Paulet*, 2 Robert. 344.

Where a testator appoints executors, and afterwards appoints a person or persons as "sole" executor or executors, the first appointment is revoked. *Re Lowe*, 3 Sw. & Tr. 478; *Re Baily*, L. R. 1 P. & D. 628.

Uncertainty.

An appointment may be bad for uncertainty, as where a testator appoints "two of my sons" or "one of my sisters." *Re Blackwell*, 2 P. D. 72; and see *Re De Rosaz*, 2 P. D. 66, as to parol evidence.

How Appointment may be qualified.

The appointment of executor may be qualified as to time or place, or subject-matter; or the creation of the office may be conditional.

Time.

The time may be limited when the person appointed shall begin or shall cease to be executor.

Thus an executor may be appointed as at the expiration of five years after the death of the testator, or at an uncertain time, as upon the death or marriage of his son (Swinb. pt. 4, s. 17); or when he shall come of age (Went. 22); or on the death of the original executor. *Re Lighton*, 1 Hagg. 235.

Likewise an executor may be appointed for a particular period, as for five years next after the testator's death, or during minority, or during widowhood, or until death or marriage. Swinb. pt. 4, s. 17.

In these cases if the testator does not appoint a person to act before or after the time limited, an administrator *cum testamento annexo* will be appointed.

In like manner the appointment may be limited in point of place. Thus the testator may make different executors for his goods in different counties or districts, or in various countries. Swinb. pt. 4, s. 18; *Velho* v. *Leite*, 3 Sw. & Tr. 456; *Re Harris*, L. R. 2 P. & D. 83. Place.

Again, the power of an executor may be limited as to subject-matter. Thus an executor may be made of a particular thing, as of his household goods, or of his cattle, or of his debts due to him (Went. 29); and one for general and another for limited purposes. *Lynch* v. *Bellew*, 3 Phillim. 424. Subject-matter.

But though there may be separate executors of different parts of the assets, yet *quoad* creditors they are all executors and may be sued as one executor. *Rose* v. *Bartlett*, Cro. Car. 293.

Lastly, the appointment may be conditional, and the condition may be either precedent or subsequent. Conditional.

Thus the appointment may be conditional on his giving security to pay legacies, or on his proving the will within three months, or on his paying his debt due to the testator. Wms. 202.

Devolution of the Office.

An executor cannot assign the executorship. *Beddell* v. *Constable*, Vaugh. 182.

But the interest vested in him as sole executor may, generally speaking, be continued by his executor, who to all intents and purposes is the executor of the original testator. The executor of an executor represents the first testator.

So long as the chain of representation is unbroken by

any intestacy, the ultimate executor is the representative of every preceding testator.

The rule is the same though the original probate is a limited one. *Re Beer*, 2 Rob. 349.

But a limited probate will not *continue* the chain of representation. *Re Bayne*, 1 S. & T. 132.

But if the first executor dies intestate, then his administrator is not such a representative; and an administrator *de bonis non* of the original testator must be appointed.

Where a sole executor dies either before the testator or before probate, the office does not devolve, but an administrator *cum testamento annexo* must be appointed. *Wankford* v. *W.*, *post*, p. 19.

Representation survives. Where there are several executors and one dies the whole representation survives, and will be transmitted ultimately to the executor of the surviving executor, unless he dies intestate. Went. 215.

Where an executor renounces probate the representation shall devolve as if he had not been appointed executor. 20 & 21 Vict. c. 77, s. 79.

Where an executor to whom power is reserved survives his acting co-executor and does not appear when cited, the chain of executorship is continued in the executors of the acting executor without any fresh grant from the Court. *Re Reid*, (1896) P. 129.

So on the death of an executor without having renounced or taken probate, the executor of the survivor of two acting executors becomes the representative of the original testator. *Re Lorimer*, 2 Sw. & T. 471.

A grant to the attorney of an executor does not break the chain of representation. *Re Murguia*, 9 P. D. 236.

In what cases the chain is broken. The conditions under which the chain of executorship is broken in law have been thus enumerated in Tristram & Coote's P. P., p. 173, 10th ed.:—

1. When the immediate sole acting executor dies intestate or testate without appointing an executor.

2. When the survivor of the immediate acting executors dies intestate.

3. When the remote sole acting executor, to whom an executorship has been transmitted downwards *per catenam*, dies intestate.

4. When the survivor of the remote acting executors dies intestate.

5. When the remote executor or executors renounce the probate of their own testator's will, or have been cited and do not appear.

6. When the remote executor or executors die without having proved their own testator's will.

7. When of two or more executors who have died after probate taken by them, it is impossible to show which survived the other or others.

8. When one of the executors, having renounced before 1st January, 1858, has survived the other executor or executors.

Executor de son Tort.

If one who is neither executor nor administrator intermeddles with the assets or otherwise acts as executor, he thereby makes himself an executor *de son tort*.

A single act of intermeddling may be sufficient for the purpose, if it be such as may induce the creditor to think that the party so intermeddling was the rightful executor. *Mountford* v. *Gibson*, 4 East, 441, 451.

What constitutes an executor *de son tort*.

But acts of necessity do not bind. 3 Hagg. 774.

A very slight circumstance of intermeddling will make an executor *de son tort*. Indeed almost any kind of meddling, however slight, is enough.

Thus it has been said that milking the cows, even by the widow of the deceased, will constitute such an executorship (Dyer, p. 166); or taking a Bible or a bedstead. Toller, 38.

Living in the house and carrying on the trade of the

deceased was held sufficient, notwithstanding his wife (the daughter of the deceased) proved the will, and she and her husband were acting together and were in the house before the death of the testator. *Hooper* v. *Summersett*, Wight. 16.

When the will is proved or administration granted and another person then intermeddles, he will not be an executor *de son tort*, but a mere trespasser (Godolph. pt. 2, c. 8); but *secus* if he gets the goods into his hands before administration is granted to another. *Kellow* v. *Westcombe*, 1 Freem. 122.

But though there be an executor or administrator, yet if he take the goods, *claiming them as executor*, or otherwise intermeddles as *executor*, in this case, because of such claiming to be executor, he may be charged as executor *de son tort*. This, however, has been denied, and it seems now to be settled that there cannot be a lawful executor and an executor *de son tort* at the same time. *Hall* v. *Elliott*, Peake, 87; *Tomlin* v. *Beck*, 1 Turn. & R. 438.

What acts do not constitute. There are, however, many acts which a stranger may perform without being involved in such an executorship; such as locking up the goods for preservation, or making an inventory thereof, directing and defraying the expenses of the funeral, repairing his houses, or providing necessaries for his children. Godolph. pt. 2, c. 8.

If another person takes the goods of the deceased and sells or gives them to a third person, this shall charge him as executor *de son tort*, but not the third person (*Ibid.*); unless perhaps there be collusion. *Paull* v. *Simpson*, 9 Q. B. 365; comp. *Williams* v. *Heales*, L. R. 9 C. P. 177.

So a creditor who obtains payment from an executor *de son tort* does not thereby become an executor *de son tort*. *Hursell* v. *Bird*, 65 L. T. 709.

Again, where a person sets up a colourable title to the goods, or a lien, though he may not make out his title completely, he will not be charged (*Flemings* v. *Jarrat*, 1 Esp. N. P. C. 336); nor if he take them in mistake for his own (Godolph. pt. 2, c. 8); nor as agent for the executor

(*Sykes* v. *S.*, L. R. 5 C. P. 113); or for the administrator, even before the grant. *Hill* v. *Curtis*, L. R. 1 Eq. 90.

The question whether a person is executor *de son tort* or not is, when once the facts are established, a question of law. *Padget* v. *Priest*, 2 T. R. 99.

An executor *de son tort* has all the liabilities, though none of the privileges, that belong to the character of executor. *Rayner* v. *Köhler*, L. R. 14 Eq. 262; *Coote* v. *Whittington*, L. R. 16 Eq. 534; but see *Cary* v. *Hills*, L. R. 15 Eq. 79.

Liability of.

In an action by a creditor he shall be named executor generally; and if so sued, it is no answer that he is only executor *de son tort*. *Meyrick* v. *Anderson*, 14 Q. B. 719.

A lawful executor may be joined in the suit, but not an administrator. Godolph. pt. 2, c. 8.

There cannot be an administrator *de son tort*. Godolph. pt. 2, c. 8.

But though an executor *de son tort* cannot by his own wrongful act acquire any benefit, yet he is protected in all acts not for his own benefit which a rightful executor may do. *Ibid.*

Therefore in an action by a creditor of the deceased, under a plea of *plene administravit*, he shall not be charged beyond the assets which came to his hands. Dyer, 166 b; but see *Kenny* v. *Ryan*, *infra*.

So he may give in evidence, under the same plea, that he has delivered the assets to the rightful executor or administrator *before* action brought; but it is no defence where the delivery is *after* action brought (*Hill* v. *Curtis*, L. R. 1 Eq. 90), for the creditor would then have to bring a second action. 2 B. & Adol. 315.

Nor can an agent of an executor *de son tort* discharge himself by accounting to his principal. *Sharland* v. *Mildon*, 5 Hare, 469.

But the liability of one executor *de son tort* for the acts of another executor *de son tort* is not limited to the actual personal receipt of goods or money, but he may be liable

THE OFFICE OF EXECUTOR.

for the acts of another when such acts have been authorised and directed by him. *Kenny* v. *Ryan*, (1897) 1 Ir. R. 513.

An executor *de son tort* cannot plead a retainer for his own debt, even though the rightful executor or administrator assent. *Curtis* v. *Vernon*, 2 T. R. 587.

Yet if an executor *de son tort* afterwards obtain administration, he may retain. 1 Saunders, 265, n. (2).

But if administration be granted to one after he has intermeddled wrongfully, this will not purge the wrong done; and therefore a creditor may sue him either as lawful administrator or as executor *de son tort*. *Laury* v. *Aldred*, 2 Brownl. 185.

<small>His liability in an action by the rightful executor.</small>
If the rightful executor or administrator sue the executor *de son tort*, he may give in evidence, in mitigation of damages, payments made by him in the rightful course of administration. *Padget* v. *Priest*, 2 T. R. 100; *Mountford* v. *Gibson*, 4 East, 451.

But he cannot plead payment of debts to the value of the assets (*Elworthy* v. *Sandford*, 3 Hurl. & C. 336), even though such payments amount to the full value of the goods sought to be recovered. Wms. 221.

And this recouping in damages will only be allowed where there are sufficient assets to satisfy all the debts, otherwise the rightful executor might be precluded from satisfying his own debt by way of retainer. *Elworthy* v. *Sandford*, *supra*.

<small>What effect his acts have on goods aliened by him.</small>
All lawful acts which an executor *de son tort* doth are good, and shall bind the rightful executor, and shall alter the property; the reason being that creditors are not bound to seek further than him who acts as executor. *Oxenham* v. *Clapp*, 2 B. & Ad. 309, 315.

But the acts must be those of one who is acting as executor, and not a mere solitary act by one who wrongfully takes upon himself to hand over the goods (*Mountford* v. *Gibson*, 4 East, 441); and the party with whom he deals must have fair reason for supposing that he has authority to act as executor. *Thomson* v. *Harding*, 2 E. & B. 630.

Such acts, moreover, are good only when they are lawful, and such as the true representative was bound to perform. *Buckley* v. *Barber*, 6 Ex. 164.

The question how far he is bound in his character of rightful administrator by his own acts done while executor *de son tort*, will be considered hereafter.

An English company cannot, on the death of a foreign shareholder, transfer his shares and pay the dividends to the foreign executors, unless the latter take out probate in this country. *Att.-Gen.* v. *New York Breweries Co.*, (1899) A. C. 62.

If they do so, the company will be considered an executor *de son tort* and liable to pay probate duty on the assets so administered. *Ibid.*

Executor's Refusal or Acceptance of Office.

An executor may refuse the office, even though he has agreed in the lifetime of the testator to accept it. *Doyle* v. *Blake*, 2 Sch. & L. 239. Executor cannot be compelled to prove,

The time within which he must decide to accept or refuse is uncertain, and left to the discretion of the Judge. Swinb. pt. 6, s. 4.

No action lies for neglect to take out probate, and the plaintiff's only remedy is to cite the executor in the Probate Division. *Re Stevens*, (1898) 1 Ch. 162.

If he refuse, administration *cum testamento annexo* will be granted to another. *Garrard* v. *G.*, *post*, p. 15.

Where an executor dies before taking out probate, or does not appear when cited, he will be treated as if he had renounced. 21 & 22 Vict. c. 95, s. 16; *Re Lorimer*, 2 Sw. & T. 471; but see *Re Ponsonby*, *ante*, p. 3.

But if he once administer, he will be deemed to have accepted, and the Court may compel him to prove the will. *Mordaunt* v. *Clarke*, L. R. 1 P. & D. 592; *Re Stevens*, (1898) 1 Ch. 162. unless he has administered.

And if an executor have intermeddled with the estate he may be compelled, on the application of a legatee, to take up probate, though he appears an undesirable person to fill the office of executor. *Re Coates*, 78 L. T. 820.

And if any person take possession of, and in any manner administer any part of, the effects of the deceased he will be liable to a penalty if he does not prove within six months of testator's death. 55 Geo. 3, c. 184, s. 37 ; 44 Vict. c. 12, s. 40 ; *Att.-Gen.* v. *New York Breweries Co.*, (1898) 1 Q. B. 205.

An executor of an executor, who has accepted the executorship of the latter testator, cannot renounce the executorship of the former. *Brooke* v. *Haymes*, L. R. 6 Eq. 25.

The Court, however, *may* accept the executor's refusal, notwithstanding he has administered. Went. 91.

After intermeddling, a renunciation is invalid and ought to be cancelled. *Re Badenach*, 3 Sw. & T. 465.

Thus if an executor apply before probate for payment of a debt, though unsuccessfully, he cannot afterwards renounce. *Cooke* v. *Stevens*, (1897) 1 Ch. 422.

The executor is liable to be sued, although administration be granted to another, if he has once administered. See *post*, Chap. XV.

But he cannot be sued by a creditor unless he has either administered or proved the will. *Mohamidu* v. *Pitchey*, (1894) A. C. 437.

What amounts to an administering. With respect to what acts will amount to an administering, two rules may be laid down, viz. :—

1. That whatever the executor does with relation to the goods which shows an intention to take upon him the executorship will regularly amount to an administration.

2. That whatever acts will make a man liable as an executor *de son tort* will be deemed an election of the executorship. *Ante*, p. 9.

Hence if he applies for payment of a debt (*Cooke* v. *Stevens*, *supra*), or seizes a stranger's goods which he supposes belong to the testator, with intent to administer, this will make him executor. Bac. Abr. Exor., E. 10.

But if he seizes the testator's goods, claiming a property in them himself, though the claim is unfounded, this will not make him executor. *Ibid.*

Where in answer to an inquiry an executor wrote that he was one of the executors, this was held sufficient evidence that he had acted. *Vickers* v. *Bell*, 10 Jur. N. S. 376.

But an executor is not to be considered as acting by merely assisting a co-executor, or acting as his agent. *Orr* v. *Newton*, 2 Cox, 274; *Stacey* v. *Elph*, 1 M. & K. 195; *Dove* v. *Everard*, 1 R. & M. 231.

An executor may renounce after he is sworn (*Jackson* v. *Whitehead*, 3 Phillim. 577); but not after he has taken probate. *Re Veiga*, 32 L. J. P. M. & A. 9. Renunciation.

Renunciation cannot be verbal, but it need not be under seal, and may be by attorney. *Re Gibson*, 1 P. & D. 105; *Re Rosser*, 3 S. & T. 490. How executor may renounce.

Until the refusal is recorded no person can take out administration (*Long* v. *Symes*, 3 Hagg. 776); and until it is recorded it can be withdrawn. *Re Morant*, L. R. 3 P. & D. 151.

Administration will not be granted on the consent of the executor. *Garrard* v. *Garrard*, L. R. 2 P. & D. 238; *Re Reid*, (1896) P. 129.

If a party renounce in person, he takes the usual oath; but if he renounce by proxy, the oath is dispensed with. If he refuse to take the oath, this amounts to a refusal of the office. Toller, 42.

An executor cannot in part refuse. He must refuse entirely or not at all. *Brooke* v. *Haymes*, L. R. 6 Eq. 25.

Where an executor renounces probate, his executorship shall wholly cease, and the representation of the testator shall be committed as if such person had not been appointed executor. 20 & 21 Vict. c. 77, s. 79; *Re Gill*, L. R. 3 P. & D. 113.

But the old practice which, in a proper case, allowed a Retracting renunciation.

co-executor to retract his renunciation, is not abrogated by this Act. *Re Stiles*, (1898) P. 12.

So where one of two executors absconded after taking probate, the Court allowed his co-executor, who had renounced, to retract his renunciation and take probate. *Re Stiles, supra.*

Semble, that retraction will not be allowed after administration has been granted. *Ibid.*

Cannot take representation in another character.

By Rule 50 P. R. (Non-contentious Business) no person who renounces probate of a will or letters of administration in one character is to be allowed to take representation in another character; but see *Re Wheelwright*, 3 P. D. 71; *Re Russell*, L. R. 1 P. & D. 634.

Where a power is given to executors they cannot exercise it if they renounce (*Crawford* v. *Forshaw*, (1891) 2 Ch. 261); but those who act may exercise the power. *Granville* v. *M'Neile*, 7 Ha. 156.

Where an executor is a creditor and neither acts nor proves, he can sue the other executor. *Rawlinson v. Shaw*, 3 T. R. 557.

Of Probate.

Jurisdiction in all matters relating to the grant and revocation of probate of wills or of administration is now vested in the Probate Division.

Executor cannot assert his title without probate.

The consequence is that an executor cannot assert his title in any other Court without showing that he has previously established it in the Probate Division, the usual proof of which is a copy of the will under the seal of the Court, which is called the probate.

This (or letters of administration with the will annexed where there is no executor) is legal evidence of the will in any question respecting personalty or realty. 60 & 61 Vict. c. 65.

The probate is, however, merely evidence. The executor

derives his title from the will itself, and the property vests in him from the testator's death. Hence the probate is said to relate back to the testator's death. *Post*, p. 42.

The executor is in a sense trustee for the legatees; and now he is also trustee for the devisees, that is, when the estate is clear, or he has assented. 60 & 61 Vict. c. 65, s. 2 (1); *Re Smith*, 42 C. D. 302; *Re Marsden*, 26 C. D. 783.

County Courts have jurisdiction in all contentious business, *i.e.* grants or revocations of grants of probate or letters of administration, provided— {County Courts.}

1. The deceased lived at his death in the district where the application is made.

2. His personal estate, without deducting debts, was under 200*l.*, and his real estate under 300*l.*, exclusive of charges. *Davies* v. *Brecknell*, L. R. 2 P. & D. 177.

The Probate Court may remit cases to the County Court. 20 & 21 Vict. c. 77, s. 59; 21 & 22 Vict. c. 95, s. 12; *Slater* v. *Alvey*, L. R. 2 P. & D. 154.

As to practice, see County Court Rules, 1889, Ord. 49.

As to appeals, see 20 & 21 Vict. c. 77, s. 58; R. S. C. 1883, Ord. 59, r. 4.

And see Intestates' Widows and Children Acts, 1873 and 1875, as to the administration of small estates under 100*l.*

What the Executor may do before Probate.

The executor may do almost all the acts which are incident to his office before probate, except only some of those which relate to suits.

He may take possession of the assets and dispose of them, pay, release or receive debts, distrain for rent, and assent to or pay legacies. Wms. 251. {What acts stand good.}

He may enter on the testator's terms for years, and may now take possession of his real estate. 60 & 61 Vict. c. 65, s. 2, sub-s. 2.

And though he should die before proving the will, yet do these acts stand good. In a word, the executor's death before probate determines the executorship, but does not avoid it. *Wankford* v. *W.*, *infra*.

But if such acts are relied on for title, or sought to be enforced, the probate must be produced.

Thus, though the executor, before probate, can give a valid title to an assignee or specific legatee or devisee, yet if it be necessary to support that title by deducing it from the executor, this can only be done by producing the probate. And if the executor die before probate, letters of administration *cum testamento annexo* must be produced instead. *Post*, p. 19.

Nor is a purchaser bound to pay the purchase money till probate, because the executor cannot give a complete indemnity. *Newton* v. *M. R. Co.*, 1 Dr. & Sm. 583; and see *Re Stevens*, (1898) 1 Ch. 162.

Cannot maintain actions.

An executor cannot maintain actions before probate, except such as are founded on his actual possession; and in those actions where he relies on his *constructive* possession as executor he will, generally speaking, have to produce the probate at the trial. *Tarn* v. *Commercial, &c.*, *infra*.

But where the executor has been in *actual* possession, such possession is in itself sufficient without showing any title in any action, such as trover or trespass, where actual possession is a *primâ facie* title without reference to the circumstances under which such possession was obtained. Went. 84; *Brassington* v. *Ault*, 2 Bing. 177.

But may commence them.

But though an executor cannot *maintain* actions before probate except upon his actual possession, yet he may advance in them as far as that step where the production of probate becomes necessary. Dan. 405; *Wankford* v. *W.*, *infra*.

He may therefore *commence* an action as executor before probate, and if his title is put in issue, the subsequent probate will make the action a good one if obtained before the hearing or trial. *Ibid.*; Went. 84.

He may obtain an injunction to protect the estate, may petition in bankruptcy, or for a winding-up order, and may be sued by creditors or legatees before probate. Wms. 256 ; and see *post*, p. 20.

But the Court may at any time stay proceedings until probate is taken out. *Tarn* v. *Commercial, &c.*, 12 Q. B. D. 294.

If he die before probate, his executor cannot prove both wills and so become executor to both testators, but administration *cum testamento annexo* must be taken out to the first testator. *Isted* v. *Stanley*, Dyer, 372 a ; *Wankford* v. *W.*, 1 Salk. 308.

As to the manner of obtaining probate and the practice relating thereto, see Wms. pt. 1, bk. iv., chap. 2, and Tristram & Coote. It is only necessary to add here that probate may now be obtained of a will of realty only. 60 & 61 Vict. c. 65.

CHAPTER II.

OF THE OFFICE OF ADMINISTRATOR.

What may be done before.

WHERE there is no executor, the Court will grant letters of administration; and, as we have already seen, the jurisdiction to grant them is now vested in the Probate Division.

What may be done before administration.

The general rule is that a party entitled to administration can do nothing as administrator before letters of administration are granted to him, inasmuch as he derives his authority not from the will but from his appointment by the Court.

Thus administration must issue before the commencement of an action at law by an administrator, even though he be administrator *cum testamento annexo*. *Phillips v. Hartley*, 3 C. & P. 121.

In Chancery, however, it is sufficient to produce the letters of administration at the hearing, if the grant be alleged in the statement of claim. Daniell, 405; but see *Re Masonic, &c.*, 32 C. D. 373.

And a petition for administration in bankruptcy may be presented before the grant, it being sufficient if the legal representative is constituted before the order is made. *Re Sleet*, (1894) 2 Q. B. 797.

What cannot be done.

So an administrator cannot before administration release, nor assign a term, nor surrender a lease, nor effect a mortgage, nor give notice. Wms. 343.

Acts made valid by relation back.

Yet cases may be found where letters of administration have related back to the death of the intestate so as to give validity to the acts done before they were obtained, but it seems only in those cases where the act done is for the benefit of the estate. *Morgan* v. *Thomas*, 8 Exch. 302; *post*, p. 42.

But if work is done before administration for the benefit of the estate, not at the order of the administrator, he will not be liable. *Re Watson*, 19 Q. B. D. 234.

The right to bring actions, founded on mere possession, against wrongdoers seems to apply as much to administrators as executors. *Ante*, p. 18.

And now all rules of law relating to the effect of administration as respects chattels real and as respects the dealing with chattels real before administration, and the powers, rights, duties, and liabilities of personal representatives in respect of personal estate, shall apply to real estate so far as the same are applicable, except that some or one of several representatives cannot sell or transfer real estate. 60 & 61 Vict. c. 65, s. 2 (2). Real estate.

General Administration.

Before inquiring into the rights of those persons expressly pointed out by statute to whom administration is to be granted, it is necessary to consider the right of the husband. Husband's right to be his wife's administrator.

The husband had an exclusive right to be the administrator of his wife. *Re Lambert*, 39 C. D. 626.

This right is not affected by the Married Women's Property Act, 1882.

And it has even been held that he is the legal personal representative of his wife within the M. W. P. Act, 1882, s. 23, without taking out administration: *Surman* v. *Wharton*, (1891) 1 Q. B. 491.

The right may, however, where there is real estate, be now affected by the Land Transfer Act. See *Re Ardern*, (1898) P. 147.

This right of the husband passes to his legal representatives (*Fielder* v. *Hanger*, 3 Hagg. 769; *Partington* v.

OFFICE OF ADMINISTRATOR.

A.-G., L. R. 4 H. L. 109), unless the next of kin are entitled as by settlement or separation deed. *Re Pountney*, 4 Hagg. 289; *Allen* v. *Humphreys*, 8 P. D. 16.

A grant of administration limited to such property as the wife could not dispose of by will may still be made to a husband. *Re Donovan*, 78 L. T. 567; *Re Leman*, (1898) P. 215.

The husband, however, will be passed over in the following cases:—

If he is cited and does not appear. *Re Moore*, (1891) P. 299; and see *Re Ardern*, (1898) P. 147.

If he has deserted his wife. *Re Stephenson*, L. R. 1 P. & D. 289; *Re Shoosmith*, (1894) P. 23.

If he has been divorced. *Re Hay*, L. R. 1 P. & D. 51.

And, it would seem, if his wife has obtained a judicial separation. See 20 & 21 Vict. c. 85, s. 21.

Where it is not known whether the husband or the wife survived, administration will be granted of the estate of each to their respective next of kin. *Re Alston*, (1892) P. 142.

Of the right of the widow. The Court prefers a sole to a joint administration, and therefore will in ordinary cases prefer the widow to the next of kin.

But a joint grant to widow and next of kin will be made under special circumstances. *Re Dickinson*, (1891) P. 292.

And where a good cause is shown the widow will be passed over and administration be granted to the next of kin.

Thus if she has barred herself of all interest in her husband's estate by settlement.

Or if she is a lunatic. *Ante*, p. 3.

Or if she has misconducted herself. *Re Stevens*, (1898) P. 126.

Or if she is divorced; and in that case she need not be cited. *Re Nares*, 13 P. D. 35.

But her having married again is not a valid objection. *Webb* v. *Needham*, 1 Add. 494.

Nor is it any objection that she has been judicially separated from her husband by reason of his misconduct, or at all events not without notice. *Re Ihler*, 3 P. & D. 50.

And administration will be granted to her executor. *Re Bryant*, (1896) P. 159; *Re Teece*, ibid. 6.

Subject as above, the right to letters of administration as regards personalty accrues, generally speaking, to the next of kin, or some or one of them as the Court may think fit, in the following order:— *(The right of the next of kin.)*

Children.
Grandchildren.
Remoter descendants.
Father.
Mother.
Brothers and sisters.
Grandfathers and grandmothers.
Uncles, aunts, nephews, nieces, and great-grandparents.
Cousins.

If the next of kin is a married woman and renounces, the grant is made to her husband. *Haymes* v. *Matthews*, 1 Sw. & T. 460.

As to principles which guide the Court in making election between several next of kin in equal degree, see Wms. 362. *(Where there are several next of kin in equal degree.)*

The grant is not always made to him whom the majority of the parties interested desire. *Re Stainton*, 2 P. & D. 212; *Sawbridge* v. *Hill*, ibid. 220.

The whole blood is preferred to the half blood unless material objections can be proved. *Stratton* v. *Linton*, 31 L. J. P. & M. 48.

A son is preferred to a daughter; but this rule may be met by another, viz. that the grant will be made *priori petenti*. *Cordeux* v. *Trasler*, 34 L. J. P. M. & A. 127.

Cæteris paribus, a man accustomed to business will be preferred. *Williams* v. *Wilkins*, 2 Phillim. 100.

The fact that next of kin is also a disputed creditor is not in his favour. *Webb* v. *Needham*, 1 Add. 494.

A grant will not be made to a bankrupt; and a husband's right will not vest in his trustee in bankruptcy. *Re Turner*, 12 P. D. 18.

Where the sole next of kin was a lunatic and the committee renounced, the Court granted administration to a stranger. *Re Hastings*, 4 P. D. 73.

Where next of kin is abroad he must be cited before the grant will be made to another. Wms. 365.

Creditor, when entitled.
If none of the next of kin take out administration, a creditor may by custom do it, and so may an executor of a creditor, and though his claim is statute-barred. *Coombs* v. *C.*, 1 P. & D. 288.

But a creditor will not be granted administration to defeat the right of retainer of the next of kin unless he can prove the existence of assets in the jurisdiction. *Re Foy*, 78 L. T. 49.

For want of both creditors and next of kin desirous of taking out administration, the Court may grant it to any person at its discretion. *Re Mayer*, L. R. 3 P. & D. 39; *Re Moore*, (1892) P. 145.

Or it may grant to a stranger letters *ad colligenda bona*. *Re Ashley*, 15 P. D. 120.

Although a next of kin may have intermeddled and made himself liable as executor *de son tort*, he cannot be compelled by the Court to take upon himself the office of administrator. *Re Fell*, 2 S. & T. 126; *Re Davis*, 4 S. & T. 213.

A grant may be made to the attorney of the next of kin if resident abroad, or if effects are under 20*l*. Wms. 376.

Administration may be taken out here to an intestate domiciled abroad where there are assets in this country; and though distribution is to be regulated according to the law of the domicil, the assets in this country must be administered here. *Preston* v. *Melville*, 8 Cl. & Fin. 1.

The administrator in the country of the domicil is, however, entitled to call on all limited administrators to pay over the net surplus. *Eames* v. *Hacon*, 16 C. D. 407.

Administration was refused to a colonial official administrator. *Re Reitz*, 3 Hagg. 766.

Heir.
But now real estate of persons dying after the 1st

January, 1898, devolves upon the personal representatives, and letters of administration may be granted in respect of real estate only. 60 & 61 Vict. c. 65, s. 1.

And where a person dies possessed of real estate the Court shall, in granting letters of administration, have regard to the rights of persons interested in his real estate; and his heir, if not one of the next of kin, shall be equally entitled to the grant with the next of kin. 60 & 61 Vict. c. 65, s. 2 (4).

The grant may be made to the heir without giving notice to the next of kin if there is no personal estate; but where the title of the heir is doubtful, or the amount of personalty is large as compared with the realty, such notice should be given. *Re Barnett*, (1898) P. 145.

The Land Transfer Act, 1897, does not bind the Crown, and therefore the legal estate in escheated land does not, under sect. 1, vest in the Solicitor to the Treasury as the Crown's nominee. *Re Hartley*, (1899) P. 40. Crown.

Persons incapable of being administrators include not only those who have already been mentioned as disqualified for the office of executor (*ante*, pp. 2, 3), but also bankrupts. *Ante*, p. 23. Who cannot be administrators.

But an alien is not disqualified. *Ante*, p. 2.

If the next of kin be a minor the grant will be made to another during his minority (*post*, p. 28), even though by the law of the country of domicil the minor is entitled. *Re Orleans*, 1 S. & T. 253.

Coverture is no incapacity; and a married woman may now take administration without the consent of her husband, and in all respects act as if she were a *feme sole*.

Administration cum testamento annexo.

Where there is a will but no appointment of executors, or the appointment fails, the Court will grant administration with the will annexed.

OFFICE OF ADMINISTRATOR.

In such cases no one has a legal right of preference; and the Court has a discretion in the choice of an administrator according to its own practice.

The practice may be summarised as follows :—

To person having greatest interest. The rule is to consider who has the greatest interest in the effects of the deceased, and regard must now be had to the rights of the persons interested in the real estate. Wms. 400.

Hence the residuary legatee, if there be one, is preferred to the next of kin or legatees; and the same preference will, it is thought, now be given to a residuary devisee. *Ibid.*

And this is so even where there is no present prospect of any residue, and also where he is only residuary legatee in trust. *Ibid.* 401.

His personal representatives have the same right where the residuary legatee has a beneficial interest and is not a mere trustee. *Ibid.* 402.

If there is no residuary legatee, or he declines, administration is usually granted to the next of kin. *Ibid.* 403.

If the next of kin decline, it may be granted to a legatee or to a creditor. *Ibid.* 404.

Citation. In all cases where a party has a prior title to a grant he must be cited before administration is committed to any other person. *Ibid.* 386; *Re Harper*, (1899) P. 59.

Where the testator dies after 1st January, 1898, possessed of real estate, the Court shall, in granting letters of administration, have regard to the rights and interests of persons interested in his real estate, and the heir-at-law, if not one of the next of kin, shall be equally entitled to the grant with the next of kin. 60 & 61 Vict. c. 65, s. 2 (4).

It would seem, therefore, that in such cases the preference given to a residuary legatee would be extended to a residuary devisee.

Administration de bonis non.

If a sole executor dies before proving the will, administration *cum testamento annexo* must, as we have seen, be granted although he may have administered in part.

But if a surviving or sole executor dies after probate intestate *administration de bonis non* becomes necessary, that is, administration of the goods of the original testator left unadministered by the former executor. Death of sole executor intestate.

So if the original testator dies abroad and his executor proves the will there, and then dies, having appointed his own executor who proves the latter will here, administration *de bonis non* must be obtained in this country. *Re Gaynor*, L. R. 1 P. & D. 723. Where will is proved abroad.

Where the estate had been administered except as to one legacy, the Court granted administration with will annexed *de bonis non* without requiring the representative of the executor or residuary legatees to be cited. *Re King*, 8 P. D. 162; and see *Re Wilde*, 13 P. D. 1. Where estate administered except one legacy.

Such administration *de bonis non* will be committed *cum testamento annexo*, and will be granted to the person entitled according to the principles already stated with regard to administration *cum testamento annexo*. *Akers* v. *Dupuy*, 1 Hagg. 473.

In many instances it is obvious he will be a different person from the representative of the deceased executor; but if the executor were also beneficial residuary legatee his representative will likewise be entitled to administration *de bonis non* to the original testator. *Ante*, p. 26.

Where power is reserved to one of two executors, and the acting executor dies, administration *de bonis non* cannot be granted, as upon the non-appearance to a citation of the executor to whom power was reserved, the claim of executorship would be continued in the executors of the acting executor without any fresh grant. *Re Reid*, (1896) P. 129.

Death of sole administrator.
Upon the death of a sole or surviving administrator, whether testate or intestate, the Court must appoint an administrator *de bonis non*. 2 Black. Comm. 506.

As regards the person to be appointed administrator *de bonis non* in that event, it was formerly laid down that there was no distinction between an original and a *de bonis non* administration. But the rule now is that the grant ought to follow the interest. *Re Pountney, ante*, p. 22.

But the statutes only regard the next of kin at the time of the death of the intestate, and not at the time a second grant is wanted. *Almes* v. *A.*, 2 Hagg. App. 155.

If therefore such next of kin are dead the Court will in ordinary cases grant administration to him who has the greatest interest in the effects of the original intestate. *Ibid.*

And on this ground an executor of the deceased administrator will be preferred to his next of kin. 2 Hagg. App. 150, 153.

Administration durante minore ætate.

If the person appointed sole executor, or the person entitled to administration, be within age, administration *durante minore ætate* is granted.

When necessary.
But if there are several executors and one is of full age, no administration of this sort is granted, because he who is of full age may execute the will. *Ante*, p. 2.

It has, however, been held differently in the case of several next of kin of equal degree entitled under an intestacy. *Cartwright's Case*, 1 Freem. 258.

It is discretionary in the Court to grant this sort of administration to such person as it shall think fit. *West* v. *Willby*, 3 Phillim. 379; *Rex* v. *Bettesworth*, 1 Barnard. 370, 425.

Guardian.
In the exercise of this discretion it was the practice to grant administration to the guardian.

In the appointment of guardian a distinction exists

between an infant under seven and a minor over that age, the latter having power to nominate his own guardian. Toller, 100; Wms. 418.

The guardianship was generally granted to the next of kin of the child. But the Court has a discretion and may pass them over. *Quick* v. *Q.*, 33 L. J. P. & M. 177; *Re Gardiner*, 9 P. D. 66; *Re Webb*, 13 P. D. 71.

But there are many cases where the Court has refused to grant administration to the guardian, as where he is very poor. *Havers* v. *H.*, Barnard. C. C. 23. [*When guardian is excluded.*]

Or very old. *Re Ewing*, 1 Hagg. 381.

Or where the estate is insolvent. *West* v. *Willby*, 3 Phillim. 374. *Secus*, if the estate is solvent. *John* v. *Bradbury*, L. R. 1 P. & D. 245.

The practice above stated has been applied and somewhat varied by P. R. (Non-contentious) 1862, rr. 33—36.

Where the minor is a foreigner the Court will not follow the grant of the country of domicil if contrary to the law of this country. *Re Orleans*, 1 S. & T. 253; but see *Re Da Cunha*, 1 Hagg. 237. [*Where minor a foreigner.*]

The guardian of a minor next of kin is entitled to a grant of administration during the absence abroad of the administrator. *Re Lee*, (1898) 2 Ir. R. 81.

An administrator during the minority of a sole executor has the same powers as one appointed during the minority of the next of kin. 38 Geo. 3, c. 87, s. 7.

If administration be granted during the minority of several infants it determines upon the coming of age of any one of them. 4 Burn, E. L. 385. [*Limit of.*]

But if one dies before he comes of age this will not determine the administration. *Jones* v. *Strafford*, 3 P. Wms. 89.

The limit to the administration of an administrator *durante minore ætate* is the minority of the person, and there is no other limit. *Re Cope*, 16 C. D. 49.

He has all the powers of an ordinary administrator, including power to sell the estate for payment of debts

(*Ibid.*), or even in due course of administration, although not necessary for payment of debts. *Re Thompson*, (1896) 1 Ir. R. 356.

And he may exercise a power of sale given by a testator to his executors or administrators. *Monsell* v. *Armstrong*, 14 Eq. 423; but see *Re Robinson*, L. R. Ir. 3 C. D. 429.

Liability of administrator. If an executor *durante minore ætate* has duly administered the assets and paid over the surplus to the executor of full age, he is not chargeable to creditors. But he is liable to creditors if he has committed a *devastavit*, even though he obtain a release from the infant when of full age. Wms. 425.

It is said, however, that he can only be called to account, after the administration is determined, by the executor and by no other person. *Fotherby* v. *Pate*, 3 Atk. 603; Bac. Abr. Exors. (B. 1) 2.

A decree for administration may be made against an administrator *durante minore ætate*. *Sewell* v. *Ransford*, 21 W. R. 244.

Administration pendente lite.

20 & 21 Vict. c. 77. By the Court of Probate Act, 1857, s. 70, it is enacted that, pending any suit touching the validity of the will of any deceased person, or for obtaining, recalling or revoking any probate or grant of administration, the Court may appoint an administrator, and such administrator shall have all the rights and powers of a general administrator, other than the right of distributing the residue, and shall be subject to the control of the Court and act under its direction.

And may appoint a receiver. Sect. 71.

Such an administrator may be appointed on the application of a person not a party to the suit. *Tichborne* v. *T.*, 1 P. & D. 730; *Re Evans*, 15 P. D. 215.

A caveat entered against probate is not a *lis pendens* for the purpose of appointing such an administrator. *Salter* v. *S.*, (1896) P. 291.

Nor is a petition in reference to the person appointed executor. *Grant* v. *G.*, 1 P. & D. 654.

Where an executrix proved her husband's will and died leaving a will which was disputed in a suit, the Court appointed an administrator *pendente lite* to the estate of the husband. *Re Fawcett*, 14 P. D. 152.

Before granting such administration the Court must be satisfied as to the necessity and also as to the fitness of the proposed administrator. *Bellew* v. *B.*, 34 L. J. P. M. & A. 125; *Northey* v. *Cock*, 1 Add. 329.

But the Court will not appoint such an administrator where there is a person who can discharge the duties of such an administrator, as an executor or surviving partner. *Mortimer* v. *Paull*, L. R. 2 P. & D. 85; *Horrell* v. *Witts*, L. R. 1 P. & D. 103.

Such an administrator will be appointed, when just and proper, although a receiver has been appointed in Chancery. *Tichborne* v. *T.*, 1 P. & D. 730.

The practice was to appoint such an administrator in all cases where the Court of Chancery would appoint a receiver. *Bellew* v. *Bellew, ubi sup.*

The Court, unless by consent, never appoints any of the litigant parties, but selects an indifferent nominee. *Colvin* v. *Fraser*, 2 Hagg. 613; *De Chatelain* v. *Pontigny*, 1 S. & T. 34; *Queen's Proctor* v. *Williams*, 2 S. & T. 353. {Who may be administrator.}

Such administrators are the appointees of the Court, and not merely the agents of the persons nominating them. 1 Hagg. 222.

The Court may direct that such administrators shall receive out of the personal and real estate of the deceased such remuneration as the Court thinks fit. 20 & 21 Vict. c. 77, s. 72.

The functions of an administrator *pendente lite* commence from the date of the order of appointment, and terminate with a decree in favour of the will. *Wieland* v. *Bird*, (1894) P. 262. {Functions of.}

But if the decree is appealed from, his duties do not

cease until the appeal is disposed of. *Taylor* v. *T.*, 6 P. D. 29.

Such an administrator may, without any leave of the Probate Division, be sued in the Chancery Division by a creditor of the deceased in the same way as a general administrator. *Re Toleman*, (1897) 1 Ch. 866.

Chancery Division will not appoint a receiver.
The Court of Chancery will not appoint a receiver where an administrator *pendente lite* has been appointed by the Probate Division. *Veret* v. *Duprez*, 6 Eq. 329; *Hitchen* v. *Birks*, 10 Eq. 471.

And an action in the Chancery Division for a receiver *pendente lite* in the Probate Division will be transferred to the latter division. *Barr* v. *B.*, W. N. 1876, 44.

So a receiver was refused in Chancery where letters of administration had been granted to the defendant. *Re Ivory*, 10 C. D. 372.

And on the other hand the Probate Division will not interfere with an administrator who is acting under the direction of the Chancery Division. *Tichborne* v. *T.*, L. R. 2 P. & D. 41.

Administration durante absentiâ.

If the executor or next of kin be out of the jurisdiction the Courts have always had the power, before probate obtained or administration issued, to grant to another a limited administration *durante absentiâ*.

But when probate was once granted and the executor had gone abroad, the Courts did not feel authorised to grant another administration.

38 Geo. 3, c. 87.
To remedy this it was provided by 38 Geo. 3, c. 87, that at the expiration of twelve months after the testator's death, if the executors or executor to whom probate has been granted are or is out of the jurisdiction, such special administration as therein mentioned may be granted on the application of any creditor, next of kin, or legatee.

And by the Court of Probate Act, 1857, s. 74, the above statute shall apply in like manner to all cases where letters of administration have been granted and the administrator is out of the jurisdiction.

It will be noticed that the foregoing apply only to absence *after* probate or grant of letters. As to absence before, see Court of Probate Act, 1857, s. 73. *Ante*, p. 3.

And by the Court of Probate Act, 1858, s. 18, the provisions of the Act of Geo. 3, and the Court of Probate Act, 1857, are extended to all executors and administrators residing out of the jurisdiction whether it be or be not intended to institute Chancery proceedings.

The above Acts apply to the case of an executor of an executor. *Re Grant*, 1 P. D. 435.

To whom made.

A grant has been made to the personal representatives of a legatee. *Re Collier*, 2 S. & T. 444.

And to an assignee in bankruptcy of an administrator out of the jurisdiction. *Re Hammond*, 6 P. D. 104.

A grant was made to a new trustee substituted by the Court of Chancery for an executor who had gone abroad. *Re Hampson*, L. R. 1 P. & D. 1.

Where the applicant is residuary legatee and his interest is undetermined, the grant will be made under 38 Geo. 3, c. 87; but where a particular sum is set aside for, and is actually payable to, the applicant, the grant can be made under 21 & 22 Vict. c. 95, s. 18. *Re Ruddy*, L. R. 2 P. & D. 330.

Such an administration would seem to be at an end the moment the executor returns. *Secus* as to an administration granted *durante absentiâ* to the attorney of an executor. *Re Cassidy*, 4 Hagg. 360.

The authority of an administrator *durante absentiâ* does not become actually void, but only voidable, on the death of the executor. *Taynton* v. *Hannay*, 3 B. & P. 26. As to the proper course in such an event, see Wms. 438.

Such an administrator may sell leaseholds, but he must

prove that his principal is alive. *Webb* v. *Kirby*, 7 D. M. & G. 376.

Such an administrator is accountable to the executor or administrator. *Slaughter* v. *May*, 1 Salk. 42.

Administration durante dementiâ.

<small>Where sole representative is insane.</small> If an executor becomes lunatic, a grant of a temporary administration with the will annexed will be made. Toller, 99.

Where a sole executor or administrator becomes a lunatic, it is the practice to make a limited grant to his committee during his lunacy.

But by consent of the committee administration may be granted to a residuary legatee.

The practice where a grant has been made to a next of kin who has become insane appears to be as follows:—

Where a lunatic has been so found and a committee appointed, the grant is made to the committee. *Re Cooke*, (1895) P. 68.

Where he is not so found, but under s. 116 of the Act of 1890 a person has been appointed with general authority over the lunatic's property, such person is treated as a committee. *Ibid.*

If the person appointed under s. 116 has only limited powers, he is not in the same position as a committee and not entitled to a grant. *Ibid.*

Where there is no committee, and no person in the position of a committee, the grant is made to another of the next of kin for the use of the lunatic during the lunacy. *Ibid.*

<small>Where one of several is lunatic.</small> Where one of two executors becomes lunatic, the probate is revoked and a fresh one granted to the sane executor. *Re Marshall*, 1 Curt. 297.

Where one of two administrators becomes insane, the

grant is revoked and a fresh one granted to the sane administrator. *Re Phillips*, 2 Add. 335 ; *Re Newton*, 3 Curt. 428.

Other limited Administrations.

Again, an administration may be granted limited to *Ad litem.* commencing or substantiating proceedings in Chancery. *Burdon* v. *Morgan*, L. R. 2 P. & D. 371.

But the appointment of an administrator *ad litem* is now in many cases unnecessary, for by Ord. 16, r. 46, the Court may appoint some person to represent the estate or proceed in the absence of any such person.

Limited administrations may also be granted in respect of time, place, and object. *Time, place, or object.*

Thus a limited administration may be granted till a will be transmitted to England or till a lost will be found (*Re Metcalfe*, 1 Add. 343 ; *Re Brown*, 80 L. T. 360 ; *Re Campbell*, 2 Hagg. 555), or until the heir could be cited. *Re Roberts*, (1898) P. 149.

There may also be a grant limited to certain specific effects. *Re Dodgson*, 1 S. & T. 259 ; *Re Prothero*, L. R. 3 P. & D. 209.

But this sort of grant is exceptional, and should not be made without strong reason. *Re Somerset*, L. R. 1 P. & D. 350.

The Court will grant letters of administration to the *cestui que trust* of a trust fund limited to that fund, after the death of the trustee, on the consent of his personal representatives. *Re Ratcliffe*, (1899) P. 110.

Administration will be granted for a particular object, as to assign a term, or to a particular legacy (Wms. 445), or to convey certain leaseholds. *Re Butler*, (1898) P. 9.

And lastly, administration may be granted limited to the effects in one particular country or place. *Re Mann*, (1891) P. 293.

Such limited administrations ought not, generally

speaking, to be granted without the renunciation of the party entitled to the general grant, or a citation of such party. Wms. 449.

Bond.

Except the Crown solicitor, all administrators must give a bond to the Court, with, if required, one or more sureties, for duly administering the estate.

Court cannot dispense with. The Court cannot dispense with the bond; but it has a discretion as to the amount of the penalty. *Re Powis*, 34 L. J. P. & M. 55; *Re Stacpoole*, 2 S. & T. 316; *Re Goold*, 34 L. J. P. & M. 105.

Where there has been an administration during minority, and the minor on coming of age takes out administration, he must give the same security as the original administrator. *Abbott* v. *A.*, 2 Phillim. 578.

Where the estate has been partly administered, the bond may be given in double the amount of the unadministered estate. *Re Halliwell*, 10 P. D. 198; *Re Oakey*, (1896) P. 7.

There are cases in which some one other than the administrator will be allowed to execute the bond: where, for instance, the administrator is abroad. *Re Ross*, 2 P. D. 274.

The husband need not join in the bond on a grant to the wife. *Re Ayres*, 8 P. D. 168.

Sureties. Where the property is in Court, sureties may be dispensed with. *Re Wilcocks*, 67 L. T. 528; *Re Leach*, 80 L. T. 170; and see *Re Cope*, 15 P. D. 107.

Or the amount may be reduced. *Re Cormack*, (1891) P. 151; and see *Askew* v. *A.*, *Ibid.* 174; *Re Paxton*, 14 P. D. 40.

Sureties cannot be discharged, and others substituted for them. *Re Stark*, L. R. 1 P. & D. 76.

Where the estate does not exceed 50*l.*, one surety is enough. Tristram & Coote, p. 102.

And also where a husband administers to his wife. *Ibid.*
A company has also been accepted as sole surety. *Re Hunt*, (1896) P. 288.

The administrator of a foreign subject, resident abroad, may, if deceased left no debts in England, or by leave of the Judge, give a bond with foreign sureties. Tr. & Co. 101.

In all other cases sureties residing in the United Kingdom or Channel Islands or Isle of Man are required except by leave. *Ibid.; Re Scott*, (1895) P. 342.

In ordinary cases sureties do not justify. Tristram & Coote, 103. Justifying security.

But as a rule the Court will direct justifying security to be given if a legatee or next of kin apply for it, at least to the extent of their shares. *Ibid.*

Creditors have no right to require the sureties to justify unless a strong case is made out. *Ibid.* 104.

Where there is not a personal service of the decree on the party having a prior claim to the grant, justifying securities are required. Wms. 460.

The Court may, where there has been a breach of the bond, order an assignment for the purpose of suing on it. 20 & 21 Vict. c. 77, s. 83; *Re Young*, L. R. 1 P. & D. 186; *Re Cartwright, Ibid.* 422. Assignment of bond.

As to what is a breach, see *Dobbs v. Brain*, (1897) 2 Q. B. 97; *Bolton v. Powell*, 2 D. M. & G. 1, 17.

Where a second bond has been given, the surety under the first bond cannot be sued until an action has been brought on the second bond. *Re Irving*, 1 P. & D. 658.

A bond by a creditor to administer without preference to his own debt does not prevent retainer. *Davies v. Parry*, (1899) 1 Ch. 602.

CHAPTER III.

EFFECT OF PROBATE AND LETTERS OF ADMINISTRATION.

IT was a legal consequence of the exclusive jurisdiction of the Probate Court in deciding on the validity of wills of *personalty* and granting administration that its sentences should be conclusive evidence.

As to what facts probate is conclusive.
Hence a probate, even in common form, was conclusive both in law and equity as to the appointment of the executor and the validity and contents of the will so far formerly as it extended to personal property. And this rule will now apply to all wills whether of personal or real estate. 60 & 61 Vict. c. 65, s. 1; and see 20 & 21 Vict. c. 77, s. 64.

In short, without the *constat* of the Probate Court no other Court will take notice of the rights of representation to personalty or now even of realty. *Pinney* v. *Hunt*, 6 C. D. 100.

The probate cannot be impeached even on the ground of fraud (*Griffiths* v. *Hamilton*, 12 Ves. 307); and payment to an executor who has obtained probate of a forged will is a good discharge, notwithstanding the probate be afterwards declared null. Wms. 466; but see *Ex parte Jolliffe*, 8 Beav. 168.

Again, letters of administration even if irregularly granted are valid till revoked. *Mohamidu* v. *Pitchey*, (1894) A. C. 437.

And as long as letters of administration remain in force they are conclusive evidence as to who is the next of kin. *Re Ivory*, 10 C. D. 372.

The probate is also conclusive as to every part of the will

THE EFFECT OF PROBATE AND ADMINISTRATION.

in respect of which it has been granted. 1 P. Wms. 388.

But for the purpose of construing a will the Court will look at the original will as well as the probate. *Re Harrison*, 30 C. D. 390; *Compton* v. *Bloxham*, 2 Coll. 201; *Manning* v. *Purcell*, 7 D. M. & G. 55. *In what cases equity will interfere.*

But though Courts of Equity are bound to receive probate, yet they will in certain cases affect with a trust a bequest obtained by fraud, and in such cases the Court will either convert the wrongdoer into a trustee or oblige him to consent to a revocation by the Probate Court. *Barnesley* v. *Powell*, 1 Ves. Sen. 119, 284, 287.

Again, though the Court must accept the probate, it will in certain cases so construe the will as to render it ineffectual. *Walsh* v. *Gladstone*, 1 Phil. C. C. 294; *Concha* v. *Concha*, 11 App. Cas. 541; and see *Re Parker*, 1894, 1 Ch. 707, where the Court disregarded a limited grant of probate made for a particular purpose.

The probate formerly was only evidence as to wills of personal estate. But in the year 1857 an Act was passed which provided for the citation before the Probate Court of the heir of the testator and the devisees of his real estate; and such heir and devisees, when cited, were bound by the proceedings; but this occurs only when a contest is expected or actually takes place. In all ordinary cases a will so far as it affects real estate has not hitherto required to be proved. Wms. R. P. 236.

But now as regards persons dying after 1st January, 1898, probate and letters of administration may be granted in respect of real estate only, although there is no personal estate (60 & 61 Vict. c. 65, s. 1 (3)); and the persons interested in the real estate are entitled to take out administration. *Ibid.* s. 2 (4); *Re Barnett, ante*, p. 25.

And since all real estate will devolve after the above date on the personal representatives, it seems to follow that probate will in all cases be evidence of wills of real estate.

Revocation of Probate or Administration.

As to what are sufficient grounds for revocation, see Wms. 487, 491.

With regard to the effect of revocation on the intermediate acts of the former executor or administrator, the Court of Probate Act, 1857, provides that all payments and reimbursements under revoked probates or administrations are to be valid (sect. 77), and that all persons making payments or transfers *bonâ fide* upon any probate or administration shall be indemnified (sect. 78).

Grant: void or voidable.
There is a distinction on this subject between grants which are void and such as are merely voidable. Wms. 501.

If the grant be *void*, the mesne acts, except in so far as they are protected by the above statutes, shall be of no validity. *Ibid.*

It would seem, however, that, as between the rightful representative and the alienee, the act of alienation, *if done in the due course of administration*, shall not be void. *Graysbrook v. Fox*, Plowd. 282, 283.

If the grant be only *voidable*, then another distinction arises between the case of a suit by citation which is to revoke and an appeal which is to reverse. Wms. 502.

In case of an appeal all intermediate acts are ineffectual, except those protected by the above Act. Wms. 503.

But if the suit be by citation, all lawful acts done by the first administrator shall be valid, even though done with intent to defeat the second administrator, or *pendente lite*. *Ibid.*

It may perhaps be laid down as a general test of whether an administration is void or voidable, that, where the grant is in derogation of the right of an executor, it is void; but where the administration is granted by the proper jurisdiction, and is only in derogation of the right of the next of kin or residuary legatee, it is merely voidable. Wms. 504; but see 227.

A grant of letters of administration obtained by

suppressing a will containing no appointment of executors is not void *ab initio*. *Boxall* v. *B.*, 27 C. D. 220.

Where letters of administration are revoked, the administrator will not get his costs of administration suit instituted by him with knowledge that another person claimed to administer. *Houseman* v. *H.*, 1 C. D. 535; and see *Re Dean*, 21 C. D. 581.

An executor who has proved cannot take steps to revoke the probate (*Re Chamberlain*, 1 P. & D. 316); but an administrator may, as seen by the bond.

CHAPTER IV.

THE ESTATE OF EXECUTORS AND ADMINISTRATORS.

The Quality of the Estate.

Estate of executor.
As the interest of an executor in the estate of the deceased is derived exclusively from the will, so it vests in him from the moment of the testator's death.

The law knows no interval between the testator's death and the vesting of the right in the executor, and as soon as he obtains probate his right is considered as accruing from that period. *Whitehead* v. *Taylor*, 10 A. & E. 210.

Estate of administrator.
On the other hand, an administrator derives his title wholly from the Court. He has none until the letters of administration are granted, and the estate vests in him only from the time of the grant. *Woolley* v. *Clark*, 5 B. & A. 746; 21 & 22 Vict. c. 95, *post*, p. 44.

Accordingly no right of action accrues to an administrator until he has sued out letters of administration.

Thus, if the Statute of Limitations has not begun to run during the lifetime of the intestate, it does not begin to run until letters of administration have been taken out. *Murray* v. *E. I. Co.*, 5 B. & A. 204; *Burdick* v. *Garrick*, L. R. 5 Ch. 233, 241.

Relation back.
This proposition must, however, be taken with some qualification, for it is clear that for some purposes the letters of administration relate back to the time of the death. Went. 115; *ante*, p. 20.

Thus an administrator may have an action of trover or

trespass for the goods of the intestate taken by one before the grant; otherwise there would be no remedy for this wrongdoing. *Tharpe* v. *Stallwood*, 5 M. & G. 760; *Foster* v. *Bates*, 12 M. & W. 233.

And if any one, acting on behalf of the intestate's estate, makes a contract before the grant, the administration will relate back in order that the estate may not lose the benefit of the contract. *Bodger* v. *Arch*, 10 Ex. 333.

And so if services have been rendered for the benefit of the estate under a contract with the person who becomes administrator and who ratifies the contract, the estate of the deceased is liable for such services. *Re Watson*, 19 Q. B. D. 234.

Further, where the administrator might maintain trover for a conversion between the death and the grant, he may waive the tort and recover as on a contract. *Welchman* v. *Sturgis*, 13 Q. B. 552.

So the grant will have the effect of vesting leasehold property in the administrator by relation, so as to enable him to bring actions in respect of it for all matters affecting the same subsequent to the death, and so as to render him liable to account for rents and profits from the death. *Rex* v. *Horsley*, 8 East, 410; *Patten* v. *P.*, 1 Al. & N. 493.

So, too, real estate will now vest in the administrator as from the death of the intestate. 60 & 61 Vict. c. 65, s. 1. But it is conceived that he would not be deemed in possession until entry in the same way as chattels real. *Post*, p. 44.

But the relation back will not effectuate a legal proceeding. Therefore it will not make good a distress or an assignment. *Bacon* v. *Simpson*, 3 M. & W. 87; *Keene* v. *Dee*, 1 Al. & Nap. 496, n.

Again, although an executor *de son tort* cannot plead a retainer for his own debt, yet if he obtains administration he may retain. *Curtis* v. *Vernon*, 3 T. R. 587, 590; and see *ante*, p. 12.

But the relation back will not divest any right legally

vested in another between the death and the grant. *Rex* v. *Horsley*, 8 East, 405.

The rule that a party cannot be made a trespasser by relation is only applicable where the act complained of was lawful at the time. *Tharpe* v. *Stallwood*, 5 M. & G. 760.

<small>Relation back where deceased had only a special property.</small> Where an uncertificated bankrupt was allowed to retain possession of goods acquired after the bankruptcy, his administrator might maintain trover against a third party who had sold the goods between the death and the grant. *Tyson* v. *Chambers*, 9 M. & W. 460.

But there is no such relation back as to chattels in which the deceased had no personal interest, but held merely as the administrator of another, and his representative could not maintain trover even against a mere wrongdoer. *Elliott* v. *Kemp*, 7 M. & W. 306.

<small>Statute runs from death.</small> By the Statute of Limitation (3 & 4 Wm. 4, c. 27), s. 6, it is enacted that for the purposes of the Act an administrator claiming the estate or interest of the deceased shall be deemed to claim as if there had been no interval between the death and the grant.

Until letters of administration are granted, the personal estate of the intestate vests from his death in the Judge of the Probate Court. 21 & 22 Vict. c. 95, s. 19.

<small>Distinction between chattels real and personal as to vesting in possession.</small> All movable goods, though in ever so many different and distant places, vest in the executor in possession on the testator's death. Went. 228.

But it is otherwise of things immovable, as leases for years of land; for of these the executor or administrator is not deemed to be in possession before entry. *Ibid.*

So of leases for years of a rectory, consisting of glebe lands and tithes for years, it may be doubtful if actual possession can be without actual entry into the glebe land. Went. 929.

But a *reversion* of a term which the testator granted for a part of the term, is in the executor immediately by the death of the testator. *Trattle* v. *King*, T. Jones, 170.

And in case of a lease for years of tithes only, it was

held that the executor, though in never so remote a place, should instantly upon the setting out thereof be in actual possession to maintain action of trespass for taking them away. Went. 229.

Quære, whether entry will be necessary in the case of freeholds devolving on the executor under the Land Transfer Act, 1897.

An executor or administrator has his estate as such in *auter droit* merely—that is, as the minister or dispenser of the goods of the dead. Quality of estate of representatives.

If, therefore, he becomes bankrupt, with any property in his possession belonging to the deceased, distinguishable from his own property, it is not distributable under the bankruptcy. Bankruptcy Act, 1883, s. 44. Where he becomes bankrupt.

The trustee cannot seize even *money* which can be distinguished and ascertained to belong to the deceased. *Farr* v. *Newman*, 4 T. R. 621, 648.

And under the bankruptcy of an executor directed to carry on a trade with a limited sum, the general assets are not liable beyond that sum. *Ex parte Garland*, 10 Ves. 110.

But where goods are allowed to remain in the possession of the administrator or the person entitled to administration for a length of time, and that person becomes bankrupt, such goods will be deemed to be in the order and disposition of the bankrupt with the consent of the true owners, and will belong to the trustee. *Fox* v. *Fisher*, 3 B. & A. 185; *Re Thomas*, 1 Phill. 159; *Kitchen* v. *Ibbetson*, 17 Eq. 46; and see Bankruptcy Act, 1883, s. 44 (2), iii.

The bankruptcy of an executor may operate as a forfeiture of a lease of the testator. 1 C. M. & R. 405.

Where a trustee in bankruptcy possesses himself of effects belonging to the bankrupt as executor only, the Court will order the return of such effects to the bankrupt, or appoint a receiver. *Ex parte James*, L. R. 9 Ch. 609; *Ex parte Simmons*, 16 Q. B. D. 308.

Where a bankrupt is executor and residuary legatee and

refuses to get in the assets, the Court will assist the trustee in bankruptcy to collect them in the name of the executor. *Ex parte Butler*, 1 Atk. 213.

Execution for debt of executor. The goods of a testator in the hands of his executor cannot be taken in execution for a judgment against the executor in his own right. *M'Leod* v. *Drummond*, 17 Ves. 168; *Kinderley* v. *Jervis*, 22 Beav.; but see *Quick* v. *Staines*, 1 B. & P. 295.

So if an executor dies indebted, leaving to his executor goods which he had as executor, these are not assets liable to the payment of his debts, but only for the payment of the first testator's. Went. 194.

But after a lapse of six or seven years equity will not restrain by injunction a creditor of an executor from taking in execution property of the testator which is assets in equity. *Ray* v. *R.*, Coop. 264.

But a lapse of three months is not sufficient. *Gaskell* v. *Marshall*, Mood. & R. 132.

The fact that an executor has carried on the business in his own name, and that the testator's assets employed in it are ostensibly the executor's own property, will not entitle a judgment creditor of the executor to take in execution the testator's assets. *Re Morgan*, 18 C. D. 93.

Lapse of time and an enjoyment of the assets in a manner inconsistent with the trusts, coupled with the consent of the beneficiaries, may, however, raise an inference of a gift of the assets to the executor, and entitle his judgment creditor to take them in execution. *Ibid.*

But when the possession and the time which has elapsed are in accordance with the trusts of the will, no such inference can arise. *Ibid.*

Conversion of assets to own use. In some cases the property which the executor or administrator has at first in a representative character may become his own to his own use.

Thus, where an executor mixed the testator's money with his own, the property in the specific coin was of necessity altered, and a creditor could not at law take such money in execution. Went. 196.

But in equity, if an executor pay the testator's money to his own account at his banker's, the person for whom he holds the money can follow it and have a charge on the balance in the banker's hands. *Re Hallett*, 13 C. D. 696.

Again, it was a rule of law that an executor had a right to acquire as a purchaser an absolute title to specific chattels by intending so to deal with them and by paying the testator's debts to an amount exceeding the value of those chattels.

But this is not so in equity, and the executor has under such circumstances no absolute right to the property. *Hearn v. Wells*, 1 Coll. 333.

Again, it has been said that if the debt due to the executor from the testator amount to the full value of all his effects in the executor's hands, there is a complete transmutation of the property in favour of the executor. Toller, 239.

This, however, appears to be doubtful, though he can in such a case retain the whole of the assets without realising them. *Re Gilbert*, (1898) 1 Q. B. 282.

So in the case of a lease of the testator, if the executor pay the rent out of his own purse, the profits to the same amount were at law held to be his. Went. 200.

If the testator's goods be sold under a *fieri facias*, the executor may buy them from the sheriff and so make them his own. *Ibid.*

As an executor may assent to his own legacy, and so vest it in himself, so an administrator who is entitled as one of the next of kin may appropriate to himself his own share of residue. *Elliott v. Kemp*, 7 M. & W. 313.

There is no merger of an estate which a man holds Merger. as executor or administrator with one which he holds in his own right, at all events so far as regards the claims of creditors upon the assets of the deceased. Wms. 562.

The question of merger is of little importance since the Judicature Act, 1873, s. 25.

But it may be stated that, in the absence of special circumstances, a term held by a person in his own right does not merge in the reversion held by the same person as administrator. *Chambers* v. *Kingham*, 10 C. D. 743.

The Quantity of the Estate.

The whole estate vests.

Both at law and equity the whole personal estate of the deceased vests in the executor or administrator, and in the case of a person dying after 1st January, 1898, his real estate also, except copyholds and customary freeholds. 60 & 61 Vict. c. 65, s. 1.

Except joint estates.

But the property, whether real or personal, which the deceased had with a right in any other person to take by survivorship does not pass to his executor or administrator.

In cases, however, of joint estate or possession where there is no survivorship, as in the case of co-parceners or partners, the estate of the deceased will devolve upon his executor or administrator. *Post*, p. 73.

As we have seen, the real estate as well as the personalty now devolves upon the personal representative of any person dying after the 1st January, 1898; but even before that date an executor or administrator might in some instances be seised of real property of the deceased as trustee, or be *ex officio* invested with a power of disposing of it, and a mere charge of debts gave them an implied power of sale.

Again, under the doctrine of equitable conversion real estate directed to be sold or contracted to be sold was considered in equity as personalty, and passed to the personal representative as part of his assets, and they could convey to the purchaser. Conveyancing Act, 1881, s. 4.

Real estate now devolves on representatives.

Now, however, by the Land Transfer Act, 1897, both real and personal estate, of persons dying after 1st January,

1898, will devolve upon the same personal representative, whose powers in respect of personal estate shall apply to real estate (sect. 2 (2)), and real estate shall be administered as if it were personal estate (sect. 2 (3)) ; but the order in which real and personal assets are now administered shall not be altered (sect. 2 (3)), and subject as aforesaid the personal representatives shall hold the real estate as trustees for the persons by law beneficially entitled thereto (sect. 2 (1)).

Hence it follows that on the death of any person after 1897 the whole of his property vests in his personal representatives, with the exception of (1) joint property with a right of survivorship in another person, and (2) copyholds or customary freehold, whether held beneficially or otherwise.

The Estate of Several Executors or Administrators.

If there be several executors or administrators, they are regarded in the light of an individual person. They have a joint and entire interest in the effects of the deceased, including chattels real, and now in the real estate also (60 & 61 Vict. c. 65, s. 1), which interest is incapable of being divided, and in case of death will vest in the survivor without any new grant by the Court.

Consequently, if one of two executors or administrators grant or release his interest in the assets to the other, nothing will pass, because each was possessed of the whole. So, if one of several executors release but his part of the debt, the whole is discharged. Godolph. pt. 2, c. 16, s. 1.

So if two men hold a lease as executors, and one of them grant all his interest in the lease, the whole term will pass, because each has an entire authority and interest ; and for the same reason no partition can be made between them. Dyer, 23 b.

But if one of several sell the goods, he alone can

maintain an action for the price, or if one contracts he must sue alone. *Heath* v. *Chilton*, 12 M. & W. 632.

But one of several cannot sell or transfer real estate. 60 & 61 Vict. c. 65, s. 2 (2).

Since each has an entire interest, it follows that the act of one in possessing himself of the effects is the act of the others, so as to entitle them to a joint interest in possession, and a joint right of action, but not so as to create a joint personal liability. 4 Tyrwh. 563; but see *Heath* v. *Chilton*, *supra*.

They cannot for the same reason maintain an action in right of the deceased upon a contract made by the defendant with one of themselves. *Rose* v. *Poulton*, 2 B. & Ad. 822.

And see *post*, Chap. VIII.

The Estate of the Executor of an Executor, of an Administrator de bonis non, etc.

An executor of an executor, in however remote a series, has the same interest in the effects of the first testator as the first and immediate executor.

As to the devolution of the office, and when the chain is broken, see *ante*, p. 7.

Administrator de bonis non.
An administrator *de bonis non* is entitled to all the personal estate not administered by the first executor or administrator.

And wherever assets are in the hands of a third person at the death of an administrator or executor intestate, the administrator *de bonis non* may sue for their recovery. *Langford* v. *Mahony*, 4 Dr. & War. 81, 107.

There is such a privity of estate between the former executor or administrator and the administrator *de bonis non*, that the latter will be compelled to carry the agreements of the former into execution. *Hirst* v. *Smith*, 7 T. R. 183.

If the original executor or administrator has fraudulently aliened the assets for his own use in collusion with the vendee, such assets will be considered in equity as unadministered, and will pass to the administrator *de bonis non*, who may have the sale set aside. *Cubbidge* v. *Boatwright*, 1 Russ. C. C. 549.

If the property in any of the effects has been changed by the original representative, and has vested in him in his individual capacity, such effects will go to his own representative, and not to the administrator *de bonis non*. *Drue* v. *Baylie*, 1 Freem. 462; but see *Skeffington* v. *Budd*, 9 Cl. & F. 220, 248.

Again, the administrator *de bonis non* is entitled to all debts due and owing to the original testator or intestate; but in this instance also the original executor or administrator may have so altered the property in a *chose in action* as to transmit it to his own personal representative. *Barker* v. *Talcot*, 1 Vern. 433.

But when the substituted cause of action is such that the first representative may sue in his representative character, the right of action devolves upon the administrator *de bonis non*. *Catherwood* v. *Chabaud*, 1 Barn. & Cres. 150, 156.

With respect to enforcing judgments obtained by the original representative, the rights of the administrator *de bonis non* would seem now to be governed by R. S. C., Ord. 42 and 23.

If the original representative, in his own name, brings trespass for goods taken out of his possession which were the deceased's, and dies, his own representative must take execution; but in the case of an executor of an executor he shall hold proceeds of the execution as assets of the first testator, and in the case of a representative of an original administrator, or of an administrator of an original intestate executor, he shall be compelled in equity to pay them to the administrator *de bonis non*. *Yaites* v. *Gough*, Yelv. 33.

Married woman executrix.

The Married Women's Property Act, 1882, places a married woman, whenever married, in the position of a *feme sole*; and as under sect. 24 the husband of an executrix or administratrix is under no liability unless he has intermeddled, there ceases to be any reason for his administering in his wife's right for his own safety.

CHAPTER V.

PERSONAL ESTATE IN POSSESSION.

Chattels Real.

CHATTELS real are transmitted in the same manner as chattels personal—that is, they go in the first place to the executors for the payment of the testator's debts, for which purpose any one without the others has an absolute power to dispose of them. But if bequeathed they pass to the legatee without any assignment by the mere signification of the executor's assent. Burton, 306; *Re Culverhouse*, (1896) 2 Ch. 251. Chattels real.

All personal chattels vest in the executor in possession upon the testator's death. But it is otherwise of chattels real, as for instance a term of years; for of these the executor or administrator is not deemed to be in possession before entry. This is the principal distinction between chattels real and chattels personal. Wentw. 228; *ante*, p. 44. Vest on entry.

Almost the only chattels real occurring in practice are terms of years and next presentations. As to the latter, see Wentw. 173; *Rennell* v. *Lincoln*, 7 B. & C. 147; and *post*, p.74.

Chattels real, though not of much importance in themselves, have become of some interest in consequence of the Land Transfer Act, 1897, which provides that on the death of any person after 1st January, 1898, his real estate shall devolve on his personal representative as if it were a chattel real, and that all enactments and rules of law relating to the effect of probate or letters of administration Real estate now devolves like chattels real.

as respects chattels real and as respects the dealing with chattels real before probate or administration shall apply to real estate so far as the same are applicable, except that some or one of several representatives cannot sell or transfer real estate. Sect. 2 (2).

Real estate, therefore, unlike real chattels, is not to be disposed of by some or one only of several representatives. But it will pass, by the mere assent of the executors, to the devisee without conveyance. Sect. 3 (1).

The chattels real which went to the executor or administrator were not confined to leases for years of lands, but extended to chattel interests in incorporeal hereditaments, such as leases for years of commons, tithes, fairs, markets, and the like.

<small>Terms of years.</small>

Formerly only leases and terms of a chattel quality— that is, chattels real—went to the executor or administrator, but he had no interest in the freehold terms or leases. All leases and terms, however, of a person dying after 1897, now vest in his representative.

A lease for years made to a man and his *heirs* went to his executor, and so did a lease for years made to a corporation sole and his *successors*. Co. Lit. 46 b.

And so did the estate of a tenant from year to year. *James* v. *Dean*, 11 Ves. 393.

Even when a term for years is specifically devised, it will in the first instance vest in the executor for the usual purposes to which the assets shall be applied, and the legatee has no right to enter without the executor's assent. *Post*, Chap. XI.

This proposition also applies to real estate of any person dying after 1st January, 1898. 60 & 61 Vict. c. 65.

If the testator had a term for years, this vests in his personal representative, and he cannot refuse it though it be worth nothing, for the executorship or administratorship is entire and must be renounced *in toto* or not at all. *Billinghurst* v. *Spearman*, 1 Salk. 297 ; *Ackland* v. *Pring*, 2 M. & G. 937.

But he may, it seems, surrender a lease which is a *damnosa hereditas. Reid* v. *Tenterden,* 4 Tyr. 111; and see 4 Tyr. 120, n.

As to his liability under the covenants of a lease where there are no assets, see *post,* Chap. XIV.

Estates *pur autre vie* and mortgage estates are not, strictly speaking, chattels real, but may be conveniently dealt with here.

With respect to estates *pur autre vie* where there is no disposition by will and no special occupant thereof, they will go to the personal representative; and if they come to the executor or administrator either by reason of special occupancy or by virtue of the Act (1 Vict. c. 26, s. 6), they shall be assets in his hands and go in the same manner as personal estate. *Reynolds* v. *Wright,* 2 D. F. & J. 590.

<small>Estates *pur autre vie.*</small>

An estate *pur autre vie* where the heir is special occupant is, however, real estate, and will, it seems, devolve as such under the Land Transfer Act, 1897. *Post,* p. 74.

With regard to mortgages, the mortgage debt always went to the personal representative, even where the legal estate went to the heir or devisee.

<small>Mortgages.</small>

And by the Conv. Act, 1881, all estates vested in any person solely by way of mortgage must devolve on the personal representative of any person dying after 31st December, 1881.

But a mortgagee might, as between his real and personal representative, by declaration convert the mortgage as well as any other part of his personal estate into land and make it pass accordingly. Wms. 603.

And though as to persons dying after 1st January, 1898, their real and personal representative will be the same, yet questions will still arise as between the persons beneficially entitled to the real and personal estate respectively, for the Land Transfer Act does not alter the rights of the persons beneficially entitled.

So, too, where a mortgage merges, questions may still arise as between the persons entitled to the personal estate and those entitled to the real estate.

Where a sale takes place in the lifetime of the mortgagor, the surplus is personal estate; where after his death, it is real estate. *Bourne* v. *B.*, 2 Ha. 35.

Where land was devised to executors for payment of debts, they took only a chattel interest; but under 1 Vict. c. 26, s. 30, the whole estate of the testator passes unless a definite term or estate is given to them. And now all freehold real estate vests in them. 60 & 61 Vict. c. 65.

Personal representatives may also become entitled to chattels real by condition or remainder. And also to contingent and executory interests therein. Fearne, 554; *post*, p. 71.

Chattels Real of Wife.

By sect. 1 (1) of the Married Women's Property Act, 1882, a married woman can now hold or dispose of by will or otherwise any property as her separate property as if she were a *feme sole*, without the intervention of any trustee.

By sect. 2 every woman married after 1st January, 1883, can hold and dispose of as if she were a *feme sole* all property belonging to her at the time of marriage or acquired after marriage.

And by sect. 5 every woman married before 1st January, 1883, can in the same manner hold and dispose of all property her title to which accrues after the Act.

Women, however, married before 1st January, 1883, in addition to the powers conferred by the Act, still retain the same power to dispose of chattels real settled to their separate use, or (if married after 9th August, 1870) of chattels real acquired by them as next of kin of an intestate, as they possessed before the Act. Sects. 19 and 22.

The effect of this Act is, it seems, to extend the power which before the Act a married woman had of disposing of such chattels real as were settled to her separate use, and to give the same power to a woman married before

1st January, 1883, in respect of any chattels real her title to which accrues to her after that date, and to a woman married on or after 1st January, 1883, in respect of all chattels real whensoever her title to them may accrue. Wms. 607.

It follows that, if the wife survive her husband, his executor or administrator has no right whatever to such chattels as by the statute are made the separate property of the wife, but the property remains in and survives to the wife. *Ibid.*

And if the husband survive the wife, it would seem that in respect of those chattels real over which a wife by the statute has a complete power of disposal as a *feme sole*, if she dies intestate without disposing of them, her husband has a right to them as her administrator; and to establish his title he must take out administration to her. *Ibid.; Hope* v. *Hope,* (1892) 2 Ch. 336. But see *Surman* v. *Wharton,* (1891) 1 Q. B. 491.

The Act does not affect the devolution of the wife's property, but only the *jus mariti.* The effect of the Act appears to be merely (1) that the husband is deprived of the power of divesting his wife of her chattels real during coverture; and (2) that if she does not alien them in her lifetime or by will, and the husband survive, he will take such chattels real as are affected by the Act as her administrator. Wms. 606.

As to the law relating to chattels real of wife previous to the M. W. P. Act, 1882, see Wms. 608.

CHATTELS PERSONAL IN POSSESSION.

Chattels Animate.

Such chattels animate as are tame and domestic, as horses, dogs, kine, sheep, poultry, and the like, pass to the personal representative; but *secus*, generally speaking,   Domestic animals.

with regard to wild animals, in which a man can have no property transmissible to his representatives. Black. Comm. 390.

A qualified property may, however, subsist in the latter class *per industriam hominis* by a man's reclaiming or taming them, though if they become wild again the property ceases; or *propter impotentiam* by reason of their being unable to get away; and these shall go to the executors or administrators. *Ibid.*; Wentw. 143.

Game.

Deer in a legal park—*i.e.* a park by grant or prescription—conies, partridges, and other game are considered as incident to the freehold, and will now pass to the personal representative as real estate, though deer may be so tame as to pass as chattels personal. *Morgan v. Abergavenny*, 8 C. B. 768; *Ford v. Tynte*, 2 J. & H. 150.

If, however, the deceased had only a term for years in the land, the deer, conies, and other game will go to the executor or administrator as personal estate—that is, he will have a right to take as many as he pleases during the term, provided he leaves enough for stores; otherwise it would be waste. Co. Lit. 58 a; but see 7 Ves. 488.

Chattels Vegetable.

Trees.

Growing trees and plants are incident to the inheritance, and will pass to the representative as real estate. They may, however, by grant or reservation, be divided from the land, although in fact they remain annexed to it, and will pass to the personal representative of the vendor or purchaser as personal estate. Wentw. 148.

When trees are severed they will, generally speaking, if timber, either by law or custom, go to the owner of the first estate of inheritance. If not timber they will, in general, go to the tenant, and consequently his personal representative. *Herlakenden's Case*, 4 Co. 63.

Fruit and other produce follow the soil, and go to the heir until severed from the trees. Wentw. 146.

Emblements, which are the corn and other annual crops, go to the personal representative as against the heir, but not as against a joint tenant or a purchaser or devisee. *Emblements.*

The rule also applies to every one who has an uncertain estate or interest, if his estate determines by the act of God before severance. Thus the personal representative of a tenant for life is entitled to emblements to the exclusion of the remainderman or reversioner, because in this case the estate of the tenant is determined by the act of God. Co. Lit. 55 b.

The personal representatives of an incumbent of a benefice are likewise entitled to emblements of the glebe lands; but an incumbent who resigns is not so entitled. *Bulwer* v. *Bulwer*, 2 B. & Ald. 470.

The representatives of a tenant in dower, a tenant by the curtesy, and a tenant at will are entitled to emblements. Co. Lit. 55 b.

Where there is a right to emblements, there is a right to free entry in order to cut and carry them away. Co. Lit. 56 a.

The executors of a landlord tenant for life are entitled to a charge on the holding for compensation paid by them under the Agricultural Holdings Act, 1883, s. 29. *Gough* v. *G.*, (1891) 2 Q. B. 665. *Compensation for improvements.*

Chattels Personal Inanimate.

These are all the movable inanimate goods and effects of the deceased, and pass to his personal representative as personal estate; and, though specifically bequeathed to a legatee, will not vest in him till the executor has assented. *Chattels personal.*

The right, however, of the personal representative to some of these is barred to some extent in favour of certain *What do not pass to executor.*

special claimants : 1. Heirlooms in respect of the heir or successor 2. Fixtures in respect of the heir, or devisee, or remainderman, or reversioner. 3. Paraphernalia in respect of the widow.

Heirlooms.

Heirlooms are such goods and personal chattels as go by *special custom* to the heir along with the inheritance, and not to the personal representative of the last proprietor.

Heirlooms are not devisable (Co. Lit. 185 b) ; though the owner may dispose of them during his life as he may of timber. Blackst. ii. 429.

They are not land, but movables (*Ibid.* ii. 17) ; and therefore are not affected by the Land Transfer Act, 1897. *Post*, p. 75.

Besides heirlooms, there are chattels in the nature of heirlooms which go in the same way to the heir. Wms. 635.

Chattels may also be devised or limited in strict settlement, so as to be transmissible like heirlooms. But they will be the absolute property of the first person seised in tail, and on his death devolve on his personal representatives. *Scarsdale* v. *Curzon*, 1 J. & H. 40. But see Jarman, ii. 548, 3rd ed., as to how this way may be obviated.

A sale of heirlooms may be made under the Settled Land Act, 1882, s. 37.

Although no testator can exempt any part of his personal. estate from payment of debts, yet when he directs certain effects to be treated as heirlooms it is the duty of the executors as far as possible to preserve them, and, unless compelled, not to apply them in the payment of debts. *Clarke* v. *Ormonde*, 1 Jacob, 114.

Although it is the general rule that chattels of a corporation sole cannot go in succession, yet there are exceptions, not only in the case of choses in action, but in cases of chattels which go to the successor of a corporation sole in the manner of heirlooms. Thus the ornaments of the chapel of a preceding bishop belong to the succeeding bishop. Wms. 639.

Fixtures.

As between the personal representative and the heir, the old rule, *Quicquid plantatur solo, solo cedit*, still obtains with some rigour in favour of the inheritance, and against the right to disannex anything which has been affixed thereto. <small>As between heir and executor.</small>

This rule has been somewhat relaxed with regard to trade fixtures; but it has been laid down in the House of Lords that the principle upon which a departure has been made from the old rule in favour of trade has no application to a case between the heir and executor. *Fisher v. Dixon*, 12 Cl. & F. 312, 328.

The rule is most strict between the heir and the executor.

This rule has been also relaxed with regard to fixtures set up for ornament or domestic convenience. *Beck v. Rebow*, 1 P. Wms. 94; *Harvey v. Harvey*, 2 Stra. 1141.

But on the other hand the old rule has been adhered to. *Colegrave v. Dias*, 2 B. & C. 76; *King v. St. Dunstan*, 4 B. & C. 686; *Bain v. Brand*, 1 A. C. 762. The law on this point is by no means settled.

As between executor and devisee, there seems no doubt that if it is apparent that the intention was that the fixtures should go with the freehold they will pass to the devisee, although they are of such a sort that the executor might have been entitled to them against the heir. *Wood v. Gaynon*, 1 Ambl. 395; *Norton v. Dashwood*, (1896) 2 Ch. 497. <small>As between executor and devisee.</small>

Executor of tenant for life and remainderman.

As between executor of a tenant for life and remainderman, the rule is more favourable for the executors. Especially as regards trade fixtures. *Lawton* v. *Lawton*, 3 Atk. 13; *Dudley* v. *Warde*, 1 Ambl. 113.

With regard to the right of the executor of tenant for life against remainderman to ornamental fixtures, not a single case is to be found; but since the law is more favourable to the executor of tenant for life than to the executor of tenant in fee, it is clear that all cases which support the right of the latter, *à fortiori* support the right of the former.

Paraphernalia.

The Married Women's Property Act has not abolished the general law as to gifts of paraphernalia. *Tasker* v. *T.*, (1895) P. 1.

A wife may therefore still acquire paraphernalia by gift from her husband, so as to exclude his executors or administrators.

Donations mortis causâ.

Before leaving the subject of the estate of personal representatives in the chattels personal in possession, it may be well to mention another species of interest in the property of the deceased which vests neither in the personal representative nor the heir.

This is a *donatio mortis causâ*. Where a man lies in extremity, or being surprised with sickness and not having an opportunity of making his will, but lest he should die before he could make it he gives with his own hands his goods to his friends about him: this, if he dies, shall operate as a legacy; but if he recovers, then the property reverts to him. *Hedges* v. *Hedges*, Prec. Chanc. 269.

Of such a gift there are three essentials: 1. The gift must be with a view to the donor's death. 2. It must be conditioned to take effect only on the death of the donor by his existing disorder. 3. There must be a delivery, and the donor must part with the dominion as well as possession.

Probate of it is not necessary, nor is the executor's assent. But it is liable to duty and to the debts of the testator upon deficiency of assets.

See further on this subject, Wms. 681; Rop. Leg. c. 1; Brett, L. C. 31.

CHAPTER VI.

CHOSES IN ACTION.

Generally.

What actions survive.
ALL personal actions founded upon any obligation, contract, debt, covenant, or other *duty* which the deceased might have brought, survive to his personal representatives.

The executor or administrator is the only representative of a deceased that the law will regard in respect of his property, and no word introduced into a contract or obligation can transfer to another his exclusive rights derived from such representation.

This representation in matters of contract is so complete that, generally speaking, it is not necessary that the executor or administrator should be named in the terms of the contract, except where personal considerations are of the foundation of the contract, as in cases of principal and agent and master and servant. *Farrow* v. *Wilson*, L. R. 4 C. P. 745.

Actions for tort.
Notwithstanding the old rule, *Actio personalis moritur cum personâ*, an executor or administrator may now have an action for all injuries to the personal estate whereby it has become less beneficial to him, whatever the form of action may be. 1 Saund. 217, n. (1).

Thus he may have an action for trespass or trover; an action to recover the price paid by the intestate for valueless shares (*Twycross* v. *Grant*, 4 C. P. D. 40; but see *Re Duncan*, (1899) 1 Ch. 387); an action to restrain the infringement of a trade mark and damages (*Oakey* v. *Dalton*, 35 C. D. 700); an action for falsely and maliciously publishing a statement calculated to injure the right of property in a trade mark. *Hatchard* v. *Mege*, 18 Q. B. D. 771; and other actions of a like kind. See *post*, Chap. XIV.

But he cannot maintain an action merely because the person injured incurred in his lifetime some expenditure of money in consequence of the personal injury. *Pulling* v. *G. E. Ry.*, 9 Q. B. D. 110, 112.

Actions for tort to the person or to the freehold of the testator do not as a general rule survive. Went. 166; but see *Williams* v. *Breedon*, 1 Bos. & Pull. 380.

But it has been thought that this is not the case with regard to chattels real. Went. 169.

It is conceived, therefore, that actions for tort to the freehold will now survive, since freeholds now devolve upon the representative.

By 3 & 4 Wm. 4, c. 42, s. 2, the personal representative may, within a year after the death of the testator, bring an action for injury to real estate committed within six months before the death, and the damages shall be part of the personal estate. *Quære* whether this applies to chattels real.

An action for damages for obstruction to ancient lights lies against executors or administrators, though the obstruction was completed more than six months before the death of the obstructor. *Jenks* v. *Clifden*, (1897) 1 Ch. 694.

By Lord Campbell's Act (9 & 10 Vict. c. 93), an action is maintainable against any person causing death through wrongful act, neglect, or default. The action is to be for the benefit of certain relations, and shall be brought by the personal representative. Sect. 2. The cause of action is beyond that which the deceased would have had. *Pym* v. *G. N. Ry.*, 4 Best & Sm. 406. Executors can bring an action in Chancery Division for declaration as to the persons entitled to the money. *Bulmer* v. *Bulmer*, 25 Ch. D. 409.

By 27 & 28 Vict. c. 95, where no action is brought by personal representative, it may be brought by persons interested.

Judgment and satisfaction under Lord Campbell's Act is not a bar to a second action for damage to the personal estate. *Leggott* v. *G. N. Ry.*, 1 Q. B. D. 599.

In like manner a personal representative can sue for compensation under the Employers' Liability Act, 1880, and Workmen's Compensation Act, 1897.

Actions *ex quasi contractu*.   If a personal representative can show that damage has accrued to the personal estate by the breach of an express or implied promise, he may sustain an action at common law, although the action is in some sort founded on a tort. *Alton* v. *M. Ry. Co.*, 19 C. B. N. S. 213, 242; *Bradshaw* v. *L. & Y. Ry.*, L. R. 10 C. P. 189; and see *Leggott* v. *G. N. Ry., supra*.

The rule that the personal representative may sue on all contracts with the testator *broken in his lifetime* must be understood with some qualification.

No action it seems is maintainable upon an express or implied promise to the deceased, where the damage consisted entirely of injury to the deceased and without any injury to his personal estate. *Chamberlain* v. *Williamson*, 2 M. & S. 408; and see *Finlay* v. *Chirney*, 20 Q. B. D. 494.

A further qualification is in respect of actions upon covenants real, which in many cases survive to the heir of the covenantee, even where he takes nothing by descent. Fitz. N. B. 145.

But if such a covenant is broken in the lifetime of the testator or intestate, it would seem that the rule was that the personal representative might sue upon it. But see *King* v. *Jones*, 4 M. & S. 188.

It is conceived, however, that the right to sue upon covenants real will now descend to the personal representatives and not to the heir, since the freeholds now devolve upon the former.

It seems now, however, that an executor may sue on a

contract broken in the testator's life even where there is no damage to the personal estate. *Raymond* v. *Fitch*, 2 C. M. & R. 588; *Ricketts* v. *Weaver*, 12 M. & W. 718.

An action will lie for an executor or administrator upon a promise made to the deceased for the exclusive benefit of a third party. *Bafield* v. *Collard*, Sty. 6.

Particular Instances.

Where the Representative is entitled to Choses in Action.

An annuity is so far considered personal property that, although granted to a man and his heirs, it is not a hereditament within the Statute of Mortmain. But on the other hand it partakes of the nature of real estate in that, when granted with words of inheritance, it descends to the heir to the exclusion of the executor. Wms. 718. *Annuities.*

Unless, however, words of inheritance are employed it will pass to the executors. *Parsons* v. *Parsons*, L. R. 8 Eq. 260, where an annuity was given to A. B. *for ever*. See also *Stafford* v. *Buckley*, 2 Ves. Sen. 170; *Aubin* v. *Daly*, 4 B. & Ald. 59.

Shares in companies are generally personal estate (Companies Act, 1862, s. 22); but shares in some of the old canal companies have been held to be real estate. *Shares.*

Stock in the public funds is personal property; and though it was at one time doubted, it is now settled that, like all other personal property, it is assets in the hands of the executor, and till he assents the legatee has no right to the legacy. 33 & 34 Vict. c. 71, s. 23. *Stock.*

An interest in the testator's literary property and also certain works of art may devolve on the personal representative, pursuant to several statutes. Wms. 724. *Copyright.*

An interest may also vest in him by virtue of a patent granted to the testator; and by the Patents Act, 1883, s. 34, an application may be made by the personal representative to patent an invention of the testator. *Patent.*

F 2

Rent.

Where a man seised in fee makes a lease reserving rent, the whole rent which becomes due after his death shall go to his heir, even though expressly reserved to his executors. But if a lessee for years make an underlease the rent accruing after his death shall go to his personal representative even though reserved to the heir.

Where no reversion is left in the lessor and the rent is reserved to his executors, administrators, and assigns, it will go to them and not to the heir. *Jennison* v. *Lexington*, 1 P. Wms. 555.

If the rent be reserved for years and be severed from the reversion, it may then go to the personal representative although the reversion goes to the heir. *Knolle's Case*, Dyer, 5 b.

Arrears of rent accrued in the lifetime of the deceased shall in all cases go to the personal representative as part of his personal estate. Went. 129.

By the Apportionment Act, 1870, all rents are apportionable.

Servants.

By the death of a master his servant is discharged, and therefore the executors or administrators of the former can bring no action to enforce the contract of service after his death. Wentw. 141.

Nor has the executor or administrator, generally speaking, any interest in an apprentice bound to the deceased. *Post*, 168; and see *Ferns* v. *Carr*, 28 C. D. 409.

Copyhold fines.

If the lord of a manor admit a copyholder, but die before the fine be paid, it will go to his executors. So also of reliefs and heriots. Co. Lit. 47 b.

In the case of a sole corporation no chose in action can go in succession (*Fulwood's Case*, 4 Co. 65 a); but by custom it may.

Formerly, although the deceased had in his lifetime assigned his choses in action, still upon his death they vested in his personal representative because they were not assignable. Now, however, they are assignable. Jud. Act, 1873, s. 25 (6).

The executor of a bankrupt is not entitled to his choses in action, for they are vested in the trustee in bankruptcy. Bankruptcy Act, 1883, s. 50 (5).

The personal representative of a wife cannot apparently recover arrears of pin-money or arrears of alimony. Wms. 735.

Right of Personal Representative to Choses in Action as respects Husband and Wife.

The result of the Married Women's Property Act, 1882, ss. 1, 2, 5, 19, is that, with regard to such property as by sects. 2 and 5 is made the separate property of the wife, the husband will not be able, if he survive her, to claim such property *jure mariti*, but only as administrator of his wife, and this equally whether the property consists of chattels in possession or choses in action, and whether or not the choses in action have been reduced into possession.

As to the law relating to women married before the Act and acquiring title before that date, see Wms. 737.

Where Action accrues after Death of Testator or Intestate.

Upon the death of the testator or intestate, if any injury is done to his goods, his personal representative may bring an action for damages for the tort, either in his own name or in his representative capacity, and whether he ever had actual possession or not. *Hollis* v. *Smith*, 10 East, 295; 2 Saund. 47, n.; *Fraser* v. *S. C. Co.*, 1 Ad. & E. 354.

Actions for torts done in executor's time.

As already stated, these actions may be maintained although the injury was done before probate or administration granted. *Ante*, p. 43.

An executor as such may maintain ejectment where the testator had a lease for years or from year to year upon an ouster after his death. *Slade's Case*, 4 Co. 95 a.

So an executor or administrator may sue as such as well as in his own name, upon a contract made with him in his representative capacity. And this he may do not only in cases where the consideration flows from the deceased, but also where it flows directly from himself as executor. Thus an executor may sue as such not only on an account stated with him as executor concerning money due to the testator, but also on an account stated with him as executor concerning money due to him as executor. Wms. 762.

It is now firmly established that wherever the money recovered will be assets the executor may sue for it and declare in his representative character. *Abbott* v. *Parfitt*, L. R. 6 Q. B. 346.

But it is not established that *all* the executors may join in suing on a contract whether they all made the contract or not. *Heath* v. *Chilton*, 12 M. & W. 632.

Where an administrator as such has paid that which he ought not he may in the same character recover it back again. *Clark* v. *Hougham*, 2 B. & C. 149.

An executor or administrator may bring an action on a judgment recovered by him as such, and he may sue either in his representative capacity or in his own name. *Crawford* v. *Whittal*, Dougl. 4, n. (1).

Suits accruing in time of executor on contracts made with testator.

In many cases an action on which the deceased himself could not have sued, may accrue to the executor or administrator in his own time, upon a contract made with the testator or intestate in his lifetime.

It has already appeared that where a cause of action accrued in the lifetime of the testator on a contract made to him, without naming his executors, or to him and his *assigns*, such *chose in action*, generally speaking, is transmitted to the executor (*ante*, p. 64), and the executor can also sue on such contract, although the action does not accrue till after the death of the testator.

Thus if A. covenants with B. to make him a lease, and B. dies before it is made, his executor as such may have an action on the covenant. *Chapman v. Dalton*, Plowd. 286.

So if A. covenant to grant a lease to B. and his *assigns*, and B. dies before the grant of the lease, it must be made to his executors as his assigns, or they may bring covenant. Went. 215.

Likewise a right to sue which never existed in the deceased may accrue to his representative by remainder or by reason of a condition made to the deceased. Went. 181.

The pledgor has his whole life to redeem, unless called upon by the pledgee to redeem, and on his death, without such a demand, his personal representative may redeem. Story's Eq. § 1032; *Kemp v. Westbrook*, 1 Ves. 278. {Executor of pledgor.}

Executory and Contingent Interests.

Contingent and executory interests, whether in real or personal estate, are transmissible to the representatives of a party dying before the contingency, upon which they depend, takes effect. Fearne, 554; Wills Act, 1837, s. 3.

And such interests, though they do not vest in possession, may vest in right so as to be transmissible to executors or administrators. *Chauncey v. Graydon*, 2 Atk. 616; *Peck v. Parrott*, 1 Ves. Sen. 236.

But it is obvious that where the contingency is the endurance of the life of the party entitled till a particular period, the interest itself will be extinguished by the death before that period arrives, and will not be transmissible to his executors or administrators.

The executor or administrator of the object of a power cannot be an appointee under it. Thus, where a wife has power to appoint among children, and one dies before appointment, no part can be appointed to the executor or administrator. *Maddison v. Andrew*, 1 Ves. Sen. 59.

Of the Continuing of Actions.

The practice with respect to the continuance of suits when the cause of action survives to the executor or administrator of the deceased is now regulated by R. S. C., Ord. 17.

As to death after judgment and before execution, see R. S. C., Ord. 42, r. 23.

The authority of an arbitrator is determined by the death of either party; but *quære* whether the death of one party of one side does so. *Re Hare*, 6 Bingh. N. C. 163. But by special reference an award may be made available for or against the personal representative. *Tyler* v. *Jones*, 3 B. & C. 144. Only, however, where the cause of action survives for or against the personal representative. *Bowker* v. *Evans*, 15 Q. B. D. 565. *Aliter* where the cause of action has been determined and damages only are referred for assessment. *Chapman* v. *Day*, 48 L. T. 907.

The authority of a solicitor in a cause is determined by the death of his client, consequently further proceedings must be made by the personal representative. *Palmer* v. *Reiffenstein*, 1 M. & G. 94.

By 22 & 23 Vict. c. 35, s. 26, no trustee, executor or administrator doing any act *bonâ fide* under a power of attorney is to be liable by reason of death or other avoidance of the power.

CHAPTER VII.

REAL ESTATE.

REAL estate now devolves upon personal representatives as if it were a chattel real, notwithstanding any testamentary disposition. 60 & 61 Vict. c. 65, s. 1. *What real estate passes.*

But this does not include property vested in the deceased with a right in any other person to take by survivorship. *Ibid.* Therefore the estate of a coparcener is not within this exception and will pass under the Act. See *Re Matson*, (1897) 2 Ch. 507.

Nor does it include copyholds nor customary freeholds where admission is necessary. *Ibid.*

The section applies to real estate over which the deceased executes by will a general power of appointment, though it has no application to limited powers.

Whether this is so where the appointment fails by the death of the appointee in the testator's lifetime depends upon the intention of the testator. *Re Pinède*, 12 C. D. 667.

Real and personal property, therefore, over which a general power is exercised, become assets for payment of debts.

And this appears to be the case where the donee is a married woman. *Re Ann*, (1894) 1 Ch. 549, 555.

But personal property subject to a general power does not pass to the executor *virtute officii*, and therefore, it seems, still remains equitable assets only. See *Jenney v. Andrews*, 6 Madd. 264.

It is assumed that equitable as well as legal estates will

pass, notwithstanding the marginal note speaks only of the "legal interest." 11 C. D. 460.

The term real estate ordinarily includes incorporeal hereditaments, such as advowsons, tithes, commons, offices, dignities, franchises, annuities charged on land, and rent-charges. It would seem, therefore, that these will pass, with, however, some obvious limitations.

It has been suggested that the true criterion of what real estate passes under the Act is to be found in the words "notwithstanding any testamentary disposition," or, in other words, that the true test is whether the estate is devisable. There is much force in the suggestion, and it has the merit of avoiding several difficult questions.

There is little doubt that a vested remainder, whether present or future, will pass to the representative just as a chattel real in remainder does. Went. 189.

And just as contingent and executory estates and possibilities in chattels real, accompanied by an interest, pass to the personal representative of a person dying before the contingency takes effect, so it would seem similar interests in freeholds will pass in the same way. Fearne, 554. *Ante*, p. 71.

An estate *pur autre vie* where the heir is special occupant will, it is thought, pass under this sub-section. Comp. sect. 4 of Conv. Act, 1881; Wolst. 24; and see *Re Sheppard*, (1897) 2 Ch. 67. *Ante*, p. 55.

Money to be invested in land must in any case pass to the personal representative; but he will, it seems, hold it as real estate.

An advowson will pass to the representative as real estate, but not the right to nominate, unless the living be vacant. Cripps, 456.

So, too, rent-charges will pass.

Formerly representatives were only liable for arrears of rent-charge accrued during lifetime of deceased, because the land out of which it arose did not pass to them (*Eton Coll. v. Beauchamp*, 1 C. C. 131); but now, since the land itself devolves upon them, they will apparently be liable as terre-tenant, so long as they are in possession.

Rights of entry, which are devisable, will, it is thought, pass. See *Pemberton* v. *Barnes*, (1899) 1 Ch. 544.

The widow's right to dower will, it is thought, be excepted from real estate so passing. *Spyer* v. *Hyatt*, 20 B. 621.

Heirlooms, not being real estate and not being devisable, will not, it is thought, pass under the Act. *Ante*, p. 60.

An annuity to A. "and his heirs" is a hereditament; but *quære* whether it will pass under this section.

Chattels real will continue to pass under the old law; but *quære* whether they are "land" within sect. 3.

As real estate will now devolve like a chattel real, it will not, it is thought, vest in possession until entry by the personal representative.

The Act, though in its title and preamble purporting to establish a real representative, does not in terms authorise the appointment of real representatives, but merely provides that the personal representative shall be also the real representative. As to titles of Acts, see (1899) 1 Ch. 1. Whether separate executors can be appointed of real estate.

It is conceived, therefore, that a testator could not appoint separate executors of his real estate, as being contrary to the spirit and policy of the Act. See *Re Parker*, (1894) 1 Ch. 707; *Re Ardern*, (1898) P. 147.

But in any case they would have to convey as personal representatives in order to imply a covenant against incumbrances.

It will be seen that the vesting is to take place on the death. Sect. 1 (1). But where there are no representatives the legal estate will vest in the heir-at-law, until divested by the constitution of legal representatives. *John* v. *J.*, (1898) 2 Ch. 573, 576. When vesting takes place.

Sed quære, whether this applies to executors.

The Act does not bind the Crown; and, therefore, real estate vests in the Crown by escheat, and not in the Treasury Solicitor. *Re Hartley*, (1899) P. 40. Crown.

Probate and letters of administration may now be granted Probate of real estate.

in respect of real estate only, although there is no personal estate. Sect. 1 (3).

And in granting letters of administration the Court will have regard to the rights of persons interested in the real estate, and the heir, if not one of the next of kin, shall be equally entitled to the grant with the next of kin. Sect. 2 (4).

All rules, orders and instructions, and the existing practice of the Court with respect to non-contentious business, shall, so far as the circumstances of each case will allow, be applicable to grants of probate and administration made under the Land Transfer Act, 1897. Rule of 20th November, 1897.

It is conceived that wherever there is realty, it will always be necessary to cite the heir, even where the husband is entitled to administration. See *Re Roberts, infra*.

Under special circumstances the husband was passed over and administration granted to the heir. *Re Ardern*, (1898) P. 147.

Where there is no personalty the grant will be made to the heir in general terms without giving notice to the next of kin. *Re Barnett*, (1898) P. 145.

Where the heir cannot be found, a grant *ad colligenda* with power to deal with the real estate will be made until the heir can be cited. *Re Roberts*, (1898) P. 149.

Before a creditor can obtain administration it will now be necessary to cite the heir as well as the next of kin.

In future the old rule that a will of a married woman merely exercising a power over real estate, though appointing an executor, was not entitled to probate will be altered. See *Re Tomlinson*, 6 P. D. 209.

Jurisdiction is now given by the Act to grant administration to real estate. Sect. 1 (3).

The devolution of the estate of representatives will now apply to real estate. See *ante*, p. 7.

Dealings before probate.

All enactments and rules of law relating to the effect of probate or letters of administration as respects chattels real, and as respects the dealings with chattels real before probate or administration, and the powers of personal representatives in respect of personal estate, apply now to real estate, so far as applicable. Sect. 2 (2).

Executors can now, therefore, take possession of the real estate and deal with it, and can *commence* actions before probate, but probate would be necessary before the hearing or before they can give a good title.

The powers of administrators over real estate before letters are far more restricted, and they cannot sell or mortgage before the grant of administration.

As to what executors can do before probate, see *ante*, p. 17; and as to what administrators can do before administration, see *ante*, p. 20.

The rules of law with respect to the payment of costs of administration and other matters relating to the administration of personal estate apply now to real estate so far as applicable. Sect. 2 (2). *Administration.*

The costs of administration are now therefore, it would seem, to be borne by both the real and personal estate. But see sect. 2 (3), *infra*.

The heir or devisee need not now in the first instance be made a party to an administration suit of real estate, at least before the assent of the representative has been given.

And real estate is to be administered in the same manner, subject to debts, costs, and expenses, and with the same incidents as personal estate; but not so as to affect the order in which real and personal assets respectively are now applicable for the payment of debts or legacies, or the liability of real estate to be charged with legacies. Sect. 2 (3).

The principal effect of this seems to be that all freehold real estate will be charged with the payment of debts, though not in exoneration of personal estate.

Although the effect of the Act is to create a mixed fund, it is conceived that the saving proviso in sect. 2 (3) will leave the legacies primarily chargeable upon the personalty

78   REAL ESTATE.

in the absence of any express direction to the contrary. See *Re Board*, (1895) 1 Ch. 499.

The powers, rights, duties, and liabilities of personal representatives in respect of personal estate shall apply to real estate, so far as applicable, as if it were a chattel real. Sect. 2 (2).

Powers over real estate.
It follows that the personal representatives will, in all cases, have power to take possession of the real estate, distrain for rent, sell or otherwise dispose of it, and generally deal with it as if it were personal estate.

But all the representatives must join in a sale or transfer (sect. 2 (2)), the Act thus placing them, as regards the sale of real estate, in the position of trustees.

And a judgment for administration not registered as a *lis pendens* would not prevent such sale or mortgage. *Berry* v. *Gibbons*, 8 Ch. 747.

It is submitted that a sale of freeholds after twenty years will now be subject to the same rule as leaseholds. See *Re Venn and Furze*, *post*, p. 88.

Having regard to *Re Harkness and Allsopp*, (1896) 2 Ch. 358, it would seem that a married woman cannot convey real estate vested in her by the Act as legal personal representative, except with the concurrence of her husband and by deed acknowledged.

Whether representatives have power to lease seems doubtful, but it is assumed that they can to the extent indicated below.

In dealing with leaseholds they may grant an underlease, if necessary for the due administration of the property, but cannot give an option of purchase, though advantageous to the estate. *Oceanic Co.* v. *Sutherberry*, 16 C. D. 236.

The latter part of this rule will now, no doubt, apply to freeholds, and by analogy the executors will now be entitled to grant a lease where it is necessary for the due administration of the assets.

But *quære* whether a lease would be a transfer within sect. 2 (2).

It would seem that a personal representative may now retain for his debt out of real estate. Sect. 2 (3), and *post*, p. 117. {Retainer.}

But an executor being also trustee for sale of realty cannot set off a debt due from the heir against real estate descended to him. *Milnes* v. *Sherwin*, 33 W. R. 927. And the principle of this decision does not seem to be affected by the Land Transfer Act.

For the purpose of the Statute of Limitations, time begins to run against an administrator claiming a chattel real, not from the grant, but as from the date of the death of the intestate. 3 & 4 Wm. 4, c. 27, s. 6; *Re Williams*, 34 C. D. 558. And the same rule will now apply to real estate which vests in him as representative. {Statute of Limitations.}

At any time after the death of the owner of any *land*, his personal representatives may assent to any devise contained in his will, or may convey the *land* to any person entitled thereto. Sect. 3. {Assent.}

Quære whether "land" includes copyholds or leaseholds.

Real estate, being now liable for payment of debts, will not therefore vest in the heir or devisee until the assent express or implied of the representatives, or a conveyance by them.

He will, however, have an inchoate right, which will pass to his representatives as real estate. *Post*, p. 132.

The assent will relate back to the death, and so confirm any intermediate dealings. *Post*, p. 134.

Assent to a tenant for life will be deemed an assent to remainders, and *vice versâ*. *Post*, p. 135.

Entry on land by a representative who is also a devisee will not of itself be proof of assent. Burton, 306.

As regards real estate, the assent of all the representatives would seem to be necessary. Sect. 2 (2).

The assent of a married woman representative seems open to the same objection as a conveyance by her. *Ante*, p. 78.

Assent may be given before probate, but the title of the devisee will be imperfect. *Ante*, p. 18.

But a conveyance to the heir cannot apparently be made before the grant of administration.

The assent may be retracted under certain circumstances. *Post*, p. 134.

The real estate, after payment of debts, is now distributable by the personal representatives, who hold it (subject as aforesaid) as trustees for the persons beneficially entitled. Sect. 2 (1).

The effect of this section seems to be to make the executors, directly the estate is clear, trustees 'of the real estate, and the rents and profits thereof, for the persons beneficially entitled as from the death of the testator ; and this would seem to amount to an implied assent or appropriation. The result may be that the executors may lose some of their rights, as, for instance, the right of retainer or set-off. See *Ballard* v. *Marsden*, 14 C. D. 374.

Personal representatives may now assent to a devise in the same way as they can assent to a legacy. Or they may convey the land to the person entitled as heir, devisee, or otherwise. Sect. 3 (1).

But the assent or conveyance *may* be made subject to a charge for the payment of any money which the representatives are liable to pay, in which case all liabilities of the representatives in respect of the land shall cease, except as to anything done before the assent or conveyance. Sect. 3 (1).

If, after a year from the death, the representatives fail, on request, to convey to the persons entitled, the Court may order a conveyance to be made ; or, in case of registered land, that the person be registered as proprietor. Sect. 3 (2).

The application would probably be by originating summons, and it is conceived that a vesting order might be made under the Trustee Act, 1893, ss. 29, 31.

Where the representatives are registered, a fee will not be charged for any transfer not for valuable consideration. Sect. 3 (3).

On the production of an assent in the prescribed form (see Rules, form 46), the person named therein will be registered as proprietor. Sect. 3 (4).

The representatives may, in the absence of any provision to the contrary, and with the consent of the person entitled, appropriate any part of the residuary estate in or towards satisfaction of his legacy or share, and may for that purpose value, in accordance with the prescribed provisions, the whole or any part of the property; but notice of such appropriation must be given to all persons interested in the residuary estate. Sect. 4 (1). *Appropriation.*

From the marginal note it would appear that the section refers to the appropriation of " land " only.

The section does not seem to extend the powers already possessed by personal representatives with regard to the appropriation of personal estate, which powers they now have over real estate, by virtue of sect. 2.

And as regards real estate the section will be of little practical use until the mode of ascertaining the value is prescribed by rules, which has not yet been done.

The section does not apparently apply to an intestacy. The right of an administrator to appropriate is therefore as before the Act, with the addition of a like right as to real estate. See *Barclay* v. *Owen*, 60 L. T. 220; *post*, p. 138.

A conveyance by the personal representative of real estate by way of appropriation is not a conveyance on sale within the meaning of the Stamp Act, 1891. See sect. 4 (2).

By sect. 5 nothing in Part I. of the Act is to affect any duty payable in respect of real estate, nor impose any fresh duty thereon. *Duty.*

But it may be that this only applies to the *quantum* of duty, and not to the manner of payment.

And, *quære*, whether estate duty is now a first charge on freehold real estate which passes to the executor as such, and consequently no longer comes within the letter or spirit of sect. 9 of the Finance Act.

Again, all freehold property being now in the same position as realty devised for payment of debts, the paramount power of sale of the executors must, it is thought, defeat the claim to succession duty, which is only payable on the beneficial interest.

It would follow, therefore, that the only claim for succession duty would be in respect of the surplus, and that a purchaser would not, any more than in the case of leaseholds, be bound to concern himself about the liability of the property to succession duty.

A sale by executors for the purposes of administration will, it is thought, be as free from duty as a sale for raising estate duty under sect. 9 (5).

CHAPTER VIII.

POWERS OF REPRESENTATIVES.

Of Powers generally.

AFTER the administration is granted, the power of an administrator is equal to that of an executor.

As we have already seen, an executor or administrator has the same property in the personal effects as the deceased had when living, and so he has the same power to bring actions to recover them. *Cobbett* v. *Clutton*, 2 C. & P. 471. {To bring actions.}

But an executor *de son tort* cannot bring any action in right of the deceased, except where mere possession is a *primâ facie* title. *Ante*, p. 18.

Within a convenient time, and without force, the personal representative had a right to enter the house descended to the heir to remove the goods; but now it seems he is entitled to possession of the real estate. 60 & 61 Vict. c. 65. {To enter house.}

He has also a right to take deeds or other papers belonging to the deceased; and need not give a schedule of such deeds and papers. *Cobbett* v. *Clutton*, 2 C. & P. 471.

If he cannot take possession of the assets without force, he must desist, and resort to his action. Wentw. 81, 202.

The personal representatives can distrain for arrears of rent (3 & 4 Wm. 4, c. 42, s. 37); or any one of them may distrain alone. 3 Bac. Abr. 30. {To distrain.}

If an administrator makes an underlease of a term of years of the deceased, reserving rent to himself, his executors, &c., his executors, and not the administrator *de bonis non*, shall have the rent; but it seems they cannot distrain for it (*Drue* v. *Baylie*, 1 Freem. 392, 403); because the reversion belongs to the administrator *de bonis non*; and a reversion is necessary to found the remedy by distress.

Absolute power of disposal.

The personal representative has an absolute power of disposal over the whole of the assets; and they cannot be followed by creditors, much less by legatees, even though specific. *Simpson* v. *Morley*, 2 K. & J. 71, 75; *Wolverhampton Bank* v. *Marston*, 7 H. & N. 148.

The principle is that the representative in many instances must sell in order to perform his duties, and no one would deal with him if liable afterwards to be called to account.

But not for his own purposes.

An executor or administrator purporting to act as such will generally confer a good title upon an alienee to whom he conveys or transfers a legal estate or title, and the alienee is under no obligation to see the consideration money properly applied. *Ricketts* v. *Lewis, infra.*

If an executor who is also residuary legatee sells or mortgages for his own purposes an asset to a person who has no notice of unsatisfied debts or of any ground which rendered it improper, the purchase or mortgage is valid against an unsatisfied creditor, even though such purchaser or mortgagee has acquired only an equitable interest if perfected by notice. *Graham* v. *Drummond*, (1896) 1 Ch. 968.

This rule, however, does not apply if the executor or Court still retains sufficient control over the asset to apply it for the benefit of creditors. *Ibid.*

Where there was a judgment for administration not registered as a *lis pendens*, and the executor and residuary legatee, both with notice, assigned to a *bonâ fide* purchaser for value without notice, it was held that the assignment was effectual to vest a good title in the purchaser. *Lonergan* v. *Hoban*, (1896) 1 Ir. R. 401.

But as the executor or administrator has no right to

raise money for his own purposes or otherwise than for the purpose of performing the duties of administration, so a mortgage for purposes foreign to the administration will be set aside as against a mortgagee who has notice of the purpose for which the money is raised. *Ricketts* v. *Lewis, infra.*

Thus an administrator has no power to mortgage leaseholds to raise money for repairs where there is no covenant to repair. *Ricketts* v. *Lewis,* 20 C. D. 745.

An executor as executor borrows money ostensibly for executorship purposes on the security of the testator's assets; this is a valid transaction. *Berry* v. *Gibbons,* 8 Ch. 747.

A man known to be an executor borrows on the security of the assets admittedly for his own private purposes; that is invalid. *Wilson* v. *Moore,* 1 M. & K. 337.

An executor, not known to be such, borrows money for his own private purposes on the security of that which appears to be his own property, but which is really the testator's property. This was held to be invalid, but the mortgage was an equitable one, and the question was between two equitable titles. *Re Morgan,* 18 C. D. 93.

Sales made thirty-three and twenty-seven years after the death of the testator have been enforced. *Wrigley* v. *Sykes,* 21 B. 337; *Sabin* v. *Heape,* 27 B. 553.

Sales after twenty years.

The rule that after twenty years a purchaser of real estate is put upon inquiry as to the executor's right to sell, does not apply to leaseholds. *Re Venn and Furze,* (1894) 2 Ch. 101.

And it is submitted that the rule will no longer apply to real estate which vests in the executor as such. *Post,* p. 88.

The powers of personal representatives in respect of personal estate now apply to real estate so far as applicable; but they must all join in a sale or transfer of real estate. 60 & 61 Vict. c. 65, s. 2 (2).

It is thought, therefore, that personal representatives have now in all cases a power to sell real estate for payment of debts, just as they had before the Act where there was a charge of debts or legacies.

But a charge of legacies on land devised beneficially in fee or in tail did not give executors a power of sale. *Re Rebbeck*, (1894) W. N. 68.

Mortgage. The personal representative may in his discretion and for executorship purposes mortgage the assets, even though an administration decree has been made. *Berry* v. *Gibbons*, L. R. 8 Ch. 747.

Or may pledge a part of them. *Russell* v. *Plaice*, 18 Beav. 28.

He may also effect a mortgage of leaseholds to a building society with a power of sale. *Cruikshank* v. *Duffin*, 13 Eq. 555; *Thorne* v. *T.*, (1893) 3 Ch. 196.

He may also assign the book-debts of the testator to one of the creditors, to secure the payment of his debt, and give him a power of attorney to collect them. *Vane* v. *Rigden*, 5 Ch. 663.

Collusion. On a sale or mortgage by a representative the purchaser or mortgagee is not bound to see to the application of the money unless there is fraud or collusion. *Re Morgan*, 18 C. D. 93.

But where there is fraud or collusion the transaction cannot stand, and will be set aside.

What will amount to a case of fraud will appear from the following:—

A sale cannot stand if the property be sold at a fraudulent undervalue. *Scott* v. *Tyler*, 2 Dick. 725; *Ewer* v. *Corbett*, 2 P. W. 149; *M'Mullen* v. *O'Reilly*, 15 Ir. Ch. R. 251.

The executor cannot sell or pledge the assets for raising money to carry on the testator's business. *McNeillie* v. *Acton*, 4 D. M. & G. 744.

Though he may sell or pledge any part of the property actually employed in the business. *Devitt* v. *Kearney*, 13 L. R. Ir. 45.

An administrator has no power to mortgage leaseholds of the intestate under leases not containing repairing covenants in order to raise money for repairing the property, and such a mortgage will be set aside as against a mortgagee who has notice of the purpose for which the money is raised. *Ricketts* v. *Lewis*, 20 C. D. 745.

Nor may he sell or pledge in order to pay or secure his own debt. *Scott* v. *Tyler, supra*; *Jones* v. *Stöhwasser*, 16 C. D. 577; *Hill* v. *Simpson*, 7 Ves. 169; *Re Morgan, ante*, p. 85.

Or for a debt wrongfully contracted by him as executor. *Collinson* v. *Lister*, 20 Beav. 356.

But if the executor be also the specific or residuary legatee he may dispose of assets in payment of his own debt. *Taylor* v. *Hawkins*, 8 Ves. 209; *Mead* v. *Orrery*, 3 Atk. 235; *Storry* v. *Walsh*, 18 Beav. 559.

But not if he is specific or residuary legatee *jointly* with others or subject to charges under the will. *Bonney* v. *Ridgard*, 1 Cox, 145; *Hill* v. *Simpson*, 7 Ves. 152, 170. And see *Re Queales*, 17 L. R. Ir. 361.

Nor can he so pay his own debt if the creditor has express notice that any debt remains unsatisfied. *Whale* v. *Booth*, 4 T. R. 625, n.; *Hall* v. *Andrews*, 20 W. R. 799.

So if the purchaser or mortgagee has legal evidence that the advance is meant to be applied to the private purposes of the executor, the transaction cannot stand. *M'Leod* v. *Drummond*, 17 Ves. 152.

And if a person owe money to a testator's estate, and be apprised that the executor means to misapply it, he cannot safely hand it over. *Stroughill* v. *Anstey*, 1 D. M. & G. 648.

A purchaser cannot purchase from the executor a chattel specifically bequeathed, if he has notice that there are no debts unpaid. *Ewer* v. *Corbett*, 2 P. W. 149. And see *M'Mullen* v. *O'Reilly*, 15 Ir. Ch. R. 251.

Mere lapse of time, though more than twenty years, does not give rise to the presumption that all the debts have been paid and that the executor has ceased to be executor. *Charlton* v. *Durham*, L. R. 4 Ch. 438.

So where there had been a lapse of thirty-five years from the testator's death, and no allegation of debts, it was held that the executor could still give a receipt. Lewin, 531; *ante*, p. 85.

But as to real estate the rule is that after twenty years the executors, selling under a charge of debts, must show that there are debts still unpaid. *Re Tanqueray-Willaume*, 20 C. D. 465; *Re Ryan*, 17 L. R. Ir. 42.

This rule, however, does not apply to a sale of leaseholds (*Re Venn and Furze*, (1894) 2 Ch. 101); and it is submitted that the *ratio decidendi* of *Re Venn and Furze* clearly applies to freeholds which vest in the representative as such under the Land Transfer Act, 1897.

Where there is collusion the assets may be followed within a reasonable time (*M'Leod* v. *Drummond*, 17 Ves. 152); but in no case after twenty years. *Andrew* v. *Wrigley*, 4 B. C. C. 125.

Executor cannot purchase assets.

An executor cannot immediately, or by means of a trustee, purchase the assets from himself, and shall be considered a trustee for the persons interested, and shall account for the utmost advantage made by him out of such purchase. *Hall* v. *Hallett*, 1 Cox, 134; *Watson* v. *Toone*, 6 Madd. 153.

But an executor of a deceased partner may sell his share to the surviving partners, if it can be fairly and properly done. *Chambers* v. *Howell*, 11 Beav. 6.

A sale is not avoided merely because the purchaser *may*, at his option, become trustee or executor, if in point of fact he never does become such. *Clark* v. *C.*, 9 App. Cas. 733.

Power to assign leases.
Or underlet.

A representative may dispose absolutely of a term of years, even against a specific legatee. Bac. Abr. Leases, I. 7.

Or may grant an underlease if necessary for the due administration of the estate, but he cannot give an option of purchase at a future time. *Oceanic Steam Co.* v. *Sutherberry*, 16 C. D. 236.

But an underlease cannot be granted where a sale is

called for. *Drohan* v. *D.*, 1 Ball & B. 185; *Evans* v. *Jackson*, 8 Sim. 217.

The power to assign or underlet is restrained by a condition not to assign where the executor or administrator is named in the condition or covenant.

But if not named it is doubtful whether the restriction will extend to them, though it would seem that it will not. Wms. 810; *Seers* v. *Hind*, 1 Ves. 294.

But an administrator will be restrained, as assignee, where *assigns* are named. *More's Case*, Cro. Eliz. 26.

Equity will not afford relief against forfeiture so occasioned. Conv. Act, 1881, s. 14.

Leases, it is conceived, may now be granted of the real estate which has devolved upon the representatives, where it is necessary for the due administration of the estate; but any person taking such a lease will, it is thought, do so at the risk of having to show that it was properly granted in the due administration of the executor's office. See *Oceanic, &c.* v. *Sutherberry, supra*. {Power to lease.}

The representatives' power of disposal is not affected by the commencement of a creditor's administration action, but continues till judgment. *Neeres* v. *Burrage*, 14 Q. B. 504; *Re Barrett*, 43 C. D. 70. But see *Berry* v. *Gibbons*, *infra*. {Powers how affected by administration action.}

And it has been held that a decree for administration, without any injunction or appointment of a receiver, does not take away the power of the executor to deal with the assets. *Berry* v. *Gibbons*, 8 Ch. 747.

Nor release him from his duties. *Garner* v. *Moore*, 3 Drew. 277.

A promissory note or bill of exchange made payable to the deceased or his order, may be indorsed by his representative. {Power to indorse bills.}

And may be indorsed in such terms as to negative personal liability. Bills of Ex. Acts, 1882, s. 31 (5).

Where a payee of a note indorsed it, but died before delivery, delivery by his executors without any indorsement by them was held inefficacious. *Bromage* v. *Lloyd*, 1 Exch. 32.

Where the drawee of a bill is dead, presentment for acceptance may be made to his personal representative. Bills of Ex. Act, 1882, s. 41 (1, c). The holder now has an option, and presentment is excused, and a bill may be treated as dishonoured by non-acceptance where the drawer is dead. *Ibid.*, s. 41 (2, a).

Where the drawee or acceptor of a bill is dead, and no place of payment is specified, presentment for payment must be made to a personal representative, if such there be and can be found. *Ibid.*, s. 45 (7).

If a person indebted to another gives him a blank acceptance for a certain sum, and the donee subsequently dies, his administrator may fill up the paper as a bill payable to drawer's order, insert his own name as drawer, and enforce payment against the acceptor. *Scard* v. *Jackson*, 24 W. R. 159.

Cannot sell by attorney.

Delegatus non potest delegare. Therefore where a power of sale is given to executors they cannot sell by attorney. *Combe's Case*, 9 Co. 75. But see now 60 & 61 Vict. c. 65, s. 2 (2).

Re-insurance.

Formerly re-insurances were illegal, though the personal representatives might re-insure. But now by 30 & 31 Vict. c. 23, ss. 3, 4, Sch. D., they are legal, without any necessity for their appearing to be re-insurances on the face of them.

Election.

An executor may in some cases claim by election; as where the testator at the time of his death was entitled out of several chattels to take his choice of one or more to his own use. Toller, 174.

Compromise.

By the Trustee Act, 1893, s. 21, an executor or administrator may pay or allow any debt or claim on any evidence he thinks sufficient; and may accept a composition, compromise, abandon, submit to arbitration, or otherwise settle any debt or claim in good faith.

This power may now, it seems, be exercised with respect

to real estate devolving on the personal representatives under the Land Transfer Act, 1897. See *Abdullah* v. *Rickards*, 4 Times R. 622.

The power to compromise applies as much to a legatee as to debts owing to or from the testator's estate. *Re Warren*, 82 W. R. 916.

The section does not authorise executors to enter into a compromise with respect to the validity of the will or the testamentary power of the testator. *Abdullah* v. *Rickards*, 4 Times R. 622.

A compromise by executors of a debt due from one of themselves would not, it seems, be upheld unless it would clearly benefit the estate. *De Cordova* v. *De C.*, 4 A. C. 692; *Stott* v. *Lord, infra*.

The question to be considered is whether the representatives have acted in good faith; and it is not for them to show that the transaction was a proper one, but for those impeaching it to show its impropriety. *Re Brogden*, 38 C. D. 546.

Powers of One of Several Representatives.

Co-executors, however numerous, are regarded in law as one person; and therefore the acts of one are deemed to be acts of all.

Hence a release of a debt by one is valid, and shall bind the rest. *Jacomb* v. *Harwood*, 2 Ves. 267; *Herbert* v. *Pigott*, 2 C. & M. 384. But see *Stott* v. *Lord, infra*.

So a receipt by one is a good discharge, though he forges the signatures of his co-executors. *Charlton* v. *Durham*, 4 Ch. 433.

So one may settle an account, and in the absence of fraud it will be binding on the others, though dissenting. *Smith* v. *Everett*, 27 Beav. 446.

. So one may probably indorse a bill of exchange. Chalmers, 5th ed. 127; *Reg.* v. *Winterbottom*, 2 C. & K. 37.

So a grant or surrender of a term by one is good. *Simpson* v. *Gutteridge*, 1 Madd. 616.

And the attornment of one shall be the attornment of the other. *Ibid*.

So the acknowledgment by one is sufficient to bind the estate and prevent the Statute of Limitations running. *Re Macdonald*, (1897) 2 Ch. 181.

But an acknowledgment by one executor and trustee against the will of the other, that more than six years' interest is due upon a mortgage, cannot be treated as the act of the two as regards the real estate, so as to prevent the statute running. *Astbury* v. *A.*, (1898) 2 Ch. 111.

Semble, such an acknowledgment would be effectual in the case of a claim against the personal assets. *Ibid*.

So the sale or gift by one of several executors of the goods of the deceased is the sale and gift of them all. Touchst. 484.

And the purchaser of a specific legacy from one executor who is also the legatee is not bound to inquire whether the other executors have given their assent. *Cole* v. *Miles*, 10 Ha. 179.

But where one of two executors, erroneously believing that he was acting with the authority of the other, contracted to sell leaseholds, it was held that the purchaser could not enforce specific performance of the contract. *Sneesby* v. *Thorne*, 7 D. M. & G. 399.

And one executor cannot enter into a contract, for one executor is not the agent of another to bind him by contract. *Turner* v. *Hardey*, 9 M. & W. 770.

One executor cannot without the authority of the Court sell or transfer real estate. 60 & 61 Vict. c. 65, s. 2 (2).

Quære, whether this applies to a mortgage.

Where a compromise by one executor was against the will of his co-executors, and had the effect of relieving him from a liability which he was under to the testator's estate, it was set aside. *Stott* v. *Lord*, 8 Jur. N. S. 249.

Payment by a debtor, for the express purpose of

discharging his debt to an estate, to his own agent, who happens to be, but not to the debtor's knowledge, one of the executors of the estate, is not sufficient to discharge the debtor. *Miller* v. *Douglas,* 56 L. J. Ch. 91.

In a company under the Companies Act a valid transfer may no doubt be made by one of two executors, who are noted as executors but not registered as shareholders, subject to any provisions in the articles. Buckley.

But if in a company under the Companies Clauses Acts the names of the executors are placed on the register, even though under the description of executors, they become joint shareholders in their individual capacity, and any transfer must be made by all of them. *Barton* v. *L. & N. W. Ry.,* 24 Q. B. D. 77, *post,* p. 162.

And a transfer by one to which the signature of the other is forged does not pass a moiety of the shares or stock, but is inoperative altogether. *Barton* v. *N. S. Ry.,* 38 C. D. 458.

One executor cannot therefore transfer railway shares or stock, since these are governed by the Companies Clauses Act. *Barton* v. *L. & N. W. Ry., supra.*

The Bank of England require all the executors who have proved to join in any transfer of stock standing in the name of their testator. 33 & 34 Vict. c. 71.

One executor can assent to a legacy, and even his single assent to his own legacy will vest the complete title in himself. *Cole* v. *Miles,* 10 Ha. 179.

And one executor can retain for his own debt; and also out of a legacy to his co-executor in respect of a *devastavit* by the latter. *Sims* v. *Doughty,* 5 Ves. 243; *post.*

One may take possession of the effects so as to cause a joint possession, but not so as to attach a liability or impose a charge on the others, as if one takes possession and enjoys a term, such enjoyment is not the enjoyment of all so as to render them chargeable. *Nation* v. *Tozer,* 1 C. M. & R. 172.

And so though one may dispose of the assets so as to

bind all, he is not their agent so as to bind them by his contracts. *Turner* v. *Hardey, supra.*

How far a *devastavit* by one will affect the others, see *post*, p. 183.

One of several administrators stands on the same footing as one of several executors. *Jacomb* v. *Harwood*, 2 Ves. Sen. 267; *Smith* v. *Everett*, 27 Beav. 454.

The powers of a deceased executor or administrator go to the survivor or survivors (Trustee Act, 1893, s. 22); and where one renounces, those who prove can exercise the powers alone. *Crawford* v. *Forshaw*, (1891) 2 Ch. 261.

But if a sole executor renounces, the power is extinguished. *Att.-Gen.* v. *Fletcher*, 5 L. J. Ch. 75.

The question whether some or one of several executors could exercise a power to sell land has been much discussed. Wms. 821. But see now L. T. Act, s. 2 (2), and as to copyholds. *Peppercorn* v. *Wayman*, 5 De G. & S. 230.

Now, however, as to persons dying after 1st January, 1898, the freehold real estate vests in the personal representatives, and cannot be sold by some or one of them without the authority of the Court. L. T. Act, s. 2 (2).

Quære, whether a power given to persons *nominatim* would survive, or indeed could be exercised at all, after the Land Transfer Act, 1879.

All executors must join in bringing actions, even though some be infants. *Smith* v. *S.*, Yelv. 130. But where one only has proved, he may sue alone. D. C. P. 224. If all have proved, and one sue alone, the defendant may apply to the Court to have the others joined as co-plaintiffs.. R. S. C., Ord. 16, r. 11.

Generally speaking, one executor cannot sue or be sued by his co-executor, nor after the death of one can his executor be sued by the survivors for a debt due to their testator. Wentw. 75.

But where an executor is also a creditor and does not prove, he can sue the other executor. *Rawlinson* v. *Shaw*,

3 T. R. 557. And he can also sue to protect himself. *Gleadow* v. *Atkin*, 2 C. & J. 548; *Miles* v. *Durnford*, 2 De G. M. & G. 641; *Robinson* v. *Harkin*, (1896) 2 Ch. 415.

Executors may agree that one of them shall hold the land devised to them in trust at a fixed rent, and may distrain for arrears. *Cowper* v. *Fletcher*, 34 L. J. (N. S.) Q. B. 187. But the rent must be a fair occupation rent. *De Cordova* v. *D.*, 4 App. Cas. 692.

Powers of Executor of Executor, Administrator de, &c.

In all cases, except of special trust or authority, the executor of an executor stands in the same position as the first executor. {Executor of executor.}

But where a power is of a kind that indicates a personal confidence, it must *primâ facie* be understood to be confined to the individual to whom it is given, and will not, except by express words, pass to others to whom, by legal transmission, the same character may happen to belong. *Cole* v. *Wade*, 16 Ves. 27; *Re Cooke*, 4 C. D. 454.

The numerous cases on the question whether a power is a personal confidence, or transmissible with the office or estate, are almost all cases of power to sell land. The question, however, has ceased to be of much importance since the Conv. Act, 1881, s. 30, and Trustee Act, 1893, s. 22. But see *Re Ingleby, &c.*, 13 L. R. Ir. 326.

And now the question as regards power to sell freeholds will not arise in the future, as the personal representatives will have a statutory power to sell real estate. 60 & 61 Vict. c. 65.

As to power to lease and other powers, see *Robson* v. *Flight*, 4 D. J. & S. 608; Farwell, 452.

An administrator *de bonis non* becomes by the grant the only personal representative of the original deceased, and with respect to the estate left unadministered he has the same powers as the original representative. *Catherwood* v. *Chabaud*, 1 B. & C. 154.

With regard to special and limited administrators, see *ante*, p. 28, *et seq.*

A *feme covert* executrix or administratrix is now in the position of a *feme sole*, and can sue without giving security for costs. *Threlfall* v. *Wilson*, 8 P. D. 18.

But she cannot convey real estate to a purchaser, except with the concurrence of her husband, and by deed acknowledged. *Re Harkness*, (1896) 2 Ch. 358, *ante*, p. 78.

CHAPTER IX.

PAYMENT OF DEATH DUTIES.

Estate Duty.

By the Finance Act, 1894, an estate duty, substituted for probate duty, is now payable in all cases where the death took place after 1st August, 1894. Representatives must pay.

One of the first duties of a legal representative is to pay the death duties.

The executor shall, to the best of his knowledge and belief, specify in appropriate accounts annexed to the Inland Revenue affidavit all the property in respect of which estate duty is payable. Sect. 8 (3).

Where the executor does not know the amount or value of any property, he may state in the Inland Revenue affidavit that he does not know the amount or value thereof and that he undertakes when ascertained to bring in an account thereof. Sect. 6 (3).

The executor or administrator, or any person intermeddling with the personal property, must pay the estate duty in respect of all personal property, wheresoever situate, of which the deceased was competent to dispose, on delivering the Inland Revenue affidavit. Finance Act, 1894, s. 6 (2), s. 22 (1, d).

This includes property over which the deceased had a general power of appointment. Sect. 22 (2).

The representative is also required, since the Land Transfer Act, 1897, by the Revenue authorities, to pay duty on all freeholds in England vested solely in the deceased, or over which he had a general power of appointment.

On what payable.
The duty is payable on the capital value of the property passing on the death of the deceased, including property which he had power to dispose of as he liked. Sect. 22 (2).

All such property, whether real or personal, settled or unsettled, is liable. Sect. 1.

For a scale of the rates of duty, see sect. 17.

A further duty of 1 per cent., called settlement estate duty, is also payable under certain circumstances. *Post.*

Where, however, the net value does not exceed 1,000*l.*, the payment of estate duty covers the settlement estate duty and legacy and succession duties. Sect. 16 (3).

Interest at 3 per cent. without deduction for income tax is payable on the duty from the death, or where the duty is payable by instalments, or becomes due at any date later than six months after the death, from the date at which the first instalment of the duty becomes due, and is recoverable in the same manner as if it were part of the duty. Fin. Act, 1896, s. 18.

Where the fixed duty is paid within a year, interest is not payable. Sect. 16 (5); but see Fin. Act, 1896, s. 18.

Property passing on the death, when situate out of the United Kingdom, is liable, if before the Act legacy or succession duty was payable thereon, or would have been but for the relationship of the person to whom it passed. Sect. 2 (2).

It is payable not only on property actually disposed of by will or passing to the next of kin, but also :—

1. Upon all gifts made by the deceased within twelve months of his death. Sect. 2 (3).

2. Upon all gifts not immediately taken into the exclusive possession of the donee whenever made. Sect. 2 (1, c) 44 & 45 Vict. c. 12, s. 11.

3. Upon the benefit accruing by survivorship of all

transfers, purchases, or investments made by the deceased in joint names. *Ibid.*

4. Upon the proceeds of policies effected by the deceased, and kept up by him, wholly or partly, for the benefit of a donee. *Ibid.; Lord Advocate* v. *Fleming,* (1897) A. C. 145.

5. Upon property so settled by the deceased that a life interest or power to revoke the settlement is reserved to the settlor. *Ibid.*

6. Upon annuities (other than a single annuity not exceeding 25*l.*, or the first granted of two or more such annuities) or other interests which the deceased either by himself alone, or in concert with some other person, purchased or provided so that a benefit arose or accrued by survivorship or otherwise on the death of the deceased. Sect. 2 (1, d); sect. 15 (1).

The estate duty payable in respect of an annuity may be paid by four equal yearly instalments. Fin. Act, 1896, s. 16.

There is, or was, however, a difference between the mode of payment of duty on real and personal estate. For whereas the representative is bound to pay estate duty on personal property, he was not so bound with regard to real estate. Sect. 6 (2).

The Act provides that he *may* pay duty on real property, if it is under his control, or if the persons acquiring it under the will request him to do so. Sect. 6 (2).

Moreover the duty on real estate may be paid by eight yearly instalments or sixteen half-yearly instalments, the first to become due twelve months after the death, with interest from the date *when the first instalment is due.* Sect. 6 (8).

If, however, the property is sold, the duty must be paid on the completion of the sale. *Ibid.*

Since all real estate (except copyholds and customary freeholds) now vests in the personal representative, it would seem that such real estate will now be under his control for the purpose of paying duty under the Act. It is submitted that sect. 5 of the Land Transfer Act relates only to the *quantum* of duty and not to the mode of payment.

It may be a saving to the estate, therefore, if the executor pay duty on the real estate by instalments. But if he takes that course he must still include in his affidavit the real estate, in order that all the property may be aggregated for the purpose of calculating the duty.

In case too much or too little duty has been paid in the first instance, a second affidavit should be made and filed. Sect. 8 (12). But no return can be made of any fixed duty.

Where the commissioners are satisfied that the estate duty cannot without excessive sacrifice be raised at once, they may allow payment to be postponed for such period, to such extent, and on payment of such interest not exceeding 4 per cent. or any higher interest yielded by the property, and on such terms as the commissioners think fit. Sect. 8 (9).

A person authorised or required to pay the estate duty shall have power, whether the property is vested in him or not, to raise such duty, interest and costs by sale or mortgage or a terminable charge. Sect. 9 (5).

There is little doubt that this could be done by the representative before probate, and even before the grant of administration.

All estate duty is payable out of the general personal estate (*Re Culverhouse*, (1896) 2 Ch. 251 ; *Salt* v. *Locker*, (1898) 2 Ch. 648) ; but settlement estate duty out of the settled property. Fin. Act, 1896, s. 19.

Settlement Estate Duty.

Where property is settled by will, that is, where it is to pass by way of succession, a further estate duty called settlement estate duty is payable upon the settled property at the rate of 1 per cent. on the capital value. Sect. 5.

It is not payable where the only life interest conferred is that of the wife or husband of the deceased. Sect. 5.

Nor where the total estate does not exceed 1,000*l*. Sect. 16 (3).

It is only payable once during the continuance of the settlement. Sect. 5.

If the will is proved in due time, it need not be paid till after probate.

It is, however, payable with interest from the death in the same manner as estate duty. *Ante*, p. 98.

Legacy and Succession Duties.

The Finance Act, 1894, has considerably altered the incidence of these duties in all cases where the testator has died after 1st August, 1894.

Neither legacy nor succession duty is now payable :—

1. Where the testator's total estate does not exceed 1,000*l*. net. Sect. 16 (3).

2. Where the legatee or successor is either a husband or wife, or a child or parent, or other lineal descendant or ancestor of the testator. Sect. 1.

Where, however, the estate exceeds 1,000*l*. and the beneficiary does not come within the above relationship, then either legacy or succession duty is payable on the capital value of the legacy, property, or other beneficial interest succeeded to.

Where the interest is a life interest, the value of that interest is, for the purpose of assessing the duty, to be capitalised according to the Government tables of the value of lives.

Legacy duty is the duty payable on personal property, except leaseholds, and succession duty is the duty payable on real property, including leaseholds.

Where the executor has to pay duty, he must deduct the amount on paying over the legacy, or must recover it from the beneficiary, or must enforce the charge on the property.

Both legacy and succession duty become payable when the legatee or successor becomes entitled in possession.

Legacy duty on personalty and succession duty on leaseholds should then be paid in full, but succession duty on real estate may be paid by instalments like estate duty. *Ante.*

In calculating succession duty on real property, the estate duty already paid in respect of the same property may be deducted from the principal value of the property.

The following are the rates of duty for both legacy and succession duty:—

Brothers and sisters of the deceased and
  their descendants . . . . . 3 per cent.
Brothers and sisters of father or mother
  of the deceased and their descendants   5 per cent.
Brothers and sisters of grandfather or
  grandmother of deceased and their
  descendants . . . . . . 6 per cent.
Any other collateral relation or stranger 10 per cent.

The husband or wife of a relative pays the same as the relative. But any relative of a husband or wife of the deceased (if a stranger in blood to the deceased) pays as a stranger.

Specific legacies are exempt, if the whole benefit taken by the legatee is under 20*l.*

But pecuniary legacies are liable, though under 20*l.*, if the testator died on or after 1st June, 1881, and so are successions to real estate after 1st June, 1889. But of course neither of these are liable where the *whole estate* does not exceed 1,000*l. Ante,* p. 101.

The executors or administrators as well as the persons beneficially entitled are personally liable for legacy duty; and trustees are, in the same manner, liable for succession duty. Heavy penalties are incurred by non-payment.

If, for any cause, the legacies cannot be paid and are retained, the duty is to be paid when they are so retained, and payment is not to be deferred till the legacies are actually paid.

Interest at 3 per cent. must be added to all such duties in arrear. Fin. Act, 1896, s. 18 (2).

No person is to pay any legacy without taking a proper receipt, showing (*inter alia*) the amount and rate of duty payable thereon.

CHAPTER X.

PAYMENT OF DEBTS.

ALTHOUGH there is no right of property in a dead body, the executor has a right to the possession of it, and any direction to the contrary contained in the will is nugatory. *Williams* v. *W.*, 20 C. D. 659.

A direction to cremate, therefore, though not illegal, is not binding on the executor. *R.* v. *Price*, 12 Q. B. D. 247.

1. Funeral expenses.

Funeral expenses, according to the condition in life of the deceased, are to be allowed before any debt or duty whatsoever. But where the estate is insolvent no more is to be allowed than is strictly necessary. *Post*, p. 173.

These expenses are to be preferred even to a debt due to the Crown. *R.* v. *Wade*, 5 Price, 627.

And have priority even in bankruptcy. Bankruptcy Act, 1883, s. 125 (7).

A husband has, it seems, a right to throw his wife's funeral expenses upon her separate estate. *Re M'Myn*, 33 C. D. 575.

Probate expenses.

The next thing to justify expense is the proving of the will or taking out administration.

The costs of an administration suit are to be considered as expenses in administering the estate, and are the first charge upon the estate. *Sanderson* v. *Stoddart*, 32 Beav. 155.

Where "testamentary expenses" are to be paid out of a specified part of the estate, that part must bear the costs of an administration suit. *Penny* v. *P.*, 11 C. D. 440. So of "executorship expenses," *infra*.

"Executorship expenses" in a will means expenses incident to the proper performance of the duty of an executor, and includes costs incurred in obtaining advice of solicitors or counsel as to the distribution, also the costs for administration of the personal estate, funeral expenses and expenses incurred by the executors for the protection of specific legacies—as, for instance, warehousing furniture specifically bequeathed—pending the distribution of the assets, and payments by the executors in discharge of debts falling due from the testator's estate after his death—as, for instance, rent due after the testator's death for a house of which he was yearly tenant. *Sharp* v. *Lush*, 10 C. D. 468.

But mortgagees are entitled to their administration costs in priority to the administration costs of the mortgagor's executor. *Re Banks*, 45 W. R. 206.

Costs of unsuccessfully opposing probate directed by the Probate Division to be paid out of the testator's estate are not testamentary expenses, but the executor's costs of defending the action are. *Re Prince*, (1898) 2 Ch. 225.

3. Payment of debts.

The third occasion of disbursement is the payment of debts. And in such payment the personal representative must be careful to observe the rules of priority, for if he pay those of a lower degree first, he must, on a deficiency of assets, answer those of a higher, of which he had notice, out of his own estate. *Harman* v. *H.*, 2 Show. 492.

So he is bound to plead a debt of a higher nature, of which he has notice, in bar of an action brought against him for a debt of a lower, and *riens ultra* if he has not assets for both; otherwise it will be an admission of assets to satisfy both debts. 1 Saund. 333 a (8).

With respect to what is sufficient notice, the representative is bound at his peril to take notice of debts of record, but of other debts he must have actual notice. Wms. 881; *Re Fludyer, post*, p. 115.

A testator cannot defeat the law as to precedence of debts by directing his executors to make an equal distribution of assets among all his creditors. *Turner* v. *Cox*, 8 Moo. P. C. 288.

Foreign assets.
Where a person domiciled in England leaves assets abroad the administration of assets is to be governed by the law of the country where the personal representative acts, and from which he derives his authority to collect them. *De Penny* v. *Christie*, (1891) 2 Ch. 63; *Carron, &c.* v. *Maclaren*, 5 H. L. C. 455.

If a person dies domiciled abroad leaving assets in this country, those assets can only be collected under an English grant of administration, and must be distributed according to the law of England, among English and foreign creditors alike. *Re Klœbe, infra*.

But if foreign assets are distributed so as to give foreign creditors priority, no doubt the English Court in distributing the English assets would be astute to equalise the payments and take care that no foreign creditor should receive anything till the English creditors had been paid an equal amount. *Re Klœbe*, 28 C. D. 175, 177.

It is the practice of the Courts in all countries to retain assets within their jurisdiction for the purpose of insuring payment of debts; and only after they are paid to allow the surplus to be remitted to the principal administrator in a foreign country. *De Penny* v. *Christie, supra*.

Solicitor's lien.
A solicitor has a lien on a fund recovered for his client before the specialty creditors of the deceased client; nor can his personal representative controvert this rule by insisting upon applying the assets in a course of administration. *Turwin* v. *Gibson*, 3 Atk. 720; *Lloyd* v. *Mason*, 4 Ha. 132.

Crown debts.
To all other debts, those due to the Crown by record or specialty have precedence; but only those due by record or specialty are so privileged. Went. 262; but see *Re Bentinck, infra*.

Thus fines for copyhold estate and arrears of rent are not so privileged; and a recognizance in Chancery, by a guardian in the matter of a minor, is not a Crown debt. Wms. 855.

But it seems that if the Crown debt and that of a subject are both inferior to debts of record, the Crown shall be preferred. *Re Bentinck*, (1897) 1 Ch. 673 ; 3 Bac. Abr. 80.

By 55 Geo. 3, c. 184, s. 45, the commissioners of stamps are authorised, in certain cases, to give credit for the duties on probates and administrations; and by sect. 48 the duty for which credit is so given shall be a debt to the Crown, and be paid in preference to any other debt whatsoever. By the same section a representative paying any debt in preference thereto is made personally liable.

It is thought that these provisions will now apply to estate duty under the Finance Act, 1894, s. 8 (1). See Hanson, 182.

Next in order are certain specific debts which are by particular statutes to be preferred to all others. Debts given priority by particular statutes.

By the Preferential Payments in Bankruptcy Act, 1888, rates and wages are to have priority when the estate is being administered in Chancery. *Re Heywood*, (1897) 2 Ch. 593 ; *post*, p. 113.

By 17 Geo. 2, c. 38, s. 3, money due to the parish by overseers is to be paid before any other debts.

But guardians are not preferential creditors against the estate of a deceased pauper for maintenance, and the executor may retain before satisfying their claim. *Laver v. Botham*, (1895) 1 Q. B. 59.

So by 59 & 60 Vict. c. 25, s. 35, the money due from an officer of a registered friendly society shall be paid in preference to any other debt or claim against his estate. *Ex parte Edmonds*, 30 W. R. 432; *Re Miller*, (20 Jan., 1893) Brabrook, 13th ed. 173 ; 51 & 52 Vict. c. 62, s. 2.

But he must receive the money by virtue of his office. *Re Aberdein*, (1896) W. N. 154.

The same rule applies to officers of savings banks. 26 & 27 Vict. c. 87, s. 14.

By 26 & 27 Vict. c. 57, provision is made for the preferential payment of regimental debts and the distribution of the effects of officers and soldiers in case of death.

Again, money due from the deceased as officer of paving commissioners under 57 Geo. 3, s. 51 (local Act), is to be paid in preference to other debts *except Crown debts.*

The words in the above Acts are very wide; sufficient as it seems to give preference against Crown debts, though perhaps they would not be so construed. 6 Ves. 99.

The 10th section of the Jud. Act, 1875, does not introduce into the administration of insolvent estates the provision of the Bankruptcy Act that all debts with certain exceptions are to be paid *pari passu*. It affects only the rights of the class of secured creditors as conflicting with those of the class of unsecured creditors, and does not affect the rights *inter se* of the members of those classes. *Re Maggi*, 20 C. D. 545; and see *Re Oriental Bank*, 28 C. D. 643, 649; *Mersey, &c.* v. *Naylor*, 9 Q. B. D. 648, 662.

The Jud. Act does not incorporate the rules of bankruptcy into administration for all purposes, but only "as to the respective rights of secured and unsecured creditors, and as to the debts and liabilities provable, and as to the valuation of annuities and future and contingent liabilities respectively." *Re May*, 45 C. D. 499, 502.

Debts of Record.

Next in priority of payment come debts of record, of which there are two sorts, viz.: (1) Judgments in courts of record; (2) Recognizances and statutes.

Judgments. Such judgments are precedent in degree not only to all debts by specialty, but to recognizances and statutes, and must be preferred by the executor or administrator whether prior in point of time or not. Therefore he must discharge a later judgment in preference to a statute or recognizance in time precedent. Went. 267.

Judgments entitled to this precedence are not only those of the High Court, but also those of any court of record.

But an order giving leave to sign judgment under Ord. 14 against the legal representative does not give priority. *Re Gurney*, (1896) 2 Ch. 863.

Nor does an order *nisi* to sign judgment. *Hanson* v. *Stubbs*, 8 C. D. 154.

By R. S. C., Ord. 17, r. 1, there shall be no abatement by the death of either party between verdict and judgment, but judgment may be entered notwithstanding the death.

By Ord. 41, r. 3, when any judgment is pronounced by the Court or a Judge in Court, the entry of the judgment shall be entered as of the day on which such judgment is pronounced, unless the Court or a Judge shall otherwise order, and the judgment shall take effect from that date; but by special leave a judgment may be ante-dated or post-dated.

By Ord. 41, r. 4, in all cases not within the last rule the entry of judgment shall be dated as of the day on which the requisite documents are left with the proper officer for the purpose of such entry, and the judgment shall take effect from that day.

Where a creditor obtained judgment against the executor on the same day that a decree was made for administration, it was held that the judgment and decree were obtained at the same time and that the judgment had no priority. *Parker* v. *Ringham*, 33 Beav. 535.

A judgment in a foreign country is considered in our Courts merely as a debt by simple contract. *Dupleix* v. *De Roven*, 2 Vern. 540; *Re Boyse*, 15 Ch. D. 591. And an Irish judgment is not entitled to priority as an English judgment. *Harris* v. *Saunders*, 4 B. & C. 411; *Ferguson* v. *Mahon*, 11 A. & E. 179. {Foreign judgments.}

But a foreign judgment, on an administration here, will be allowed any priority which it had by the law of the country under whose grant foreign assets have been remitted to England. *Ibid.*

By the Judgments Extension Act, 1868, Irish and Scotch judgments may be registered in England and then become English judgments. *Re Low*, (1894) 1 Ch. 147, 158; and see *Re Watson*, (1893) 1 Q. B. 21.

Judgment against the representative himself. A judgment against the personal representative himself is not the same as one recovered against the deceased, for it has no priority except with regard to debts of equal degree with that upon which the creditor has obtained judgment. *Re Maggi*, 20 C. D. 545; *Dollond* v. *Johnson*, Sm. & G. 301.

As between the creditor and himself, however, the representative may be compelled to satisfy the judgment *de bonis propriis*. *Abbis* v. *Winter*, 3 Swans. 579, *n*.

The executors of a judgment creditor are not entitled to a receiver or an injunction against the judgment debtor's property. *Norburn* v. *N.*, (1894) 1 Q. B. 448.

A judgment debt has no priority in bankruptcy.

Every judgment debt carries interest at 4 per cent. from the time of entry. R. S. C., Ord. 42, r. 16; *Taylor* v. *Roe*, (1894) 1 Ch. 413.

Registration. On the death of the debtor his judgment debts must be paid in full before any of his debts on bond or by simple contract. But by 23 & 24 Vict. c. 38, ss. 3, 4, in order to secure this preference the judgment must be registered or re-registered within five years before the death of the deceased in the same manner as was required in order to affect lands in the hands of purchasers or mortgagees. An unregistered judgment ranks only as a simple contract debt. *Van Gheluive* v. *Nerinckx*, 21 Ch. D. 189.

This only applies to judgments against the deceased. Therefore a judgment debt against the legal *representative*, though unregistered, is still entitled to priority. *Williams* v. *W.*, L. R. 15 Eq. 270.

Among judgment creditors there is no priority as to time or otherwise; therefore, before execution, the representative may pay whom he will first. Went. 269.

Decrees. A decree in equity, provided it were final, was equivalent to a judgment at law. *Shafto* v. *Powel*, 3 Lev. 355. But an order to account or for foreclosure was held to give no priority, even where there was an order for payment of the result of the account. *Perry* v. *Phelips*, 10 Ves. 34; *Wilson* v. *Dunsany*, 18 Beav. 293, 299.

Next in rank to judgments are recognizances and statutes. The latter, however, are practically obsolete. Recognizances.

A recognizance is an obligation entered into before some court of record or magistrate, duly authorised, with condition to do some particular act, as to keep the peace or pay a debt.

It is not a record until enrolled, and until enrolment it is not entitled to precedence. *Bothomly* v. *Fairfax*, 1 P. Wms. 334.

It is payable out of the personal estate of the debtor, in the event of his decease, next after judgment debts and before specialty debts. *Ibid.*

A sum of money due from a receiver is a debt of record, so long as the recognizance exists. *Seagram* v. *Tuck*, 18 C. D. 296.

Specialty and Simple Contract.

Formerly next in precedence in order of payment were debts by special contract, which must have been paid before debts by simple contract.

But now by 32 & 33 Vict. c. 46, in the administration of any person dying on or before 1st January, 1870, no specialty debt is to have priority, and all creditors as well specialty as simple contract shall be in equal degree and be paid accordingly out of the assets, whether legal or equitable: Provided that the Act shall not affect any lien, charge, or other security which any creditor has for payment of his debt. Hinde-Palmer's Act.

The Act does not prevent a judgment creditor from having priority, though his judgment be not registered. *Williams* v. *W.*, 15 Eq. 270.

A debt for rent has now no preference. *Re Hastings*, 6 C. D. 610; but see 51 & 52 Vict. c. 62, s. 1 (4). Rent.

Voluntary bonds.

A bond or covenant or promissory note, merely voluntary, shall be postponed to simple contract debts, but must be paid by the executor before legacies. *Dawson* v. *Kearton*, 3 Sm. & G. 186; *Re Whitaker*, 42 C. D. 119.

But the payee of a voluntary promissory note is not even in the administration of a solvent estate in the same position as the payee of a voluntary bond, so as to be entitled to claim against the estate after creditors for value. *Re Whitaker, supra*.

A voluntary bond assigned for value stands upon the same footing as a bond originally given for value, and accordingly the assignee for value of an equitable interest in the money payable under a voluntary bond is not postponed to simple contract debts. *Payne* v. *Mortimer*, 4 De G. & J. 447.

But in bankruptcy voluntary bonds are paid *pari passu* with debts for valuable consideration. *Ex parte Potinger*, 8 C. D. 621.

An executor must not pay a bond *ex turpi causâ* ; such payment would amount to a *devastavit*. *Robinson* v. *Gee*, 1 Ves. 254.

A distinction is drawn between contingent securities and those for future debts.

The rule under the old law (which may have some application to the present) appears to have been that where it was uncertain whether anything would ever become payable on the special security it should not stand in the way of simple contract deeds ; but where a sum would certainly become due, though on a future day, the special security was entitled to priority like any other obligation of its class. Wms. 871.

Under the present law, therefore, it is conceived that a debt *in futuro* would have to be met by the executor, but not a contingent debt, unless the estate was insolvent, in which case the creditor might have his debt valued and prove immediately. Jud. Act, s. 10.

As to appropriation to meet legacies *in futuro*, see *post*.

SPECIALTY AND SIMPLE CONTRACT DEBTS. 113

As to debts by simple contract, those due to the Crown shall, it seems, still be satisfied before debts due to subjects. See *Re Bentinck*, (1897) 1 Ch. 673. Debts by simple contract.

Where the estate is insolvent and is being administered in Chancery, parochial and other local rates are, equally with wages and salaries, payable in priority to all other debts. *Re Heywood*, 67 L. J. Ch. 25; (1897) 2 Ch. 593.

Damages recovered by the personal representative under 3 & 4 Wm. 4, c. 42, s. 2, for injury done by the deceased to real or personal property of another, are payable as simple contract debts.

Formerly damages for dilapidations were postponed to other debts, but they are now payable by the personal representative of the late incumbent, like other debts. 34 & 35 Vict. c. 43, ss. 29, 36.

The sum stated in the order made by the bishop as the cost of the repairs is a debt payable to the new incumbent out of the assets *pari passu* with the debts of his other creditors. *Re Monk*, 35 C. D. 583.

The question whether legacies can be paid where there is an outstanding contingent liability will be considered hereafter, as also the question whether a personal representative can be allowed payments to legatees as against creditors of whose claims he had no notice. *Post*, Chap. XI.

An executor *de son tort* may defend himself, in an action by a creditor, by showing that he has applied all the assets come to his hands in the payment of debts of equal or superior degree to those upon which the action is brought. *Ante*, p. 11.

Of Preference by the Executor.

Among creditors of equal degree the representative may pay one in preference to another. *Lyttleton* v. *Cross*, 3 B. & C. 322.

He may even after action brought confess judgment

in favour of another creditor of equal degree, or may voluntarily pay any creditor in full, though he had notice of the action. *Re Radcliffe*, 7 C. D. 733.

He may pay statute-barred debts though the estate is insufficient. But the residuary legatee, being co-defendant, may insist on the statute being pleaded. *Re Wenham*, (1892) 3 Ch. 59.

But he cannot prefer one creditor against another of a higher degree (*Re Hankey*, (1899) 1 Ch. 541); and his right of preference is not affected by 32 & 33 Vict. c. 46.

But his election may be controlled.

Thus, if one of several creditors of equal degree sue and obtain judgment against the representative, such creditor must be satisfied before the rest, and the preference of the representative is precluded.

But a voluntary payment *before judgment* is a good payment, and will be allowed. *Re Radcliffe*, 7 C. D. 733; *Vibart* v. *Coles*, 24 Q. B. D. 364.

Nothing short of an administration order will prevent the executor from paying a debt. *Re Barrett*, 43 C. D. 70.

Where a creditor sues for himself and all other creditors, no payment to any creditor made after notice of the judgment will be allowed, though the representative has a right to stand in the place of the creditor he has paid. *Jones* v. *Jukes*, 2 Ves. 518; *Irby* v. *I.*, 24 Beav. 525.

After judgment an executor cannot do any act which affects the relative rights of creditors. *Shewen* v. *Vanderhorst*, 2 R. & M. 75.

So he cannot give an acknowledgment to take a debt out of the Statute of Limitations. *Phillips* v. *Beal* (No. 2), 32 Beav. 26.

Nor pay a debt judicially declared to be barred by statute. *Midgley* v. *M.*, (1893) 3 Ch. 282.

Retainer.

An executor or administrator has a right to retain for his own debt due to him from the deceased in preference to all other creditors of equal degree. {Against debts of equal degree.}

And he may retain against creditors of a higher degree where he has no notice of the existence of such higher creditors. *Re Fludyer*, (1898) 2 Ch. 562.

This right is not affected by 32 & 33 Vict. c. 46 (*Crowder* v. *Stewart*, 16 C. D. 368), nor by sect. 10 of the Jud. Act, 1875. *Re May*, 45 C. D. 499.

But there is no retainer in bankruptcy. Therefore the right will cease from the time of his receiving notice of the petition. *Re Baker*, 44 C. D. 262, 271; but see *Re Rhoades*, (1899) 1 Q. B. 905.

An executor, therefore, who is only a simple contract creditor cannot retain against a specialty creditor. *Wilson* v. *Coxwell*, 23 C. D. 764; *Re Jones*, 31 C. D. 440; *Re Hankey*, (1899) 1 Ch. 541.

An executor's right of retainer is limited to so much of the assets as come under his control or is paid into Court during his lifetime. *Re Compton*, 30 C. D. 15; *Re Gilbert*, (1898) 1 Q. B. 282. {Against what assets.}

But if the debt due to the executor largely exceeds the assets in hand, he is not bound to realise before exercising his right of retainer, but may retain such assets in specie in satisfaction of his debt. *Re Gilbert, supra*.

If an executor asserts in his lifetime a right of retainer, but dies without having exercised it, his representatives may exercise the right for the benefit of his estate, but only as to anything which came into the actual possession or under the actual control of their testator, or which was paid into Court during his lifetime. *Re Compton*, 30 C. D. 15; *Re Jones*, 31 C. D. 440; and see *post*, 118.

An executor may retain at any time before distribution, unless perhaps there has been concealment or improper conduct on his part. *Stahlschmidt* v. *Lett*, 1 Sm. & G. 415, 420. {Time for.}

The right to retainer exists notwithstanding judgment for administration in a suit by other creditors, and notwithstanding the assets came to his hands after the judgment, and notwithstanding the bond provides that the administrator shall not unduly prefer his own debt. *Nunn* v. *Barlow,* 1 Sim. & S. 588; *Davies* v. *Parry,* (1899) 1 Ch. 602; 68 L. J. Ch. 346.

But he may, by submitting to an order for inquiries, be taken to have waived his right. *Trevor* v. *Hutchins,* (1896) 1 Ch. 844.

But the right is not affected by the fact that the executor sues on behalf of himself and all other creditors, and has submitted to account in the ordinary way. *Campbell* v. *C.*, 16 C. D. 198.

In an administration action an executor does not lose his right of retainer merely by reason of delay, if it can be explained and there are assets available. *Re Giles,* (1896) 1 Ch. 956.

None for debt bequeathed. An executor who has acquired by bequest a debt from a creditor who had proved in an administration action has no right of retainer in respect of such debt. *Jones* v. *Evans,* 2 C. D. 420.

Against receiver. There is no retainer out of assets got in by a receiver. *Re Jones,* 31 C. D. 440.

But it is otherwise where the executor hands over the assets to the receiver. *Re Harrison,* 32 C. D. 395; *Re Rhoades, supra.*

Or pays the assets into Court. *Re Giles, supra.*

Against costs. Where the fund in Court is insufficient, the right of retainer will prevail against the plaintiff's right to have the costs of suit satisfied, where the executor or administrator makes the payment in, or consents to the payment in. *Richmond* v. *White,* 12 C. D. 361; *Re Langley,* 68 L. J. Ch. 361; (1899) W. N. 23.

Against equitable assets. There is no retainer out of assets that are merely equitable. *Walters* v. *W., infra.*

For in equity all debts are equal; and a court of equity

will never assist a retainer. "Unless he can show a *legal* right to retain, equity never gives it him : if he can show a legal right, it never takes it away from him." See *Re Baker*, 44 C. D. 272.

Real estate is by 3 & 4 Wm. 4, c. 104, made assets for the payment of debts only in equity, and an executor has no right of retainer against it. *Walters* v. *W.*, 18 C. D. 182. But see now 60 & 61 Vict. c. 65, s. 2 (2) ; *ante*, p. 79. {Against real estate.}

And a trustee of an estate devised for payment of debts has no right of retainer thereout, whether he is executor or not. *Bain* v. *Sadler*, L. R. 12 Eq. 570.

The right of retainer arises only where the creditor is liable to be sued at law for a debt of the same nature ; and therefore an heir or devisee, as he could not be sued at law for simple contract debts, has no right of retainer for them. *Re Illidge*, 27 C. D. 478.

But a creditor by specialty in which the heirs were bound could sue the heir, and therefore the heir had a right of retainer. *Ibid.*

And since the executor, as real representative, can now be sued for payment of debts, it follows that he will now have a right of retainer out of real estate.

An executor or administrator may retain not only for debts which he claims beneficially, but also for those to which he is entitled as trustee. *Sander* v. *Heathfield*, L. R. 19 Eq. 21 ; see also *Bain* v. *Sadler*, *supra*. {Debt due to trustee.}

Conversely the executor or administrator may retain for debts due to another in trust for him. *Cockroft* v. *Black*, 2 P. Wms. 298 ; *Franks* v. *Cooper*, 4 Ves. 763.

An administrator *durante minoritate* may retain for his own debt, and also for that of the infant. *Franks* v. *Cooper*, 4 Ves. 764. {Administrators.}

So an administrator *durante dementia* may retain on behalf of the lunatic. *Ibid.*

If administration be granted to a creditor, as such, and afterwards repealed, such creditor shall retain against the rightful administrator. *Blackborough* v. *Davis*, 1 Salk. 38.

Under the common decree for administration against an administrator who has obtained administration as a creditor, the Master has no authority to disallow his claim to retainer, even though waived, unless there is a specific instruction to the Master to that effect. *Spicer* v. *James*, 2 M. & K. 387; *Thompson* v. *Cooper*, 1 Coll. 81. *Cf. Trevor* v. *Hutchins, ante,* 116.

By executor of executor.
An executor of a sole or surviving executor is entitled to retain either in his own right or as executor of the deceased executor, but not if he does not so survive; and only as to assets which come under the control of the original executor. *Re Compton*, 30 C. D. 15; and see *ante*, p. 115.

And in the same way the executor of an administrator-creditor may retain against the assets of the debtor. *Weeks* v. *Gore*, 3 P. Wms. 184.

Quære, whether, where an executor dies, having intermeddled, but before probate, and before any election made, his executor can retain. 3 P. Wms. 184.

By one of several.
One of three executors, who is also one of two joint creditors, has a right of retainer in respect of his joint debt. *Crowder* v. *Stewart*, 16 C. D. 368; *Re Hubback*, 29 C. D. 934.

One of two partners to whom a debt is due being made executor may retain; but if he predecease the other partner the retainer is gone, and cannot be claimed by the representative of the executor. *Burge* v. *Brutton*, 2 Ha. 373; *Talbot* v. *Frere*, 9 C. D. 575.

If two are jointly and severally bound, and one makes the obligee his executor, he may either retain or sue the survivor. *Crosse* v. *Cocke*, 3 Keb. 116.

By widow.
A widow, the administratrix of her late husband, whose estate was insolvent, was allowed to retain out of assets come to her hands as administratrix the amount of a loan to him in his business out of her separate estate. *Re May*, 45 C. D. 499. Comp. *Re Leng*, (1895) 1 Ch. 652.

De son tort.
An executor *de son tort* cannot retain even for a superior debt. *Ante*, p. 12.

But he may under 43 Eliz. c. 8—that is, where he becomes such by gift of the assets from an administrator who has obtained the grant fraudulently.

If the same person be the representative of both creditor and debtor, he may retain as representative, and it is his duty to do so. *Fox* v. *Garrett*, 28 Beav. 16 ; *Re Owen*, 23 L. R. Ir. 328.

Where two are jointly bound, one as principal and the other as surety, and the surety becomes representative of principal, he may retain. *Boyd* v. *Brooks*, 34 L. J. Ch. 605.

Surety.

The right of indemnity belonging to an executor who is surety for an unpaid debt of his testator creates an equitable debt in respect of which he may retain. *Re Giles*, (1896) 1 Ch. 956.

The executor of a surety to the Crown, who has paid the debt of his deceased principal, is entitled to the Crown's priority in the administration of the principal's estate. *Re Churchill*, 39 C. D. 174.

As a rule the right of an executor as surety to be indemnified creates a simple contract debt only, and does not entitle him to retain against specialty creditors. *Ferguson* v. *Gibson*, L. R. 14 Eq. 379 ; but see *Re Allen, infra*.

But a covenant to pay and indemnify the surety makes the latter a specialty creditor, and he can retain against other specialty creditors. *Re Allen*, (1896) 2 Ch. 345.

But the executor, in order to have a right of retainer, must have paid the debt as surety while he has the assets in his control; and if, when he pays the debt, there are no assets in his hands, there is no right of retainer. *Re Harrison*, 32 C. D. 395 ; but see *Re Allen, supra; Re Giles, infra*.

It has, however, been held that a representative as surety is entitled to retain, though he has not paid any part of the debt, or been called upon to pay it. *Re Allen, supra ; Re Giles*, (1896) 1 Ch. 956.

PAYMENT OF DEBTS.

Against co-executor. Where there are co-executors or co-administrators, each being a creditor, one cannot retain to the prejudice of the other, but they must retain rateably. 11 Vin. Abr. 72.

But one executor, who is a creditor, has a right to retain out of a balance due from himself and the other executor jointly. *Kent* v. *Pickering*, 2 Keen, 1.

Damages. Damages which are arbitrary, such as damages founded on tort, cannot be retained. *Loane* v. *Casey*, 2 W. Black. 968.

But damages for breach of pecuniary contracts, for which there is a certain standard or measure, as for breach of covenant to assign a policy, may be retained. *Re Compton*, 30 C. D. 15.

An executor is not deprived of his retainer by the fact that the amount of the liability cannot be ascertained until accounts have been taken. *Re Morris*, L. R. 10 Ch. 68.

Annuity. An annuitant administratrix can only retain for arrears, and not for the estimated value of her future annuity. *Re Beeman*, (1896) 1 Ch. 48.

Pauper. The executor of a pauper can retain against the claim of guardians for maintenance. *Larer* v. *Botham*, (1895) 1 Q. B. 59.

Statute-barred debt. An executor may retain his own just debt, though barred by the Statute of Limitations. *Stahlschmidt* v. *Lett*, 1 Sm. & Gr. 415.

But the Court will not order a fund to be paid out in order to enable an executor to retain such a debt. *Trevor* v. *Hutchins*, (1896) 1 Ch. 844.

But he cannot retain for a debt barred by the Statute of Frauds. *Field* v. *White*, 29 C. D. 358.

Set-off against Legacies.

An executor or administrator may set off against a legacy or distributive share of personal estate debts presently due by the legatee or next of kin to the estate. *Taylor* v. *T.*,

20 Eq. 155; *Rees* v. *R.*, 60 L. T. 260; *White* v. *Cordwell*, 20 Eq. 644.

And this is so though the debt is statute-barred. *Re Akerman*, (1891) 3 Ch. 212; but see *Dingle* v. *Coppen, infra*.

The principle, however, does not apply to specific devises, nor to bequests of specific leaseholds or chattels. *Ibid.*

But it does apply to moneys in the executor's hands representing property specifically bequeathed. *Taylor* v. *Wade*, (1894) 1 Ch. 671.

The rule also applies though the legatee has assigned his legacy for value. *Knapman* v. *Wreford*, 18 C. D. 300; *Re Jones, infra*.

The right also arises though the legatee has become bankrupt, where the bankruptcy occurs after the death. *Cherry* v. *Boulthee*, 4 M. & C. 442; *Hodgson* v. *Fox*, 9 C. D. 678 : *Re Watson*, (1896) 1 Ch. 925.

But if the debt is proved in the bankruptcy the right of set-off is lost. *Stammers* v. *Elliott*, 3 Ch. 195; *Re Binns*, (1896) 2 Ch. 584; and see *Re Orpen*, 16 C. D. 202, where only the composition was allowed to be set off.

The right is also gone where a fund has been appropriated to meet a trust legacy. *Ballard* v. *Marsden*, 14 C. D. 374.

An executor may set off against the legacy of a co-executor the amount of a *devastavit* committed by the latter. *Sims* v. *Doughty*, 5 Ves. 243.

And an administrator may set off the costs of a probate action ordered to be paid by the next of kin. *Re Jones*, (1897) 2 Ch. 190.

The principle that executors may set off a statute-barred debt has no application where the debtor is claiming a legal right, and not merely the testator's bounty. *Dingle* v. *Coppen*, 79 L. T. 693.

Extinguishment of Executor's Debt.

Effect of appointing creditor.

It remains to consider how far the appointment of a creditor as executor operates as an extinguishment of his claim.

The appointment alone is no extinguishment. But if the executor receives assets adequate to discharge the liability, the debt is extinguished. *Lowe* v. *Peskell*, 16 C. B. 500; *Crampton* v. *Walker*, *infra*.

Therefore, if he has no assets, he may sue the heir. Wms. 1181; but see now 60 & 61 Vict. c. 65.

The same rule applies where one of several joint debtors made the common creditor his executor (*Crampton* v. *Walker*, 31 L. R. Ir. 437); and also where the debtor appoints his creditor to be one of several executors, if the creditor administers. Wms. 1181, 1182.

So a creditor-administrator, who has no assets, may sue an executor *de son tort* for the debt due to him from the intestate. *Ibid.*

Effect of appointing debtor.

The effect in equity of appointing a debtor as executor is that the debt is considered to have been paid, and the debt is general assets for payment of debts and legacies. *Berry* v. *Usher*, 11 Ves. 90; *Simmons* v. *Gutteridge*, 13 Ves. 264; *Re Price*, 11 C. D. 163.

The appointment of a debtor as executor is clearly not sufficient of itself to annul the debt in equity. *Re Hyslop*, (1894) 3 Ch. 522.

But where there is some other equity besides the appointment, and it can be shown that the testator intended to release the debt, it will be released, even though the executor has not proved the will. *Re Applebee*, (1891) 3 Ch. 422.

CHAPTER XI.

PAYMENT OF LEGACIES.

It is obvious that the executor must take care to discharge all the debts of the testator before he satisfies any description of legacy. *Executor must pay all debts before legacies.*

And for this purpose real as well as personal property is applicable as to persons dying after 1st January, 1898.

Specifically-bequeathed property is not discharged from this liability by reason of the fact that the executor has in hand more than enough assets to pay the debts, and that the specific gifts have been made over to the specific legatees. In case of deficiency, therefore, the executor will be answerable for such legacies with interest. *Davies v. Nicolson*, 2 De G. & J. 693.

As already stated, even voluntary bonds and covenants must be paid in preference to legacies. *Ante*, p. 112. *Voluntary debts.*

With respect to contingent debts and liabilities, a question arises whether an executor can safely pay over legacies or the residue where there is an outstanding contingent liability. *Contingent debts.*

The answer is, not if he has notice; otherwise he will have no answer when the claim ripens into a certain claim. *Taylor v. T.*, L. R. 10 Eq. 477.

But as against the legatees he may claim repayment of the legacies, even though he had notice of the contingent liability at the time when he distributed the estate; but not if the liability had then ripened into a certain debt. *Jervis v. Wolferstan*, L. R. 18 Eq. 18; *Whittaker v. Kershaw*, 45 C. D. 320.

Such being the law, the executor is not bound to part with the assets, where such liabilities exist, without an indemnity or impounding a sufficient part of residue for that purpose, for otherwise he would be liable to answer damages *de bonis propriis* without any fault of his.

Where, however, the estate is administered in Court, the executor is perfectly safe; and if he gives the Court all the information he possesses, he will be protected from all liability. *Dean* v. *Allen*, 20 Beav. 1.

Liability on leaseholds. As regards leaseholds no indemnity is now necessary, as by Lord St. Leonards' Act (22 & 23 Vict. c. 35, s. 27), if the executor or administrator has sold the leaseholds and assigned them to a *purchaser*, setting apart a fund to answer any fixed sum covenanted to be laid out on the property, he may distribute the assets without making provision for future breach of covenant, and will not be subject to any liability. *Dodson* v. *Sammell*, 1 Dr. & S. 575.

In like manner he may avoid liability in respect of the rent and covenants contained in any conveyance on rent-charge. See sect. 28.

The section does not apply to a specific bequest of leaseholds, in which case the executor will have to rely on the indemnity of the specific legatee. *Dean* v. *Allen*, 20 Beav. 1; *Shadbolt* v. *Woodfall*, 2 Coll. 30.

Debts of which the executor had no notice. Another question is whether an executor or administrator can be allowed payments to legatees or parties entitled in distribution, as against creditors of whose claims he had no notice.

Formerly it was held that mere want of notice would not excuse an executor or administrator, if he *bonâ fide* distributed the assets; but see now Lord St. Leonards' Act, *infra*; and cf. *Re Fludyer*, (1898) 2 Ch. 562.

If, in the distribution of assets, a creditor misleads an executor, either by conduct or express authority, so as to induce him to pursue a course he would not otherwise have pursued, the creditor is precluded from complaining of an insufficiency of assets. *Re Birch*, 27 C. D. 622.

But mere laches or non-suing for any period within the statute will not deprive a creditor of his right of requiring payment. *Re Baker*, 20 C. D. 230.

And now by 22 & 23 Vict. c. 35, s. 29, where an executor or administrator shall have given such or the like notices as would have been given by the Court of Chancery in an administration suit for creditors and others to send in their claims against the estate of the testator or intestate, such executor or administrator shall, at the expiration of the time named for sending in such claims, be at liberty to distribute the assets, having regard to the claims of which such executor or administrator has then notice, and shall not be liable for the assets so distributed to any person of whose claim he shall not have had notice at the time of distribution; but nothing in the Act shall prejudice the right of any creditor or claimant to follow the assets. Lord St. Leonards' Act, s. 29.

A reasonable executor will issue advertisements as soon as possible after the death. *Re Kay*, (1897) 2 Ch. 518.

The section is not confined to creditors, but also applies to persons claiming as next of kin. *Newton* v. *Sherry*, 1 C. P. D. 246.

If proper notices are given under the Act, the representative has the same protection as in an administration by the Court; and if he continues to hold legacies as trustee he will not be liable *quâ* executor. *Clegg* v. *Rowland*, L. R. 3 Eq. 368; *Hunter* v. *Young*, 4 Ex. D. 256.

What is sufficient notice depends upon the particular circumstances of each case. *Re Bracken*, 43 C. D. 1.

But at least a month should be allowed for sending in claims. *Wood* v. *Weightman*, 13 Eq. 434; but see *Re Bracken*, *supra*.

But an executor, with notice of a claim, is not discharged by reason of the fact that the creditor does not come in in answer to the advertisements. *Markwell's Case*, 21 W. R. 135; *Scottish, &c.* v. *Beatty*, 29 L. R. Ir. 290.

How far creditor's priority is affected by administration suit.

Next, it is necessary to consider how far the laches of a creditor may affect his priority over legatees where there is an administration action.

Although the order directs that those who do not come in shall be excluded, yet it is usual to permit a creditor, he paying the costs, to prove his debt as long as there are assets undistributed. *Re Metcalfe*, 13 C. D. 236.

If a creditor does not come in until after the assets are distributed, he can still sue the legatees and bring back the fund; but he cannot affect the legatees, except by suit; and he cannot affect the executor at all. *David v. Frowd*, 1 M. & K. 210.

Where a creditor does not come in until some of the legatees have been paid in full, and there is left in Court a fund appropriated to other unpaid legatees, it seems that he is entitled to be paid out of such fund such a proportion only of his debt as would have been borne by the unpaid legacies if he had applied before the legacies were paid, and that he should be left to recover the residue from the paid legatees. *Gillespie v. Alexander*, 3 Russ. C. C. 130; *Greig v. Somerville*, 1 R. & M. 338.

But this rule does not apply where the estate is not administered by the Court. *Davies v. Nicolson*, 2 De G. & J. 693.

A creditor may come in as long as there are assets undistributed. Therefore, where a creditor omitted by mistake part of his claim, he was allowed to prove. *Re Metcalfe*, 13 C. D. 236.

Legacy to Executor.

No preference.

An executor has no preference in regard to his own legacy, though given for his trouble; and, in case of deficiency, it must abate. *Duncan v. Watts*, 16 Beav. 204.

A legacy to an executor has, therefore, no priority. Nor has an annuity. *Re Thorley, post*, p. 129.

The usual clause empowering a solicitor-executor to charge for work done is in effect a legacy of profit costs, and is liable to legacy duty. *Re White*, (1898) 1 Ch. 297, 299. *Profit costs.*

Such profit costs, therefore, have no priority, and cannot be claimed as against creditors. *Ibid.*

The presumption is that a legacy to a person appointed executor is given to him in that character, and it is for him to rebut that presumption. *Re Appleton*, 29 C. D. 893. *Presumption that it is given quâ executor.*

Parol evidence may, it seems, be admitted to rebut the presumption. *Ibid.*

The mere fact that the gift of the legacy precedes the appointment of the legatee as executor, or that the legacies to several persons appointed executors differ either in amount or subject-matter, is not enough to rebut the presumption. *Ibid.*

Nor is it enough that the legacies are given *nominatim* and not to them expressly as executors. *Reed* v. *Devaynes*, 3 Bro. 95; *Stackpoole* v. *Howell*, 13 Ves. 417; *Piggott* v. *Green*, 6 Sim. 72.

A legacy, therefore, given to an executor for his trouble is clearly annexed to the office, and cannot be claimed unless he acts. *Slaney* v. *Watney*, 2 Eq. 418. *And annexed to office.*

Where the gift is annexed to the office, it will make no difference that the executor is incapable by infirmities of acting. *Hanbury* v. *Spooner*, 5 Beav. 630; *Re Hawkins*, 33 Beav. 570.

The presumption will be rebutted where it can be gathered that the gift was intended to be in respect of relationship, as where the executor is referred to as "my brother" or "my cousin." *Compton* v. *Bloxham*, 2 Coll. 201; *Dix* v. *Reed*, 1 S. & S. 237. *Presumption rebutted.*

So, too, where the gift is to "my friend." *Re Dendy*, 3 D. F. & J. 350; *Bubb* v. *Yelverton*, 13 Eq. 131; but see *Reed* v. *Devaynes*, *supra*.

Or where the legacy is given "as a remembrance," or

"as a mark of respect." *Bubb* v. *Yelverton, supra* ; *Burgess* v. *B.*, 1 Coll. 367.

Or where the legacy is given after the death of the tenant for life. *Re Reeve*, 4 C. D. 841.

Where two legacies are given to the executor, one of which is clearly not annexed to the office, the other will, it seems, be deemed so too. *Wildes* v. *Davies*, 22 L. J. Ch. 497 ; explained 29 C. D. 896.

Where a testator gave to his executors a legacy, a ring, and a sum for mourning, it was held that though they did not act they were entitled to the rings and mourning. *Humberston* v. *H.*, 1 P. Wms. 333.

Where a testator declared that if any legatee died in his lifetime his legacy should not lapse, it was held that the legacy of the executor who predeceased the testator was saved to his representatives. *Murray* v. *Sanger*, W. N., (1873) 79.

Where a testator gave to his "friend and partner" much greater benefits than any of his other executors, it was held that the legacies were not given to him in the character of executor. *Cockerell* v. *Barber*, 2 Russ. 585.

What is a sufficient assumption of office.

What is a sufficient assumption of the office of executor to entitle him to his legacy?

If he proves the will with the intention of acting, or unequivocally manifests an intention to act, that will be sufficient. *Lewis* v. *Matthews, infra.*

Thus, if he give directions for the funeral and be prevented by death from proving the will or further entering upon his office, that is sufficient. *Harrison* v. *Rowley*, 4 Ves. 212 ; and see *Hollingsworth* v. *Grasett*, 15 Sim. 52.

So where an executor, being abroad, sent home a power of attorney to administer the estate and died before proving the will, his representative was held entitled to the legacy. *Lewis* v. *Matthews*, 8 Eq. 277.

Where a trustee died nineteen months after the testator without having acted, he was held entitled to a legacy

LEGACY TO EXECUTOR.

given for his trouble, no refusal to neglect to act, where necessary, appearing. *Brydges* v. *Wotton*, 1 V. & B. 134.

If an executor proves and *bonâ fide* acts as such any time before the real business of administering the estate is concluded, he is entitled to his legacy. *Angerman* v. *Ford*, 29 Beav. 349.

So he may entitle himself by proving after renunciation, but interest will only be payable from probate. *Ibid.*

But where an executor proved without apparently any intention of acting, and made use of the circumstance of probate to violate his trust in the grossest manner, he was held disentitled to his legacy. *Harford* v. *Browning*, 1 Cox, 302. {Misconduct may disentitle.}

It has been held that the rule that an executor is only entitled to his legacy if he acts, does not apply to a gift of residue or share of residue. *Griffiths* v. *Pruen*, 11 Sim. 202; *Christian* v. *Devereux*, 12 Sim. 264; but see *Compton* v. *Bloxham*, 2 Coll. 201; *Hollingsworth* v. *Grasett*, 15 Sim. 52. {Gift of residue.}

Where an annuity is given to an executor for his trouble, it will cease when the duties of the executor cease. *Hull* v. *Christian*, 17 Eq. 546. {Annuity.}

But it will not cease by the institution of a suit for administration, where no receiver is appointed and there are assets still outstanding. *Baker* v. *Martin*, 8 Sim. 25.

Such an annuity has no priority, and is liable to duty, even where it is given for carrying on the testator's business. *Re Thorley*, (1891) 2 Ch. 613.

A request by a testator that a handsome gratuity should be given to each of his executors is void for uncertainty. *Jubber* v. *J.*, 9 Sim. 503. {Handsome gratuity.}

Where a testator gave a specific bequest to A., and directed that in consideration thereof A. should pay his debts, and made A. his executor, it was held that if A. accepted the bequest he was bound to pay the debts, though they should far exceed the property bequeathed to him. *Messenger* v. *Andrews*, 4 Russ. 478. {Conditional gift.}

Where there is a direction that the executors shall pay the testator's debts, followed by a gift of all his real estate to them either beneficially or in trust, all the debts will be payable out of all the estate so given to them. *Re Bailey*, 12 C. D. 268, 273.

The question, however, is one of intention (*Ibid.*); and the latter decision may now be affected by the Land Transfer Act, 1897.

Legal devise. An executor's beneficial interest is liable to be applied in making good his *devastavit*, but this does not apply when the estate is legal, since the estate of a legal devisee is under no circumstances under the control of a court of equity. *Fox* v. *Buckley*, 8 C. D. 508, 511.

Quære, whether this principle is affected by the Land Transfer Act.

The assent of the executor to his own legacy is as necessary as to that of any other person. Toller, 345.

Executors previous to retaining their own legacies must transmit the particulars, with the duty offered, to the Commissioners, under a penalty for neglect. 36 Geo. 3, c. 52, s. 35.

As to payment of duties, see *ante*, p. 97.

Abatement of Legacies.

General legacies abate before specific.   In case the assets are sufficient to answer the debts and specific legacies, but not the general legacies, the latter are subject to abatement.

The abatement takes place in equal proportions; and in the case of stock the value is calculated according to the price at the end of a year from the testator's death. *Auther* v. *A.*, 13 Sim. 440.

The executor has no preference in regard to his own legacy as he has to his own debt. *Ante*, p. 126.

Generally speaking, nothing shall be abated from specific legacies. Wms. 1211.

But if a testator directs pecuniary legacies to come out of all his personal estate, and there is none except the specific legacies, they will be subject to those which are pecuniary. *Sayer* v. *S.*, Prec. Ch. 393.

A residuary legatee has no right to call upon particular general legatees to abate. *Baker* v. *Farmer*, L. R. 3 Ch. 537.

Residuary legatee cannot call on them to abate.

So if there is a simple bequest of an annuity it must be paid in full to the last farthing of the property, however great or small the income of the estate may be. *Croly* v. *Weld*, 3 De G. M. & G. 993, 996.

But it is otherwise where there is an intention that the annuity shall only come out of income. *Ibid.*; *Wormald* v. *Muzeen*, 17 C. D. 167.

The rule is that if there is a gift of a life interest and a reversion, and the estate is insufficient, each party bears the loss in proportion to his interest. But if there is a gift of an annuity and a residuary gift, the whole loss falls on the latter. *Ibid.*

Where assets have been lost after the death of the testator, the loss falls on the residuary legatee in the first instance. *Wilmot* v. *Jenkins*, 1 Beav. 401; *Baker* v. *Farmer*, *supra*.

Though among general legatees there is no preference, and all abate together, yet legacies given for valuable consideration, as for debts or instead of dower, have priority. Theobald, 660.

As between annuitants charged on personal estate and legatees there is no priority, and both must abate proportionably.

The annuity should be valued, and the annuitant will be entitled at once to the amount of the valuation. *Wroughton* v. *Colquhoun*, 1 De G. & S. 357; *Carr* v. *Ingleby*, *Ibid.* 362; *In re Sinclair*, 66 L. J. Ch. 514.

If, however, it was the intention of the testator to give priority, that intention must be carried into effect. *Re Hardy*, 17 C. D. 798.

K 2

A demonstrative legacy is not liable to abate with general legacies. *Roberts* v. *Peacock*, 4 Ves. 150.

As long as any of the assets not specifically bequeathed remain, such as are specifically bequeathed are not to be applied in payment of debts. But when the assets not specifically bequeathed are insufficient to pay the debts, then the specific legatees must abate in proportion to their value. Wms. 1224.

The question when real estate can be made to contribute to the payment of debts is no longer of the same importance since real estate has become part of the general assets by virtue of the Land Transfer Act, 1897. *Ante*, p. 77.

Executors' Assent to Legacy.

Assent necessary.
Every legatee must obtain the executors' assent to the legacy before his title as legatee can be complete, and before he can obtain possession.

The assent or a conveyance is also necessary in the case of a devisee. 60 & 61 Vict. c. 65, s. 3.

Before such assent, however, the legatee has an inchoate right which is transmissible to his representatives. Went. 69.

It seems that the consent is necessary even where the testator forgives a debt due to him. Went. 72.

Formerly it was the practice of the Bank of England to transfer stock specifically bequeathed direct to the legatee. But now by 33 & 34 Vict. c. 71, s. 23, all stock standing in the name of a deceased person shall and may be transferred by the executors or administrators of the deceased, notwithstanding any specific bequest thereof.

Even where the property specifically bequeathed is in the possession of the legatee, and the assets are fully adequate to the payment of debts, he has no right to retain it against the executor, by whom an action will lie to recover it. *Mead* v. *Orrery*, 3 Atk. 239.

It has been said that, if an executor refuse his consent without cause, he may be compelled to give it. Com. Dig. Admon. c. 8.

And as regards real estate, the Court may order a conveyance to be made at any time after a year from the death, if the representatives fail, on request, to convey to the person entitled. 60 & 61 Vict. c. 65, s. 3 (2).

There is no prescribed form of consent. It may be either express or implied; and may involve matters of law, though it is generally a question of fact. *Elliott* v. *E.*, 9 M. & W. 27; *Wilson* v. *Rhodes*, 8 C. D. 777; *Thorne* v. *Thorne*, (1898) 3 Ch. 196. *What will constitute assent.*

The assent may be inferred from expressions or acts, but they must be unambiguous.

Where more than one person takes under a bequest of specific property, an assent to the bequest to one will, generally speaking, be an assent to the others. *Stevenson* v. *Liverpool*, L. R. 10 Q. B. 81.

But where there is a bequest of a number of articles, the executor may withhold his assent as to part. *Elliott* v. *E.*, 9 M. & W. 23.

And he may assent to part only of a residuary gift. *Austin* v. *Beddoe*, 41 W. R. 619.

The assent may be presumed, as when executors die after the debts are paid, but before the legacies are satisfied. 2 P. Wms. 532. So where a legatee takes possession and retains it for a considerable time without complaint from the executor. Wms. 1230.

The assent may also be conditional, but the condition must be precedent, not subsequent, nor such as the executor had no right to impose. Went. 429. *Conditional.*

And he may assent to a devise subject to a charge for payment of money he is liable to pay. 60 & 61 Vict. c. 65, s. 3 (1).

The executor may assent before he proves the will; and even if he dies before probate, his assent will be effectual. Went. 82. *Who may give.*

PAYMENT OF LEGACIES.

And where there are several executors, the assent of any one of them is sufficient. *Ante*, p. 93.

Effect of assent. After assent, the property vests in the legatee, who may sue to recover it, even against the executor.

If he assents to a bequest of leaseholds, they will vest in the legatee without any deed of assignment (*Re Culverhouse*, (1896) 2 Ch. 251); and the executor cannot require an indemnity. *Ante*, p. 124.

The mere fact that the executor has made general payments to a legatee of leaseholds is not in itself sufficient to imply assent. *Thorne* v. *T*., (1893) 3 Ch. 196.

Where there is a specific bequest to the executor in trust, and he assents, the legacy ceases to be part of the testator's assets, and is held by the executor upon trust. *Dix* v. *Burford*, 19 Beav. 409; *Baker* v. *Farmer*, L. R. 3 Ch. 537.

But mere assent does not make the executor a trustee of a legacy given direct to the legatee. *Re Lowe*, 60 L. T. 599; and see *Buxton* v. *Campbell*, (1892) 2 Ch. 491.

Retracting assent. Generally speaking, if an executor assent to a legacy he cannot afterwards retract. Went. 415; *Mead* v. *Orrery*, 3 Atk. 238; *Ballard* v. *Marsden*, 14 C. D. 374.

But where the assent has not been completed by possession, he may, under special circumstances, retract; as where debts afterwards appear, of which he had no notice, which occasion a deficiency: 1 Rop. Leg. 3rd ed. 743.

And if that happens after assent has been completed by possession, he may compel the legatee to refund. *Doe* v. *Guy*, 3 East, 123.

He may, however, assent to a devise subject to debts. *Ante*, p. 133.

Relation back. The assent relates back to the death of the testator, so as to entitle the legatee to intermediate profits or confirm an intermediate grant. Went. 69, 445.

Executor's assent to his own legacy. The assent of the executor is as necessary to his own legacy as to that of any other person. Toller, 345.

It may in like manner be implied. And if he does

anything which shows he has assented, that will be taken as evidence of assent; but if his acts are referable to his character of executor, they are not evidence of such assent. *Doe* v. *Sturges*, 7 Taunt. 223; Com. Dig. Admon. (c. 6, 7).

It is not sufficient to constitute an implied assent to show that the Act is equally applicable to the title of legatee as to the character of executor; for if his acts are referable to his character of executor they are not evidence of assent. 7 Taunt. 217, 223; 1 Coll. 360.

Until the executor has made his election, he shall take the legacy as executor, though all the debts have been paid. Com. Dig. Admon. (c. 5).

With regard to the effect of entry by the executor into possession of a term of years bequeathed to him, the following distinction exists: Where the *entire* term is given to the executor, an entry will amount to an election to take as legatee. But where only a *partial* interest is given to him, he must do something more than enter, in order to give assent to his legacy. Wms. 1235; *Doe* v. *Sturges, supra; Att.-Gen.* v. *Potter*, 5 Beav. 164.

Effect of entry by executor.

An entry, however, in the latter case, may, when accompanied by other circumstances, amount to an election to take as legatee: as where the executor explains the entry by a declaration that he claims the estate as devisee for life. Wms. 1237.

The above will now apply to freeholds.

It is not essential for the validity of an assent to a bequest that it should confer a legal interest or affect the mere legal title. *Trail* v. *Bull*, 1 Coll. 352.

Though an assent to a particular estate is an assent to the remainder, yet an executor taking possession of goods bequeathed to him for life will not, while debts remain unpaid, be presumed to take as legatee so as to assent to the gift over. *Richards* v. *Brown*, 3 Bing. N. C. 493.

If an executor-legatee renounce probate, his assent to his own legacy will be ineffectual. *Broker* v. *Charter*, Cro. Eliz. 92.

This will also apply to an executor-devisee.

One of several executors may assent. *Ante*, p. 93.

Assent by one of several. If one of several executors be a legatee, his single assent will vest his own legacy in him; and if the legacy be given to all the executors, the assent of any one to his own proportion will be sufficient to vest the legacy in all. *Townson v. Tickell*, 3 B. & A. 31, 40.

Time for Payment.

Payable at end of a year. An executor cannot be compelled to pay any legacy within a year from the testator's death, even where the testator directs it to be paid earlier, though there is nothing to prevent him doing so, if he chooses. *Angerstein v. Martin*, 1 Turn. & R. 241; *Garthshore v. Chalie*, 10 Ves. 13; and see *post*, p. 144.

But a legatee can bring an action for administration before the year has expired. *Prosser v. Mossop*, 29 W. R. 489.

A gift over, which takes effect after the year, is payable immediately on the happening of the event. *Laundy v. Williams*, 2 P. Wms. 478.

Practice in administration actions. According to the practice in administration actions, the Court waits until all claims are settled and a clear fund ascertained, and then pays the particular legacies, with interest. *Thomas v. Montgomery*, 1 Russ. & M. 737; and see R. S. C., Ord. 55, r. 64.

But where it clearly appears that there will be a surplus, the Court will by anticipation direct proportional payments to be made to legatees. R. S. C., Ord. 50, r. 9.

Where the estate was large, and there were few debts, the Court ordered payment of annuities out of income, *before decree*. *Digby v. Boycott*, 4 Ha. 444.

Legacy subject to divesting. Where a legacy is subject to a limitation over, the divesting contingency will not prevent the legatee receiving his legacy at the end of the year from the testator's death

TIME FOR PAYMENT. 137

without giving security. *Fawkes* v. *Gray*, 18 Ves. 131; but see as to security *Colston* v. *Morris*, 6 Madd. 89.

An annuity commences from the testator's death, and the first payment shall be made at the end of the year after that event. *Houghton* v. *Franklin*, 1 Sim. & S. 392. Annuity.

Sed quære, whether this is so where the annuity is given out of residue. *Storer* v. *Prestage*, 3 Madd. 168.

But it may be expressly directed to commence within the year, as at the first quarter-day after the death, or monthly, in which case it will become due then, but will not be payable till the end of the year. *Ibid.; Irvin* v. *Ironmonger*, 2 R. & M. 531.

Where a *legacy* is given for life with remainder over, no interest is due till the end of two years. But where the bequest is of *residue*, the legatee is entitled to income in some shape or other from the death. Wms. 1243.

A legatee of chattels for life is entitled to possession of them upon signing and delivering to the executor an inventory admitting their receipt, and expressing that he is entitled to them for life. Security is not now required unless a case of danger is shown. *Slanning* v. *Style*, 3 P. Wms. 336; *Bill* v. *Kinaston*, 2 Atk. 82; *Conduitt* v. *Soane*, 1 Coll. 285.

Where legacies are directed to be invested in stock, the Court will not consider whether the executor might not have invested at an earlier period, so as to fix him with the stock he might have purchased. *Secus*, if the estate was clear, and he retained the legacy as trustee. *Byrchall* v. *Bradford*, 6 Madd. 13, 240.

It may here be added that an annuity to A. *or* his heirs or to A. for ever passes on his death to his personal representatives. *Parsons* v. *P.*, 8 Eq. 260; *Taylor* v. *Martindale*, 12 Sim. 158. Annuity to A. and his heirs.

But an annuity to A. *and* his heirs did not so pass, but went to the heir. Such an annuity, however, though it partook of the nature of real estate, was not an hereditament, but a fee simple personal, and therefore it would seem that it would not pass as real estate under the Land Transfer Act. See Co. Litt. 2 a.

Appropriation.

Legacies payable in futuro.

Although legatees cannot receive their legacies until the day of payment arrives, yet they may apply to the Court to set aside a sufficient sum to answer them when due. *Johnson* v. *Mills*, 1 Ves. Sen. 282; *Re Tredwell*, 65 L. T. 742.

Executors may appropriate specific assets to a trust share of residue, or transfer them to a legatee of a share, in advance of final division. *Re Richardson*, (1896) 1 Ch. 512; *Coles* v. *Davis*, 76 L. T. 771.

But a legatee has not an absolute right to have his future legacy brought into Court, whether it is in danger or not. *Re Braithwaite*, 21 C. D. 121.

And where the legacy is contingent the Court will not direct appropriation. *Webber* v. *W.*, 1 S. & S. 311.

Where there are contingent debts and liabilities no appropriation will be directed. *Thomas* v. *Montgomery*, 1 R. & M. 729.

Even where there is no express power, and the interests of infants are concerned, executors can appropriate specific assets to answer settled shares of residue, though it is safer to do so with the sanction of the Court. *Re Nickels*, (1898) 1 Ch. 630.

But it is incumbent on the executors to see that the securities appropriated are of sufficient value. *Re Chapman*, (1896) 2 Ch. 763, 787.

The value of shares is the market price, and the value of a mortgage debt has been taken at par. *Re Richardson*, (1896) 1 Ch. 512; *Re Lepine*, (1892) 1 Ch. 210.

An administrator has an equal right to appropriate. *Ante*, p. 81.

An appropriation once made is final; and the persons entitled to the severed property cannot afterwards claim in respect of loss, nor be called upon to make good an increase. *Fraser* v. *Murdoch*, 6 A. C. 855; *Re Richardson*, *supra*.

By the Land Transfer Act, 1897, s. 4, the personal representatives may appropriate any part of the residuary estate in or towards satisfaction of any legacy or share of residue; but they must give notice to the persons interested in the residuary estate. *Ante*, p. 81.

To whom Legacies are to be Paid.

This is of great importance to the executor, who must be careful to pay legacies to the persons who have authority to receive them.

If a legacy be given to A. to be divided between himself and his family, payment to A. is a good payment. So a legacy given to B. for her and her children's use may be paid to B. *Cooper* v. *Thornton*, *infra*; *Robinson* v. *Tickell*, *infra*. Legacy to A. and his family.

An executor cannot pay a legacy to an infant, nor to any other person for him, without the sanction of the Court, except perhaps where it is of small amount. *Dagley* v. *Tolferry*, 1 P. Wms. 285; *Walsh* v. *W.*, 1 Drew. 64. To infants.

Though he may pay it to the father or other person as trustee for the infant, where so directed. *Robinson* v. *Tickell*, 8 Ves. 142; *Cooper* v. *Thornton*, 3 Bro. C. C. 97.

But the executor may discharge himself of all liability by paying the legacy of an infant into Court under the Trustee Act, 1893, s. 42.

And this course ought to be pursued. But the payment in need not be made till a year from the death. Toller, 319.

Where executors invested an infant's legacy in Consols and tendered the amount produced by sale of the stock and dividends to the infant on coming of age, it was held that they ought to have paid the legacy into Court, and a decree was made for the amount of the legacy with 4 per cent. interest and costs. *Russell* v. *Simpson*, 18 L. J. Ch. 55.

Maintenance. An executor, as a rule, cannot apply any part of the capital of an infant's legacy towards maintenance; nor even income, unless the estate is clear. *Re Smith, infra.*

And if he makes disbursements in the schooling, feeding, or clothing of the children of the deceased, he will be liable for a *devastavit*. *Giles* v. *Dyson*, 1 Stark. N. P. C. 32.

But the Court has authorised such application where the fund was small and where there was no other means of support. *Ex parte Green*, 1 Jac. & W. 253; *Prince* v. *Hine*, 26 Beav. 634; and see *Robison* v. *Killey*, 30 Beav. 520.

An executor ought in every case to apply to the Court by originating summons before devoting any part of the capital to maintenance. And this, it is thought, should also be done even where income only is sought to be applied, unless there is express power or the case comes within the Conv. Act.

By the Conv. Act, 1881, s. 43, trustees may at their sole discretion apply the income of property held by them in trust for an infant either absolutely or contingently towards his or her maintenance, education, or benefit.

Where residue is bequeathed to an infant, and the estate is clear and the residue has been ascertained, the executor is trustee thereof within this section. *Re Smith*, 42 C. D. 302.

As to the old rules of equity with regard to maintenance independently of statute, see Wms. 1267.

Advancement. An executor ought not to apply any money towards advancement unless authorised by the will or sanctioned by the Court.

The Court, however, has less reluctance to break in upon capital for the purpose of advancement than for maintenance, since the former is regarded as an investment. *Walker* v. *Wetherell*, 6 Ves. 474.

But both with regard to advancement and maintenance the rule applies that if an executor do, without application, what the Court would have approved, he shall not be called upon to account, and forced to undo that, merely because it was done without application. *Lee* v. *Brown*, 4 Ves. 362, 369 ; *Prince* v. *Hine*, *supra*.

Even before the passing of the M. W. P. Act, 1882, a legacy given to the separate use of a married woman vested in her personally. *Feme covert legatee.*

The effect of the Act is, that women married after 1st January, 1883, are entitled to hold as separate property any legacy, and women married before that date are so entitled if their title accrues after that date.

Where, therefore, a legacy is separate property, either under the Act or independently of it, an executor must pay such legacy to the wife, who alone can give a good discharge.

As to cases where the legacy is not her separate property, and as to her equity to a settlement, see Wms. 1277.

Where a legatee is abroad, the executor may avoid all responsibility by paying the legacy into Court under the Trustee Act, 1893, s. 42. *Legatee abroad.*

An executor who receives notice that a legatee has charged his legacy must withhold all further payments to him, and the executor can create no new rights of set-off after that time. *Stephens* v. *Venables*, 30 Beav. 625. *Assignment of legacy.*

By 32 & 33 Vict. c. 23, all property of a felon vests in the administrator or curator (if any) appointed under the Act; but a legacy acquired by a convict while at large under ticket of leave is not subject to the Act. Sect. 30. *Felon.*

Where a legatee of a share of residue less than 20*l.* has died, and has no representative, the Court will distribute the legacy among the next of kin without requiring administration to be taken out. *Hinings* v. *H.*, 2 H. & M. 32. *Legacy under 20l.*

If a representative makes payment of a legacy or share to a wrong person, he must replace it, with interest at *Payment to wrong person.*

4 per cent. *Powell* v. *Hulkes,* 33 C. D. 552; *Att.-Gen.* v. *Kohler,* 9 H. L. C. 654; and see *Rogers* v. *Ingham,* 3 C. D. 351.

He must also see that instruments under which he is asked to pay money are genuine, for if they are forged he will be liable. *Eaves* v. *Hickson,* 30 Beav. 136; and see *Sloman* v. *Bank of England,* 14 Sim. 475.

He will not, however, be liable for a *bonâ fide* payment under a power of attorney merely because the donor is dead or has avoided it. Trustee Act, 1893, s. 23; Conv. Act, 1882, ss. 8, 9.

Interest on Legacies.

A specific bequest, if vested, carries all income and profits from the testator's death; and it is immaterial whether the enjoyment is postponed by the testator or not. 2 Rop. Leg. 227.

Where a legacy is charged upon real property, and no day of payment is mentioned in the will, interest will be given from the death. *Pearson* v. *P.,* 1 S. & L. 10; *Spurway* v. *Glynn,* 9 Ves. 483.

But where the legacy is payable out of the proceeds of sale of real estate, interest is payable from a year after the death. *Turner* v. *Buck,* 18 Eq. 301.

General legacies carry interest from one year after the death, unless some other period is fixed by the will. *Wood* v. *Penoyre,* 13 Ves. 333, 334.

But a legacy in satisfaction of a debt, or one given by a parent to a child, carries interest from the death. Wms. 1287.

So does a legacy to an infant, where maintenance is directed to be paid out of the interest of that sum. *Re Richards,* 8 Eq. 119.

Annuities commence from the death; but as a rule no interest will be allowed on arrears. *Torre* v. *Browne,* 5 H. L. C. 555.

But where a sum is given to executors to be laid out in the purchase of an annuity, interest will only run from twelve months after the death. *Re Friend*, 78 L. T. 222.

In some instances legacies payable *in futuro* will carry interest, although not given by a parent, where there is an intention that the legatees shall be maintained out of the property. *Boddy v. Dawes*, 1 Keen, 362.

Where a legacy is divested by death under age, the representative of the infant legatee is entitled to the interest accrued during the infant's life. *Taylor v. Johnson*, 2 P. W. 504; *Mills v. Roberts*, 1 R. & M. 555.

The usual rate of interest allowed on legacies is 4 per cent. R. S. C., Ord. 55, r. 64.

But interest at 5 per cent. will be allowed against an executor who applies assets to his own use or in trade. *Post*, p. 188.

Refunding of Legacies.

An executor cannot compel a legatee whom he has *voluntarily* paid, to refund. *Orr v. Kaines*, 2 Ves. 194.

But where the payment by the executor is under the compulsion of a suit, he can compel a legatee to refund in case of a deficiency of assets. *Newman v. Barton*, 2 Vern. 205.

So if payment has been obtained by fraud. *Coppin v. C.*, 2 P. Wms. 296.

Again, if the executor pays away the assets, and debts afterwards appear of which he had no notice, he may compel the legatees to refund. *Davies v. Nicholson*, 2 De G. & J. 693; *Andrew v. Cooper*, 45 C. D. 444; but see *Billing v. Brogden*, 38 C. D. 546. *Cf. Re Fludyer*, *ante*, p. 115.

A similar liability is imposed upon the next of kin by the Statute of Distribution, s. 5.

But he cannot compel residuary legatees to refund if he has paid over the assets with notice of a debt. *Jervis v. Wolferstan*, 18 Eq. 18.

Notice, however, of a possible remote contingent liability is not sufficient to prevent an executor recovering back the assets when such liability becomes a present debt. *Whittaker* v. *Kershaw*, 45 C. D. 320.

So notice of a liability on shares will not prevent executors calling on legatees to refund. *Ibid*.

The refunding is made, as a rule, without interest. *Gittins* v. *Steele*, 1 Swanst. 200.

An executor having by mistake made payments to an annuitant, was allowed to retain them out of subsequent payments. *Livesey* v. *Livesey*, 3 Russ. 287; but see *Hilliard* v. *Fulford*, 4 C. D. 389.

And he may recover, from the residuary legatees, legacy duty which he has been compelled to pay. *Brooke* v. *Haymes*, 6 Eq. 25.

Payment of Residue.

When the executor has paid all the debts and funeral and testamentary expenses, including costs of administration, he must pay over the surplus to the residuary legatee or his representative. *Trethewy* v. *Helyar*, 4 C. D. 53.

And he must now in like manner distribute the residuary real estate of any testator dying after 1897.

The residuary legatee has a right to insist that the executor before the end of the year from the death shall, if possible, convert all the assets into money. Wms. 1316.

But there is no rule that executors and trustees are under an absolute duty, without exercising any judgment of their own in the matter, to realise within twelve months from the death, unless realisation is required for payment of debts and legacies. *Re Chapman*, (1896) 2 Ch. 763.

He may, however, without express authority, agree with residuary legatees that they shall accept, before final division, any portion of the estate as their share. *Re Lepine*, (1892) 1 Ch. 210; *Re Richardson*, ante, p. 138.

PAYMENT OF RESIDUE.

After payment of debts and legacies, the executor must hand over the clear residue to the residuary legatee, or, if bequeathed for life, secure the capital by investing it in manner authorised by the Trustee Act, 1893, for the benefit of those ultimately entitled.

No particular mode of expression is necessary to constitute a residuary legatee. It is sufficient if the intention clearly appears by the will. As to what words are sufficient, see Wms. 1317.

The residue includes everything not otherwise effectually disposed of by the will.

This is the presumed intention of the testator, and may therefore be negatived by the terms of the will.

Thus the testator may narrow the title of the residuary legatee so as to exclude lapsed legacies, or so restrict the residue as that it may become a specific legacy.

Where the residue is bequeathed to several persons as joint tenants, the share of one dying before severance will survive. *Webster* v. *W.*, 2 P. Wms. 347.

But if given to several as tenants in common the share of one dying before the testator will go to the testator's next of kin; and if dying afterwards, shall go to the legatee's representative. *Page* v. *P.*, 2 P. Wms. 488.

Where co-executors take a residue in that character, they take as joint tenants. Therefore if one dies before severance his share will survive to the others. *Frewen* v. *Relfe*, 2 Bro. C. C. 220.

When the residue is undisposed of, the question arises whether it belongs to the executor or next of kin. *Right of executor to residue.*

By 1 Wm. 4, c. 40, an executor shall be deemed a trustee for the next of kin unless it appears by the will that he was intended to take the residue beneficially.

The Act does not affect the rights of executors where there are no next of kin, and in such a case, if there is no contrary intention, they will be entitled as against the Crown. *Re Bacon*, 31 C. D. 460; *Russell* v. *Clowes*, 2 Coll. 648.

The Crown, however, was held entitled against the executors in a recent case, but in that case the above Act and the above cases were not cited. *Re Wood*, (1896) 2 Ch. 596.

The Act did not introduce any new rule for the construction of wills. Whether an executor takes beneficially is simply a question of intention. *Williams* v. *Arkle*, L. R. 7 H. L. 606.

The Act only applies where the residue is undisposed of. It does not therefore apply where there is an express gift of residue. *Saltmarsh* v. *Barrett*, 3 D. F. & J. 279.

Where the Act does not apply as in the cases above mentioned the old law obtains under which the executors are, generally speaking, excluded from the residue in the following cases:—

1. They take only such residue as the testator did not *intend* to dispose of. They do not, therefore, take lapsed legacies. Theob. 652.

2. They do not take when they are treated as trustees. *Ibid.*

3. Nor where the testator professes to dispose of *part* only of his property. *Ibid.* 653.

4. Nor where a legacy is given to a sole trustee, executor, or equal legacies to them all. *Ibid.*

5. Nor where they are appointed because they occupy a particular position. *Ibid.* 655.

On the other hand executors have been held to be entitled: Where the gift is to them by name (*Williams* v. *Arkle*, L. R. 7 H. L. 606; *Hillersden* v. *Grove*, 21 Beav. 518); where the gift is subject to certain payments (*Parsons* v. *Saffery*, 9 Pr. 578); where, under special circumstances, a blank was left for the name of the residuary legatee (*Re Bacon*, 31 C. D. 460); and where three children were appointed and reasons given for not providing for the other children. *Harrison* v. *H.*, 2 H. & M. 237; and see *Fuge* v. *F.*, 27 L. R. Ir. 59.

CHAPTER XII.

DISTRIBUTION UNDER STATUTE.

The duties of administrators in respect of distribution of personal estate are regulated by the Statutes of Distribution, which lay down the proportions in which the parties entitled are to share.

But since administrators will now have to distribute real estate, as well as personalty, the following rules must be read as subject to the provisions of the Land Transfer Act, 1897.

That Act, however, though vesting real property in the personal representative, does not alter the destination of either real or personal property, and therefore the following principles will still hold good as regards personal estate.

The husband is entitled to the grant of administration of his wife's effects. *Ante*, p. 21. <small>Husband.</small>

If he dies before taking out administration, it shall be granted to his representatives, unless it can be shown that the next of kin of the wife are entitled to the beneficial interest as by settlement. *Ante*.

So if the husband die before having administered all her estate, the same rule applies. *Re Pountney*, 4 Hagg. 289; *Re Lambert*, 39 C. D. 626.

By the Intestates' Estates Act, 1890, where the estate of an intestate does not exceed 500*l*. net value, and there are no issue, the whole estate goes to the widow. <small>Wife.</small>

Where it does exceed 500*l*. the widow has a charge on the estate for 500*l*. with interest at 4 per cent. from the death. Sect. 2.

The above provision is to be in addition to her share of residue. Sect. 4.

The Act does not apply to cases of partial intestacy. *Re Twigg*, (1892) 1 Ch. 579.

Where there are no next of kin the widow takes one moiety and the Crown the other. *Cave* v. *Roberts*, 8 Sim. 214.

The widow's claim may be barred by a settlement before marriage. But it is otherwise where the husband by will makes provision for his wife in bar of her claims. Wms. 1360.

Subject as above, the widow takes one third and the children the remainder.

And if no issue, she takes one moiety, and the other goes to the next of kin.

Issue. After the allotment of a third to the widow the remaining two thirds go to the children or their lineal representatives.

If there is no wife, then all the estate goes to the children. See *Re Goodman*, 17 C. D. 266.

A brother or sister of the half blood is equally entitled to share with the whole blood; and a posthumous child has the same rights. Wms. 1367; and see *Blasson* v. *B.*, 2 D. J. & S. 665.

Where all the children are dead, all of them having left children, the grandchildren will take *per capita*. 2 Black. Com. 517.

Where some are living, and some dead, each having left children, the grandchildren take *per stirpes*.

But no child, except the heir, shall take without bringing his share under settlement or advancement by his father into hotchpot. Stat. of Dis., s. 5.

Next of kin. Subject to the Intestates' Estates Act, 1890, if there are no children a moiety goes to the widow and the rest to the next of kin, and if no widow the whole to the next of kin; but there is no representation after the intestate's brothers' and sisters' children. Stat. of Dis., ss. 6, 7.

The next of kin are ascertained by the same rules as

those which determine who are entitled to letters of administration. Toller, 381.

The distribution of the personal estate of an intestate is to be regulated by the law of the country in which he was domiciled at his death. Domicil.

But since the Statute of Distributions applies to foreigners domiciled in England, the proper law for determining the kindred under that statute is the international law adopted by the comity of nations. *Re Goodman*, 17 C. D. 266; and see *Andros* v. *A.*, 24 C. D. 637; *Grey* v. *Stamford*, (1892) 3 Ch. 88.

The *status* of a person claiming under the statute must be decided by reference to the law of the country where the *status* originated. *Re Goodman, supra*.

It is part of the law of England that personal property should be *distributed* according to the *jus domicilii*.

Although the Court is bound to administer according to the law of domicil, yet where the title has been adjudicated upon by the Courts of domicil, such adjudication is binding on the Courts here, even though the judgment proceeded on a mistake as to English law. *Re Trufort*, 36 C. D. 600.

Hence it appears that a different doctrine prevails with respect to *distribution* from that with respect to probate and administration, as to which the *situs* of the property decides the jurisdiction. *Ante*.

The *administration* of the estate must be in the country in which possession of it is taken, and held under lawful authority. And in administering the estate the Court will be guided by the law of domicil. *Ewing* v. *Orr-Ewing*, 10 A. C. 502.

The domicil only affects movables. Therefore leaseholds in England belonging to a domiciled Scotchman devolve according to the English Statute of Distributions. *Duncan* v. *Lawson*, 41 C. D. 394.

CHAPTER XIII.

ASSETS.

Foreign assets.

THE property of the testator shall be assets in whatever part of the world they are situate.

Where different administrations are granted in different countries, that will be deemed the principal which is granted in the country of the domicil. Wms. 1525.

But each portion of the estate must be administered where possession is taken. And the administrator there has a right to hold his assets against the home administrator, even after they have been remitted to this country.

The only mode, it seems, of reaching such assets is to require their transmission after all foreign claims have been settled. *Eames* v. *Hacon*, 18 C. D. 347, 351.

The liability of an executor or administrator to account for assets out of England would seem to depend upon his relation to the foreign assets. *Ewing* v. *Orr-Ewing*, 9 A. C. 34.

It is not apparently the duty of a representative acting in this country under a subsidiary grant to hand over the balance to the principal administrator. *Re Klœbe*, 28 C. D. 175.

Legal and equitable.

Legal assets are such as come into the hands and power of an executor or administrator *virtute officii*.

Equitable assets, on the other hand, are those the right to which or to recover which vests in the representative otherwise than *virtute officii*.

The distinction simply refers to the remedy, and in no way depends upon the legal or equitable nature of the property.

ASSETS.

The importance of the distinction lies in the fact or rule that preferential payments can only be made out of legal assets.

It will be seen, therefore, that the Land Transfer Act, 1897, makes a considerable and important change in the law in this respect, for by making real estate devolve upon the personal representatives *virtute officii* it makes all such real estate legal assets.

With the exception, therefore, of personal property appointed under a general power (*ante*, p. 73), and copyholds, all real and personal estate of the deceased would now appear to be legal assets.

It is a general rule that an executor or administrator shall not be charged with any other goods as assets than those *which come to his hands*, or might but for his own fault have so come. What assets come to hand.

Where they have come into his possession and are afterwards lost, the executor is in the position of a gratuitous bailee, and cannot be charged without wilful default. *Job* v. *Job*, 6 C. D. 562.

And generally he will not be liable where he is not at fault. Wms. 1535; *post*, p. 179.

With regard to choses in action he will not be charged with them until he has reduced them into possession. *Williams* v. *Innes*, 1 Camp. 364; *post*, p. 178.

Estates *pur autre vie*, where there is no special occupant, shall be assets in the hands of the executor or administrator, and shall go and be applied in the same way as personal estate. Wills Act, s. 6.

The absolute property of the goods must have been vested in the testator. Therefore property held by the deceased as sole trustee will of course not be assets, though it devolves upon his representative. Conv. Act, 1881, s. 30.

Where a man has a general power of appointment over a fund and actually exercises it, the fund will go to his executors as part of his assets and be liable to his debts as against the appointees. *Re Hoskin*, 6 C. D. 281.

This now applies to real estate. 60 & 61 Vict. c. 65, s. 1 (2).

In the same way the execution of a general power by will by a married woman makes the property appointed liable to her debts. *Re Ann*, (1894) 1 Ch. 549.

Primary liability of personalty.

It is a well-known rule that the personal estate is primarily liable for payment of debts; and this rule is not altered by the Land Transfer Act. See sect. 2 (3).

Consequently the heir or devisee is entitled to have the real estate exonerated by the personal estate.

But not so as to disappoint a creditor, or legatee except the residuary legatee. Wms. 1563.

The heir, however, is so entitled to the disappointment of the residuary legatee only, but the devisee to the disappointment of general legatees and to *contribution* by specific legatees. *Ibid.* 1564.

The claim in question must be the *proper debt* of the deceased, otherwise the heir or devisee must take *cum onere*. *Ibid.* 1565.

But a mortgage debt or equitable charge or lien for unpaid purchase money is not, since Locke King's Acts, 1854, 1867, and 1877, payable out of the personal estate so as to exonerate the land charged.

The same rule applies to legacies. The personal estate is the first and natural fund for the payment of them. And even where debts and legacies are charged on the real estate, yet the personal estate remains primarily liable.

But no such rule applies to specific personal estate so charged; in such a case the specific personalty will be the primary fund for the payment of debts. *Trott v. Buchanan*, 28 C. D. 446.

And so a direction to sell for payment of debts and legacies is not alone evidence of an intention to exonerate. *Forrest v. Prescott*, 10 Eq. 545.

Nevertheless a testator may, if he pleases, give the personal estate discharged from such payments. And though express words are not necessary, there must be an intention not merely to charge the real estate, but to discharge the personal estate. *Bootle* v. *Blundell*, 1 Mer. 230.

Where a pecuniary legacy is given only out of a particular fund, the legatee can only have recourse to that fund; and in this there is an essential difference between debts and legacies. Wms. 1583.

As a rule, where a testator expressly directs that a certain part of his personal estate shall be liable to payment of debts, it is an exoneration of the general personal estate. *Trott* v. *Buchanan*, 28 C. D. 446.

Where the testator directs a sale of his real estate, and the proceeds and the personal estate are *thrown into one mass* for the payment of debts and legacies, the real and personal estate must contribute in proportion to their relative amounts. *Roberts* v. *Walker*, 1 R. & M. 572; *Elliott* v. *Dearsley*, 16 C. D. 322; but see *Allan* v. *Gott*, 7 Ch. 439.

The effect of the Land Transfer Act, 1897, is to create a mixed fund for payment of debts, but it does not affect the order in which real and personal estate must contribute. Sect. 2 (3); see *Re Board*, (1895) 1 Ch. 499.

It is a general rule that if a claimant has two funds to which he may resort, a person having an interest in one only has a right to compel the former to resort to the other, if that is necessary for the satisfaction of both. But in practice the claimant on the single fund is usually protected by marshalling the assets.

Marshalling.

In the absence of a contrary intention sufficiently expressed, assets are applied in payment of debts in the following order:—

1. The general or residuary personalty, not specifically bequeathed or exonerated or exempted.

2. Real estates appropriated to, and not merely charged with, the payment of debts.

3. Real estates descended, whether acquired before or after the making of the will.

4. Real estates devised charged with the payment of debts.

5. General pecuniary legacies *pro ratâ*. *Re Salt*, (1895) 2 Ch. 203.

6. Specific and residuary devisees and specific legatees *pro ratâ*.

7. Real and personal property which the testator has power to appoint and has appointed by will.

CHAPTER XIV.

LIABILITIES OF REPRESENTATIVES ON THE ACTS OF THE DECEASED.

AN executor represents the debts and property, but not the person of the testator. *Phillips* v. *Homfray*, 24 C. D. 439. <small>In matters of contract.</small>

The right of action upon any obligation, contract, debt, covenant or other *duty* survives, and can be enforced against the representatives. *Ibid.*

Therefore they are answerable, so far as they have assets, for debts of every description due from the deceased.

So they may be sued by the lord of the manor for a relief due from the testator. *St. John* v. *Bawdripp*, Noy, 43.

So they are liable for arrears of a rent-charge accrued during life of deceased. *Ante*, p. 74.

So they are liable for negligence of a deceased attorney or sheriff. *Wilson* v. *Tucker*, 3 Stark. 154; *Gloucestershire, &c.* v. *Edwards*, 20 Q. B. D. 107.

And so they are liable on a promise by the deceased to do a collateral act which is uncertain, and rests only in damages. Bac. Abr. Exors. P. 2.

They so completely represent the deceased with respect to the liabilities above-mentioned that every contract or obligation of the deceased includes them, though they are not named in it. Went. 239.

This does not extend to cases where the contract is personal to the deceased, for there no action survives unless there was a breach in the lifetime of the deceased.

Thus a contract to write a book, instruct an apprentice, or build a lighthouse, are personal.

LIABILITY FOR ACTS OF DECEASED.

Where, however, a person contracts with a builder to erect a house on his land, and dies intestate before it is completed, the heir-at-law is entitled to have the house finished at the expense of the personal estate of the intestate. *Cooper* v. *Jarman*, L. R. 3 Eq. 98; *Re Day*, 67 L. J. Ch. 619.

Conversely, if the builder dies, his executors appear to be liable. *Quick* v. *Ludborrow*, 3 Bulst. 13.

As the authority of an agent is revoked by death, he cannot, generally speaking, sue the executor of the principal in respect of services rendered after the death. 15 C. B. 400.

If a man covenants that his executors shall pay a certain sum after his death, an action can be sustained against the executor. *Powell* v. *Graham*, 7 Taunt. 580.

Tort. Where the cause of action is founded upon any malfeasance or misfeasance, or is a tort, or arises *ex delicto*, and the plea must be not guilty, the rule is *actio personalis moritur cum personâ*; and if the person committing the injury dies, no action can be brought against his representatives.

No action, therefore, lies on a penal statute, and the executor or administrator of an executor or administrator was not at common law liable for a *devastavit* committed by the latter, though he is so now by 4 & 5 Wm. & M. c. 24, s. 12. *Coward* v. *Gregory*, L. R. 2 C. P. 153.

But an injury in the nature of a tort may be regarded as a breach of an obligation in the nature of an implied contract.

Thus where a testator was liable for repairs, deteriorations are to be regarded as breaches of an implied contract, and an action lies against the executors. *Batthyany* v. *Walford*, 36 C. D. 269. *Blackmore* v. *White*, (1899) 1 Q. B. 293.

In some cases a remedy may be had against the representatives in another form.

Thus, though an action did not lie against the executor for waste committed by the testator, yet for the benefit arising to his estate therefrom the executor was liable.

So, though an action for trespass for mesne profits could not be maintained against him, yet he is liable for occupation rent. *Infra.*

In most or all which cases the right of action is in respect of benefit to the estate, though arising from a wrongful act of the deceased.

There are, therefore, cases where the action, though arising out of a wrongful act, does not die, and where a profit thereby accruing to his estate may be followed. *Phillips* v. *Homfray*, 24 C. D. 454.

In such cases, whatever the original form of action, it is in substance brought to recover property, or its proceeds or value, and by amendment could be made such in form as well as in substance. The property, or proceeds or value, which in the lifetime of the wrongdoer could have been recovered from him, can be traced to his assets and recaptured there by the rightful owner. *Ibid.*

But it is not every wrongful act by which a wrongdoer indirectly benefits that falls under this head; the benefit must consist in the acquisition of property or its proceeds or value. Where there is nothing among the assets that in law or equity belongs to the plaintiff, and the damages are unliquidated and uncertain, the executors of a wrongdoer cannot be sued merely because it was worth the wrongdoer's while to commit the act complained of, and an indirect benefit has been reaped thereby. *Ibid.; Re Duncan, infra.*

The profits arising from a wrong done by a deceased man, which can be followed against his estate, are only such profits as take the shape of property, or the proceeds or value of property, withdrawn from the rightful owner and acquired by the wrongdoer. *Ibid.*

Two illustrations may be given: The proceeds of waste, committed by a tenant for life, can be followed into the hands of his executors and retaken from them. Thus, timber wrongfully cut, or its value, may be so followed. But no action for waste, as such, lies against the executors of a tenant for life. And see Settled Land Act, 1882, s. 28 (5).

Again, the rents and profits of land wrongfully received by other than the rightful owner may, as a rule, be recovered from the wrongdoer or his estate. But there is a sense in which the term "profits" is used to represent damages for trespass, as when an action for mesne profits is maintained to recover compensation for the bare possession wrongfully taken. An action for mesne profits in this sense will not lie at common law and apart from statute against executors, and no account would be decreed in equity, except in a case where the profits were either property, or the produce, or profits, or value of property actually received.

The purchaser from a testator of certain worthless shares in a limited company cannot prove in an administration action for damages for misrepresentation against the testator's estate on the ground that the estate might have benefited by the wrong complained of. *Re Duncan*, (1899) 1 Ch. 387.

By 3 & 4 Wm. 4, c. 42, s. 2, actions may be brought against executors or administrators for any injury done by the deceased to property, real or personal, within six calendar months before such person's death, but such action must be brought within six months after such representatives shall have taken upon themselves the administration of the estate.

Where coal had been tortiously taken, part within six months and part before, it was held that an action lay under the statute for so much as was raised within the six months, and also for money had and received for such as was raised before. *Powell v. Rees*, 7 A. & E. 426.

So a lord of a manor may sue for ore dug or timber cut. *B. of Winchester v. Knight*, 1 P. Wms. 406.

An action for obstruction of ancient lights lies against executors, even though the obstruction was completed six months before the death. *Jenks v. Clifden*, (1897) 1 Ch. 694.

The liability of the representatives of a deceased incumbent to answer for dilapidations is now governed by the Ecclesiastical Dilapidations Act, 1871. *Ante*, p. 113.

As to the extent to which they are liable, see *Percival v. Corke*, 2 Car. & P. 460; *Wise v. Metcalfe*, 10 B. & C. 299.

The representatives of a deceased trustee are liable for his breaches of trust.

They are also liable for their own (*Grayburn v. Clarkson*, L. R. 3 Ch. 605); but they may claim relief under the Judicial Trustees Act, 1896, s. 3.

In the case of a joint contract, if one of the parties die the survivors alone can be sued; and if all die the executor of the survivor is alone liable. Wms. 1615.

If a testator, being a sole defendant, dies *before* judgment, by Ord. 17, r. 1, if the cause of action survive, that is, if it does not fall within the rule *actio personalis moritur cum personâ*, the action shall not abate, but the plaintiff may (r. 4) obtain an order that the representative of the deceased be added as a party. This order may, it seems, be obtained *ex parte*.

If a testator, sole defendant, die *after* judgment, leave must, it would seem, be obtained to issue execution against the goods of the testator. Ord. 42, r. 23. This order must, it seems, be obtained on notice to the representative. *Re Shephard*, 43 C. D. 131; and see *Norburn v. N.*, (1894) 1 Q. B. 448.

If one of several defendants on a joint cause of action die before judgment, then it would seem that in a personal action the estate of the deceased is discharged from liability. Ord. 17, r. 1.

And if one of two defendants dies after judgment, and the plaintiff elects to take execution against the personalty, the execution must be against the survivor alone. So a release, given by the obligee to the representative of the deceased obligor, is no answer to an action against the survivor. *Ashbee v. Pidduck*, 1 M. & W. 564.

And if one of several defendants on a joint cause of action die after judgment, it would seem that Ord. 42, r. 23, will not, except as against the land of the deceased, apply;

because, as we have seen above, if one die execution must be against the survivor alone.

And in the same way, although under Ord. 17, r. 1, there is no abatement on death, yet it would seem that if the cause of action be joint, there is nothing in this Order to enable the action to continue against any other than the surviving defendant. Wms. 1617.

But if the contract be several, or joint and several, the executor of the deceased contractor may be sued at law in a separate action, but he cannot be sued jointly with the survivor. *Hall* v. *Huffam*, 2 Lev. 228.

Partners.

But in equity the executor of a joint contractor may be sued in the case of a partnership debt (4 A. C. 545); and he may recover against the surviving partner. *Re Hodgson*, 31 C. D. 177, 192.

A partnership creditor has concurrent remedies against the estate of the deceased partner and the surviving partner, and it makes no difference which he pursues first. *Ibid*.

Nor will the first creditor be precluded from resorting to the assets of the deceased partner by having in the first instance obtained judgment against the surviving partners. *Liverpool B. B.* v. *Walker*, 4 D. & J. 24.

By the Partnership Act, 1890, s. 9, every partner is liable jointly with the other partners, and after his death his estate is also severally liable, but subject to the prior payment of his separate debts.

Although a partnership liability will not generally be treated in equity as joint and several apart from administration, yet whenever the Court sees that in a contract joint in form the real intention was that it should be joint and several, it will give effect to such intention. *Beresford* v. *Browning*, 1 C. D. 30.

The liability remains until the debts are fully discharged. *Vulliamy* v. *Noble*, 3 Meriv. 619.

The discharge, however, may take place in various ways. Wms. 1623; Lindley, 256.

By the Partnership Act, 1890, s. 33, subject to any agreement, every partnership is dissolved by death.

By sect. 36 the estate of a deceased partner is not liable for debts contracted after the death.

By sect. 39 the representatives of a deceased partner may apply to the Court to wind up the business of the firm.

By sect. 42, where the surviving partners continue the business, the representatives of a deceased partner are entitled, in the absence of agreement, to a share of profits or interest at 5 per cent. on his share of assets; unless there is an option to purchase which is duly exercised.

By sect. 43, subject to any agreement, the amount due to the representatives of a deceased partner is a debt accruing at the date of the death.

With regard to the liabilities of the executors of share- *Shareholders.* holders, it is important to notice the following provisions of the Comp. Act, 1862:—

By sect. 16, all moneys payable by any member to the company shall be deemed a debt in the nature of a specialty debt. *Re Muggeridge*, L. R. 10 Eq. 443; *Buck* v. *Robson*, Ibid. 629; *Master, &c.* v. *Pearson*, 66 L. J. P. C. 25.

By sect. 76, if any contributory dies, his personal representatives, heirs, and devisees shall be liable to contribute, and shall be deemed contributories accordingly. As to the nature of the liability, see sect. 75.

By sect. 99, in settling the list of contributories, the Court shall distinguish those who are contributories in their own right and those who are merely representatives, and it shall not be necessary to add the heirs and devisees unless the Court thinks fit.

By sect. 105, if a representative makes default in paying moneys ordered, administration proceedings may be taken.

Unless excluded by the articles of association, the following regulations of Table A. will apply:—

Art. 12. The executors or administrators of a deceased

member shall be the only persons recognised by the company as having any title to his share. *Baird's Case*, L. R. 5 Ch. 725.

Art. 13. Any person becoming entitled to a share on death may be registered as a member.

A representative, however, may make himself personally liable in respect of the shares.

Two courses are open to him. He may have the shares transferred into his own name, and become to all intents and purposes a partner in the company. *Spence's Case*, 17 Beav. 203. Or he may within a reasonable time sell the shares and produce a purchaser who will take a transfer. *Buchan's Case*, 4 A. C. 588.

But until he accepts or transfers the shares the deceased member—that is, his estate—remains a member, and his representatives are entitled to the benefits accruing thereon, and are liable for calls in respect thereof. *New Zealand Gold Co.* v. *Peacock*, (1894) 1 Q. B. 622; *James* v. *Buena Ventura Synd.*, (1896) 1 Ch. 456.

It is open to an executor to notify to the company that he is executor, and that would not authorise the company to put him on the register so as to make him personally liable. *Ibid.*; *Re Cheshire, &c.*, 32 C. D. 301.

But if shares are once put into the names of executors individually, though offered to and accepted by them in a representative capacity, they cannot limit their liability to the assets of the testator (*Ibid.*); and if in a company under the Companies Clauses Acts the names of the legal personal representatives are placed on the register, even though under the description of executors, they become joint shareholders in their individual capacity. *Barton* v. *L. & N. W. Ry.*, 24 Q. B. D. 77; *ante*, p. 93.

Executors are entitled to produce legal evidence of their representative rights for the purpose of having their title recorded without making themselves personally liable. 4 A. C. 595.

It is not a personal acceptance of shares for executors to

receive the dividends in their representative character. *Bulmer's Case*, 33 Beav. 485.

The liability of an executor not himself a shareholder is limited to the extent of the assets.

But if he distributes the assets without providing for contingent liability on the shares, he will be personally liable. *Taylor* v. *T.*, L. R. 10 Eq. 477.

He will, however, in such a case be entitled to call upon the legatee to refund the legacy, but not any intermediate income. *Jervis* v. *Wolferstan*, 18 Eq. 18; *Whittaker* v. *Kershaw*, 45 C. D. 320.

Executors cannot protect themselves against the claims of the company by advertising under Lord St. Leonards' Act. *Markwell's Case*, (1872) W. N. 210; *Russell's Case*, 15 Sol. J. 790.

But they are not, it seems, liable for a *devastavit* for paying debts before a call is made or a claim by the liquidator. Buckley.

If executors accept from a company after their testator's death new shares, they will, as between themselves and the other contributories, be personally liable in respect of them, although they have been offered to and accepted by them in their representative character. *Duff's Case*, 32 C. D. 301; *Jackson* v. *Turquand*, L. R. 4 H. L. 305.

They have purchased the shares; whether with authority under the will or not is immaterial. They are, therefore, personally liable, and can only look to their testator's estate for indemnity. *Spence's Case*, 17 Beav. 203.

Where two or more persons are registered as joint owners of a share, they are joint tenants so far as the legal interest is concerned, and the legal title survives. And, in the absence of anything to the contrary in the articles, the liability is joint. Upon the death of one, therefore, his liability will cease. *Hill's Case*, 20 Eq. 477.

But the representatives of a deceased joint owner may be liable in respect of such obligations as attached to the

LIABILITY FOR ACTS OF DECEASED.

Director.

shares up to the time of his death. *Kirby's Case*, 15 Sol. J. 922; and see *Alexander's Case*, 15 Sol. J. 788. Actions for indemnity against loss occasioned by the misrepresentations of directors, like actions for deceit, are of a personal character; and, unless the estate of a deceased director is alleged and proved to have received some benefit from the misrepresentation, such actions do not survive against his executors. *Peek* v. *Gurney*, L. R. 6 H. L. 377; *Re Duncan, ante,* p. 158.

But the estate of a deceased director is liable in respect of claims in the nature of a breach of trust. *Ramskill* v. *Edwards*, 31 C. D. 100; *Re Sharpe*, (1892) 1 Ch. 154.

And his representatives are liable to the extent of the assets. *Concha* v. *Murrietta*, 40 C. D. 543.

The executors of a deceased director, not being officials of the company, cannot be proceeded against by summons under the Comp. Act, 1890, s. 10. *Re British Guardian Co.*, 14 C. D. 335.

Covenants.

An executor is bound by the covenants of his testator, unless they are personal. And he is answerable for breaches after the death of the testator, so far as he has assets. *Coghill* v. *Freelove*, 3 Mod. 326.

A representative may be charged as such for arrears of rent due from the deceased, so far as he has assets. Woodfall, 305.

Leases.

Although a covenant in a lease runs with the land, yet this shall not discharge the executor of the original lessee from a concurrent liability on the covenant, as far as he has assets, even although the lessor shall have accepted the assignee as his tenant. 1 Saund. 241 a.

But it is otherwise where the testator was the *assignee* of the lessee, for he, being liable only for breaches in his own time, may discharge all future liability by assignment over, even to a pauper. *Taylor* v. *Shum*, 1 B. & P. 21.

An executor therefore may be guilty of a *devastavit* in not so assigning, after offering to surrender, in such a case. *Rowley* v. *Adams*, 4 M. & C. 534.

If the executor himself assigns the term, the lessor may afterwards bring covenant against the executor, notwithstanding any acceptance of the assignee as tenant. *Coghill* v. *Freelove, supra;* but see 22 & 23 Vict. c. 35, s. 27, *infra.*

Hence an executor when he carries a lease to market has a right to require that the purchaser shall indemnify him. *Staines* v. *Morris,* 1 V. & B. 8 ; *Wilkins* v. *Fry,* 1 Meriv. 266.

But he cannot in strictness be compelled to enter into any covenant except that he has not incumbered. Key & E. 5th ed., i. 696.

The testator's estate as against an equitable tenant for life is liable for repairs down to the time of his death. *Re Betty,* (1899) 1 Ch. 821 ; *Re Gjers,* (1899) W. N. 77.

No action lies against an executor or administrator upon an *implied* covenant which is not broken till after the death of the testator. Wms. 1632.

An executor *de son tort* is liable merely on proof that the term vested in him as such ; and is liable for rent and on the covenants. *Williams* v. *Heales,* L. R. 9 C. P. 177.

For subsequent rent he may be charged as representative during the term, or personally as assignee if he has entered to take possession. Woodfall, 306.

If he takes possession, he is liable personally as assign for subsequent rent up to the letting value. *Re Bowes,* 37 C. D. 128.

The executor is not liable as assignee unless he enters and takes possession ; but if he enters, he may be made liable as assignee, though by proper pleading he may limit such liability for rent to the yearly value which the premises might have yielded. *Rendall* v. *Andrew,* 61 L. J. Q. B. 630.

But *semble* he cannot after entry limit his liability under the testator's covenant to repair. *Ibid.*

If sued personally for use and occupation, he may show that he entered as executor, that he has no assets, and that the value of the land is not equal to the rent. *Patten v. Reid*, 6 L. J. Q. B. 281.

Repairs. The testator's estate is liable for his disrepair (*ante*, p. 165); but an executor, having entered, is personally liable on a repairing covenant, though he may have no assets. *Rendall* v. *Andrewe, supra;* Woodfall, 307.

But the defence that the premises are worth nothing does not seem available in an action for non-repair. And it seems that absence of assets is equally unavailable as a defence. Woodfall, 306.

The proper course for an executor, *having sufficient assets*, to take in order to rid himself of personal liability is that pointed out by 22 & 23 Vict. c. 35, s. 27. *Ante*, p. 124.

Any act of ownership is deemed constructive entry. Woodfall, 309.

An entry by one of several executors will not enure as an entry by all, so as to render them jointly liable for use and occupation. 1 C. M. & R. 172.

An executor of a tenant from year to year has the same interest as the testator, which, it seems, continues till notice to quit is given. Woodfall, 304.

Insurance. An executor is not liable for the loss of property by accidental fire, and is not bound either to insure or continue the insurance effected by the testator. *Bailey* v. *Gould*, 4 Y. & C. 221; *Fry* v. *F.*, 27 Beav. 146; but see *Re Fowler*, 16 C. D. 723.

Nor is it the duty of the executors, as against an equitable tenant for life, to keep leaseholds insured. *Re Betty*, (1899) 1 Ch. 821, 829.

By the Trustee Act, 1893, s. 18, an executor *may*, if he thinks fit, insure any insurable property for three-fourths of the value, and pay the premiums out of income, without obtaining the consent of any person entitled to such income.

But this section does not apply to any property which an executor is bound *forthwith* to convey absolutely to any beneficiary when requested to do so. Sect. 18 (2).

Quære, therefore, whether an executor can insure real property which devolves upon him under the Land Transfer Act, 1897, and which at the end of a *year* he is bound to convey to the person entitled. Sect. 3 (2).

The Trustee Act, 1893, s. 18, does not alter the incidence of payments as between tenants for life and remaindermen. *Re Baring*, (1893) 1 Ch. 61.

Executors are liable, as against a legatee of leaseholds, for repairs and insurance down to the death of the testator, but not further. *Re Betty*, *ante*, p. 165; *Re Gjers*, *Ibid*.

Where a person has agreed to take a lease or a renewal, his executors, admitting assets, will be bound. *Stephens v. Hotham*, 1 K. & J. 571. — Renewal.

An executor who renews a lease does so for the benefit of the estate. *Kelley v. K.*, 8 Ir. Eq. 403; *Re Morgan*, 18 C. D. 93.

By the Trustee Act, 1893, s. 19, an executor of renewable leaseholds may renew if he thinks fit, and is bound to do so if required by any person interested.

By 40 & 41 Vict. c. 34, if a purchaser dies before paying the purchase-money, leaving it equitably charged by way of lien on the land, the devisee will take the land charged with the unpaid purchase-money. *Re Cockroft*, 24 C. D. 94. — Executor of purchaser.

But in cases not coming within the Act the heir or devisee will be entitled to have the purchase-money paid by the executor or administrator. Wms. 1643; Dart, 924.

Similar principles apply where a vendor dies before completion, in which case the purchase-money devolves as personal estate. *Lysaght v. Edwards*, 2 C. D. 499; *Re Thomas*, 34 C. D. 166; *Re Harrison*, *Ibid*. 214. And by the Conv. Act, 1881, ss. 4, 30, the personal representatives can convey; and see now Land Transfer Act, 1897. *Ante*, p. 74.

Where a specific legacy is pledged or charged, the legatee is entitled to have it redeemed or exonerated by the executor. *Bothamley v. Sherson*, L. R. 20 Eq. 304. — Executor must exonerate specific legacies.

But legatees of leaseholds take *cum onere*, even apart from Locke King's Acts. Hence executors may require an indemnity against dilapidations before letting the legatee into possession. *Hickling* v. *Boyer*, 3 Mac. & G. 635; *Re Betty, ante*, p. 165; *Re Gjers, Ibid*.

In the same way legatees of shares are, generally speaking, liable to pay calls. *Armstrong* v. *Burnet*, 20 Beav. 432.

Copyholds. Executors do not continue the estate of their testator in copyholds, and, therefore, they must be admitted and pay the fines. Scriven, 136. *Cf. Blackmore* v. *White, ante*, p. 156.

Incomplete gift. The Court will not compel an executor to complete a gift which has not been perfected by the testator, though he may be compelled to execute an agreement by the testator to grant an annuity. *Nield* v. *Smith*, 14 Ves. 491.

Corroboration. There is no rule of law that there must be corroboration to establish a claim advanced by a living person against the estate of a dead person. *Post*, p. 217.

Guaranty. The death of the surety does not *per se* operate as a revocation of a continuing guaranty, and his executor is liable in respect of advances made after the testator's death, unless the death has come to the knowledge of the creditor. *Harriss* v. *Fawcett*, L. R. 15 Eq. 311; *Coulthart* v. *Clementson*, 5 Q. B. D. 42.

But a guaranty, the consideration for which is given once and for all, cannot be determined by the guarantor, and does not cease on his death. *Lloyd's* v. *Harper*, 16 C. D. 290; *M. Ry. Co.* v. *Silvester*, (1895) 1 Ch. 572.

As to a husband's liability *quâ* personal representative for the antenuptial contracts of his wife, see *Re Parkin,* (1892) 3 Ch. 510.

Apprentice. On the death of an attorney his articled clerk may claim a return of part of the premium out of his assets. *Hirst* v. *Tolson*, 2 Mac. & G. 134; but see *Ferns* v. *Carr*, 28 C. D. 409.

But this is not so with regard to ordinary apprentices. *Whincup* v. *Hughes*, L. R. 6 C. P. 78.

If a man perform services for the testator, without reward, but in the expectation of a legacy, he cannot claim the legacy, but he may claim remuneration against the executor. *Baxter* v. *Gray*, 3 M. & Gr. 771; *Shallcross* v. *Wright*, 12 Beav. 558. *Work done with a view to legacy.*

If a garnishee order is made against the executors of a debtor of the judgment debtor, it ought to appear on the face of it that they are sought to be charged as executors. *Stevens* v. *Phelips*, 10 Ch. 417.

CHAPTER XV.

LIABILITY OF REPRESENTATIVES ON THEIR OWN ACTS.

Executor's liability on his own contracts.
IN many cases the executor may be sued, as executor, on a promise made by him as executor, and the judgment will be *de bonis testatoris*. *Ashby* v. *A.*, 7 B. & C. 444; *Powell* v. *Graham*, 7 Taunt. 580.

But where the defendant as executor was indebted to the plaintiff for money lent to him as executor, and the defendant as executor promised to pay, the judgment must be *de bonis propriis*. *Rose* v. *Bowler*, 1 H. Black. 108; *Farhall* v. *F.*, L. R. 7 Ch. 123.

Again, a promise by the defendant as executor for use and occupation after the death of the testator has been held to charge the defendant personally. *Wigley* v. *Ashton*, 3 B. & A. 101; but see *Atkins* v. *Humphrey*, 2 C. B. 654.

So where the defendant as executor was indebted to the plaintiff for goods sold and delivered to the defendant as executor, and defendant as executor promised to pay. *Corner* v. *Shew*, 3 M. & W. 350.

And so the common count for interest was held to charge the executor personally, for it alleged a forbearance *at his request*. But a count charging him as executor on a contract by the testator to pay interest charged him only as executor. *Bignell* v. *Harpur*, 4 Exch. 773.

In actions like the above, brought against the executor as such, a promise by him was a mere *nudum factum* unless there were assets; though it was not necessary to aver that the defendant had assets. *Powell* v. *Graham*, 7 Taunt. 580.

A promise by an executor or administrator to pay a debt of the testator or to answer damages will not make him personally liable, unless there be a sufficient consideration to support the promise. He is chargeable only as executor, and to the extent of the assets. *Reech* v. *Kennegal*, 1 Ves. Sen. 126. *Personal liability of an executor on his own promise.*

And the Statute of Frauds adds a further requisite that the promise should be in writing. 29 Car. 2, c. 3, s. 4.

A verbal promise by an administrator, *before* administration, may, however, under certain circumstances, be binding upon him afterwards. *Tomlinson* v. *Gill*, Ambl. 330; *Gregory* v. *Williams*, 3 Meriv. 590; and see *Nelson* v. *Serle*, 4 M. & W. 795.

What is a valid consideration:

If a creditor, at the request of an executor, forbears to sue him, that is a sufficient consideration to charge him personally, whether he has assets or not, at the time of the promise. Wms. 1668. *What is a valid consideration.*

An executor, promising to pay a debt at a future day, makes the debt his own (*Childs* v. *Monins*, 2 B. & B. 460); and a promise to pay interest implies payment at a future day. *Bradley* v. *Heath*, 3 Sim. 543.

Where a bill is indorsed to a person as executor, and he again indorses it, he becomes personally liable, unless he indorses it in such terms as to negative personal responsibility. 45 & 46 Vict. c. 61, ss. 31 (5), 16 (1), 26 (1).

But where the plaintiff was assignee of a debt, and the defendant, in consideration that the plaintiff would accept the defendant as his debtor, promised to pay it, this was held not a sufficient consideration. *Secus*, if the promise had been in consideration of forbearance by such assignee to sue. 1 Saund. 210, n. 1.

It would seem that having assets is a good consideration for a promise to pay a debt of the deceased, or to answer damages out of the executor's own estate. *Reech* v. *Kennegal*, 1 Ves. Sen. 126.

The consequence is, that if an executor or administrator promises in writing that, in consideration of having assets, he will pay a particular debt of the deceased, he may be sued in his individual capacity, and the judgment against him will be *de bonis propriis*. Wms. 1673.

In cases like the above, where the nature of the debt is such as necessarily to make the defendant liable personally, the judgment will be *de bonis propriis*, though he be charged as promising *as executor*. *Ibid*.

What is sufficient reduction into writing:

<small>What is a sufficient writing.</small> The Statute of Frauds, 29 Car. 2, c. 3, s. 4, enacts that no action shall be brought unless the agreement, or some memorandum or note thereof, shall be in writing, and signed by the party to be charged or some one by him authorised.

It was at one time held that the consideration as well as the promise must be in writing; but this is not now necessary. 19 & 20 Vict. c. 97, s. 3.

<small>Arbitration.</small> Where an executor submits in broad terms to pay whatever shall be awarded, and the arbitrator awards that he shall pay a certain sum, he is personally bound to perform the award, whether he has assets or not. For if he thinks fit to refer generally, without protesting against the reference being taken as an admission of assets, it will amount to such an admission. *Barry* v. *Rush*, 1 T. R. 691; *Worthington* v. *Barlow*, 7 T. R. 453; *Riddell* v. *Sutton*, 5 Bing. 200.

But the liability may depend not only on the terms of the submission, but also on those of the award.

Thus the award may direct payment out of assets, in which case the executor would not, it seems, be personally liable. *Pearson* v. *Henry*, 5 T. R. 6; *Love* v. *Honeybourne*, 4 D. & R. 814; *Re Joseph*, 1 R. & M. 486.

By 45 & 46 Vict. c. 61, s. 16, an executor can indorse bills so as to limit or negative liability. *Ante*, p. 89.

<small>Liability for acts of attorney.</small> It seems that a power of attorney given by an executor will authorise the attorney to bind his principal by accepting

bills for debts due from his testator. *Howard* v. *Baillie*, 2 H. Black. 618.

With respect to funeral expenses, if an executor or administrator gives orders for the funeral, or ratifies the acts of another who has given such orders, he is liable individually for the reasonable expenses. *Brice* v. *Wilson*, 8 A. & E. 349. *Cf. Re Watson*, 19 Q. B. D. 234; *ante*, p. 43.

Funeral expenses.

And it would seem that if an administrator, before taking out letters, orders, or sanctions orders, for the funeral, he will be bound after administration. *Lucy* v. *Walrond*, 3 Bing. N. C. 841.

It appears that the executor is liable to pay funeral expenses, even without an order on his part, if he has assets. Even if he *never receives assets* to the amount of the funeral expenses, he is liable to pay, although he did not order the funeral. Per Jessel, *Sharp* v. *Lush*, 10 C. D. 472.

Where the representative has neither given nor adopted directions for the funeral, he is liable upon an implied promise, at least where no other person is liable upon an *express* contract. *Brice* v. *Wilson*, 8 A. & E. 349, n. (c).

There seems, however, to be some doubt whether the representative is personally liable on the implied promise. *Corner* v. *Shew*, 3 M. & W. 356; but see *Sharp* v. *Lush*, *supra*.

It would seem from *Reg.* v. *Price*, 12 Q. B. D. 247, that cremation is legal, and, therefore, the representative would be entitled to, and liable for, the expenses in the same manner as burial expenses. See *Williams* v. *W.*, 20 C. D. 659; *ante*, p. 104.

With respect to the liability of representatives carrying on business, the general principle is that a trade is not transmissible, but is put an end to by the death of the trader. Executors, therefore, have no authority in law to carry on the trade of their testator, and if they do so, except under the Court, they run great risk, even though directed by the will to do so.

Trade.

If the business prospers, the profits go to the estate, and the executor derives no benefit. If it loses, he will, on failure of assets, be personally responsible for the debts contracted in the business since the testator's death to the extent of his own property, also in his person, and he may be proceeded against as a bankrupt, though only a trustee. *Ex parte Garland*, 10 Ves. 110; *Re Johnson*, 15 C. D. 548.

But if the executor has wronged the estate, if he has put the assets in his own pocket, the creditors cannot stand in his place. *Ibid.*; *post*, p. 216.

A direction to carry on trade does not authorise the employment of more property than was employed in it at the death. To justify executors in employing more, there must be the most positive and distinct authority for that purpose in the will itself. *Kirkman* v. *Booth*, 11 Beav. 280; *Land* v. *Land*, 48 L. J. Ch. 311.

If it is impossible to carry on a trade with only the assets engaged in it at the death, the executors should apply to the Court for directions.

Under the bankruptcy of an executor directed to carry on trade with a limited sum, the general assets beyond that sum are not liable. *Ex parte Garland*, *supra*; *Cutbush* v. *C.*, 1 Beav. 184.

If a testator's business is properly carried on by his executors, in accordance with the will and with the assent of creditors, in the interest of creditors and beneficiaries, the executors are entitled (in priority to testator's creditors) to be indemnified out of the estate against liabilities properly incurred in carrying on the business. *Dowse* v. *Gorton*, (1891) A. C. 190; *Re Brooke*, (1894) 2 Ch. 600; *Kidd* v. *K.*, (1894) W. N. 73.

An executor cannot, without special authority, carry on the trade except for the purpose of winding it up; but he may, and in some cases must, complete the contracts of his testator, and continue a going concern for the purpose of selling to the best advantage. *Collinson* v. *Lister*, 20 Beav. 356, 365; *Garrett* v. *Noble*, 6 Sim. 504; *post*, p. 201.

If an executor, without any authority, trades with the assets, the testator's estate will not be liable in case of his bankruptcy, but the estate can prove for such assets as have been lost by the executor in the trade. *Ex parte Garland*, 10 Ves. 110.

Again, the testator may qualify the power of the executor to carry on trade, and limit it to a specific part of the assets, in which case the rest of the assets will not be liable. *Supra*.

Where the executrix and sole residuary legatee continued the business ostensibly as her own, the assets of the business in her hands were held not to be impressed with any trust in favour of the testator's creditors. *Re Fells*, 4 C. D. 509.

A distinction must, however, be taken between executors actively trading and executors merely sharing profits of a trade. *Holme* v. *Hammond*, L. R. 7 Ex. 218; Partnership Act, 1890, s. 2 (3).

The tendency of the decisions is to establish the doctrine that no person who does not hold himself out as a partner is liable to third persons for the acts of persons whose profit he shares, unless he or they are really partners *inter se*. Lindley, 57.

Devastavit.

It remains to consider what violation or neglect of duty will make the representative personally liable. *Devastavit.*

But it must be remembered that he may obtain relief in a proper case under the Judicial Trustees Act, 1896, s. 3. *Post*, p. 182.

This misconduct is called in law a *devastavit*, or wasting of assets, for which executors or administrators shall answer out of their own pockets, as far as they had, or might have had, assets. Bac. Abr. Exors. 1.

An executor is personally liable in equity for all breaches of the ordinary trusts which in courts of equity are Executor liable for breach of trust.

considered to arise from his office. *Re Marsden*, 26 C. D. 783.

If he accepts the office, he accepts the duties of the office, and in that sense becomes a trustee, and the circumstance of taking probate is in itself an acceptance of the trust. Therefore an executor who proves the will must do all which he is directed to do as executor, and cannot say that, though executor, he is not clothed with a trust. *Re Marsden, supra;* and see *ante*, p. 17.

Executors and administrators may be guilty of a *devastavit*, not only by a direct abuse of the assets, as by spending or converting them to their own use, but also by such negligence and wrong administration as will disappoint the claimants to them.

Abuse of assets.

An example of direct abuse is the application of the assets in payment of the executor's own debt to a third party, or where the executor collusively sells them at an undervalue. Went. 302.

Mal-administration.

Instances of mal-administration are the misapplication of assets in undue expenses, or the payment of debts out of their legal order, or the assent to or payment of a legacy when the fund is not sufficient for creditors. *Ante*, 124.

Paying debt of inferior degree.

But it is not a *devastavit* to pay a debt of an inferior degree before one of higher, of which the executor had no notice. *Ante*, pp. 105, 124.

But want of notice did not excuse the executor if the assets were originally sufficient, although he *bonâ fide* paid the assets to the legatees or parties entitled. *Hill* v. *Gomme*, 1 Beav. 540. But see now 22 & 23 Vict. c. 35, s. 29; *ante*, p. 125.

If the executor surrenders, or otherwise fails to preserve a term of years where the land is of greater yearly value than the rent, it is a *devastavit*. And, on the other hand, if the rent be greater, and the testator was *assignee* of the term, the executor may be guilty of a *devastavit* in not exonerating the estate by surrendering or assigning it. *Ante*, p. 164.

Formerly an executor compounding or releasing a debt was answerable for the same.

But now by the Trustee Act, 1893, s. 21, an executor or administrator may pay or allow any debt or claim on any evidence that he thinks sufficient. *Ante*, p. 90.

Compounding.

And may, if he thinks fit, accept any composition or security, and may allow time for payment, and may compromise, compound, abandon, submit to arbitration, or otherwise settle any debt, account, claim, or thing relating to the estate, without being liable for any loss occasioned by anything so done by him in good faith.

This applies only where there is no contrary intention; but it applies to all executorships and administratorships whether constituted before or after the Act. Sect. 21 (4).

An executor will be guilty of a *devastavit* if he applies the assets in payment of a claim which he is not bound to pay. *Shallcross* v. *Wright*, 29 Beav. 576.

Unnecessary payments.

So if he pays a bond *ex turpi causâ*. *Ante*, p. 112.

Or if he makes disbursements for the maintenance of the children of the deceased. *Ante*, p. 140.

But he will be allowed a reasonable time for breaking up the testator's domestic establishment. *Field* v. *Peckett*, 29 Beav. 576.

An executor may also pay a debt due from his testator though barred by the Statute of Limitations, and notwithstanding the personal estate is insufficient (*Lowis* v. *Rumney*, 4 Eq. 451; *Re Rownson*, 29 C. D. 358); but *quære* whether he can do so against the declared wish of his co-executor. *Midgley* v. *M.*, (1893) 3 Ch. 282.

But he may not pay a debt barred by the Statute of Frauds. *Re Rownson, supra.*

He is not compellable to plead the Statute of Limitations; though any person interested may do so after judgment. *Shewen* v. *Vanderhorst*, 2 R. & M. 75; *Phillips* v. *Beal*, 32 Beav. 26; *Re Barrett*, 43 C. D. 70; *Re Wenham*, (1892) 3 Ch. 59.

The Court will not interfere with an executor before

judgment, except to prevent waste. *Re Wells*, 45 C. D. 569; *Bethell* v. *Abraham*, L. R. 17 Eq. 24; and see *Berry* v. *Gibbons*, 8 Ch. 747.

Negligence. Such acts of negligence or careless administration as defeat the rights of creditors, or legatees, or parties entitled in distribution, amount to a *devastavit*.

Generally speaking, if an executor omit to sell property when it ought to be sold, and it be afterwards lost without any fault of his, he is liable. *Phillips* v. *P.*, 2 Freem. 11; *Taylor* v. *Tabrum*, 7 Sim. 28; *Fry* v. *Fry*, 27 B. 144.

There is, however, no rule that even with regard to risky securities there is an absolute unvarying obligation on executors to call them in within twelve months, regardless of the opinion of the executors as to the advisability of doing so. *Re Chapman*, (1896) 763, 782.

It is not the duty of executors to realise mortgages created by the testator, when the realisation is not required for any testamentary purpose, and when the securities themselves are not in any peril. *Ibid.* 778.

Executors will, however, be liable if they delay the payment of debts payable with interest. *Seaman* v. *Everard*, 2 Lev. 40; *Dornford* v. *D.*, 12 Ves. 130, n.

Or if they omit to sue for a debt, whereby it becomes barred or lost. *Caney* v. *Bond*, 6 Beav. 486; *Grove* v. *Price*, 26 Beav. 103; *Billing* v. *Brogden*, 38 C. D. 546; and see *Collins* v. *Rhodes*, 20 C. D. 280.

Or if they suffer rent to be in arrear. *Tebbs* v. *Carpenter*, 1 Madd. 296.

The liability is the same whether the loss arises from omitting to call in a debt, or allowing a balance to remain in the hands of a co-executor. *Styles* v. *Guy*, 1 Mac. & G. 422.

But an executor need not take steps to enforce payment, if such steps would be fruitless. *Re Brogden*, 38 C. D. 546.

And if he is satisfied on reasonable grounds that he could not maintain an action, he will not be guilty of default, and will be excused. *Re Roberts*, 76 L. T. 479.

Executors are liable for allowing assets to remain on improper investment, as for instance, upon personal security. *Bullock* v. *Wheatley*, 1 Coll. 131; but see *Re Laing*, (1899) 1 Ch. 132.

So they are liable for not converting shares within the year (*Grayburn* v. *Clarkson*, L. R. 3 Ch. 605); unless they have power to postpone. *Brindley* v. *Partridge*, 13 C. D. 654.

If the representatives refuse to take the necessary steps to get in the estate, the proper course is to apply for leave to take proceedings in their names. *Walker* v. *W.*, 20 W. R. 162.

Where executors, having refused an offer, afterwards sold for a considerably smaller sum, they were charged with the loss. *Taylor* v. *Tabrum*, 6 Sim. 281; *Fry* v. *F.*, 27 Beav. 144.

But where executors act *bonâ fide* and no neglect is proved, they will not usually be held liable. *Rowley* v. *Adams*, 2 H. L. C. 725; *Buxton* v. *B.*, 1 M. & Cr. 80; *Hughes* v. *Empson*, 22 Beav. 181; *Powell* v. *Evans*, 5 Ves. 843; *Marsden* v. *Kent*, 5 C. D. 598. *Re Chapman*, *supra*.

Where assets come to the hands of the executor, and are afterwards lost to the estate, he is in the position of a gratuitous bailee and cannot be charged without wilful default. *Job* v. *J.*, 6 C. D. 562.

<small>Loss of assets.</small>

Thus if assets are stolen or lost by casualty, as by fire, the executor will not be charged. *Bailey* v. *Gould*, 4 Y. & Coll. 221; *Jones* v. *Lewes*, 2 Ves. Sen. 240.

<small>Loss by casualty.</small>

It seems that executors are not bound either to insure or continue the insurance of their testator, though they may do so under the Trustee Act, 1893, s. 18. *Ante*, p. 166.

But they will be liable if they allow a policy of life insurance to drop without any sufficient reason, even after a decree for administration has been made. *Garner* v. *Moore*, 3 Drew. 277.

Where an executor or administrator improperly advances

money on a mortgage which would at the time of the investment be a proper investment for a smaller sum, the security will be deemed an authorised investment for such smaller sum, and the representative will only be liable to make good the sum advanced in excess thereof with interest. Trustee Act, 1893, s. 9; *Re Walker*, 59 L. J. Ch. 386. And see sect. 8 as to what should be done before investing on mortgage.

An executor cannot, after an order for administration, invest on mortgage or otherwise deal with the assets except by leave of the Court. *Widdowson* v. *Duck*, 2 Meriv. 494, 499; but see *Berry* v. *Gibbons*, 8 Ch. 747; *Re Mansel*, 33 W. R. 727.

<small>Loss by loans on personal security.</small>

A representative lending money of the deceased on personal security is guilty of a breach of trust and personally liable for any loss. But see *Forbes* v. *Ross*, 2 Cox, 116; *Re Laing*, (1899) 1 Ch. 132.

Even when the executors are authorised to lend on personal security, a loan from one to the other is a breach of trust. *Stickney* v. *Sewell*, 1 M. & Cr. 8; but see *Warwick* v. *Richardson*, 10 M. & W. 284.

<small>Keeping money in hand.</small>

An executor is not justified in unnecessarily keeping money in hand, but should invest it in authorised securities.

The authorised securities are set forth in the Trustee Act, 1893, ss. 1—7.

The power to invest in these securities is not confined to moneys awaiting investment. *Hume* v. *Lopes*, (1892) A. C. 112.

<small>Not converting property given for life.</small>

Where personal property is bequeathed for life with remainder over, and not specifically, it is the duty of the executor with certain exceptions to convert it into authorised securities; and the tenant for life is entitled only upon that principle. *Dimes* v. *Scott*, 4 Russ. C. C. 195; *Mackenzie* v. *Taylor*, 7 Beav. 467; *Wightwick* v. *Lord*, 6 H. of L. 217.

And the executor will be liable for such non-conversion

unless there was an express discretion as to investment. *Baud* v. *Fardell*, 7 D. M. & G. 628.

Where executors fail to invest as authorised they are chargeable with the whole amount of the trust fund, together with interest. *Robinson* v. *R.*, 1 D. M. & G. 247.

Unauthorised investments.

But they are not liable for continuing to hold an investment which has ceased to be an investment authorised by the will or by law. Trustee Act, 1894, s. 10; *Re Medland*, 41 C. D. 476.

Executors ought not, without great reason, to permit money to remain upon unauthorised security longer than is absolutely necessary (*Powell* v. *Evans*, 5 Ves. 839; *Bullock* v. *Wheatley*, 1 Coll. 130); but where they have acted in the honest exercise of their discretion they will not be liable (*Buxton* v. *B.*, 1 M. & C. 80; *Marsden* v. *Kent*, 5 C. D. 598); nor where they have an absolute discretion to postpone. *Re Norrington*, 13 C. D. 654; *Gray* v. *Siggers*, 15 C. D. 74.

Where they have neglected to realise assets outstanding on an improper investment, there is no fixed period at which the loss is to be calculated. It depends on the nature of the property. *Hughes* v. *Empson*, 22 Beav. 181; *Grayburn* v. *Clarkson*, L. R. 3 Ch. 606.

It is not the duty of an executor to call in money invested on real security where no risk is apparent, nor to convert leaseholds unless under particular circumstances. *Howe* v. *Dartmouth*, 7 Ves. 150; *Re Medland*, 41 C. D. 476; *Midgley* v. *Crowther*, (1895) 2 Ch. 56; *Re Chapman*, (1896) 2 Ch. 763.

By the Land Transfer Act, 1897, s. 3 (2), after one year from the death, a person entitled to freehold property may apply to the Court for an order on the personal representative to convey it to him.

Generally speaking, if an executor appoints another to receive money, and he receives it, it is the same thing as if the executor had received it; and consequently,

Employing agents.

appointing another to receive who does not repay, is a *devastavit*. Wms. 1719.

But this is not so where, *necessarily*, in the ordinary course of business, and acting with reasonable care, they employ agents. *Clough* v. *Bond*, 3 M. & C. 496; *Speight* v. *Gaunt*, 9 A. C. 1.

But the agent must not be employed, nor act, outside the ordinary scope of his business. *Re Brier*, 26 C. D. 238; *Fry* v. *Tapson*, 28 C. D. 268; *Jobson* v. *Palmer*, (1893), 1 Ch. 71; *Mara* v. *Browne*, (1896) 1 Ch. 199; *Re Turner*, (1897) 1 Ch. 536.

The liability of personal representatives for the acts of their agents is now considerably modified by the Trustee Act, 1893, ss. 17, 24.

And by the Judicial Trustees Act, s. 3, the Court has power to relieve executors from liability where they have acted honestly and reasonably. *Re Second, &c., post*, p. 183.

<small>Retaining money in bank.</small> A representative is justified in depositing money for temporary purposes in a bank of good credit, but it should be paid to a separate account. *Swinfen* v. *S.*, 29 Beav. 211; *Ex parte Kingston*, 6 Ch. 632.

And he is not liable for loss in the event of failure of the bank, unless the same happens through his own wilful default. Trustee Act, 1893, s. 24.

The Act, it will be seen, does not extend its indemnity to cases of wilful default, and the representative is therefore still liable :—

If he allows money to lie in the bank when he ought to have invested it. *Moyle* v. *M.*, 2 R. & M. 710.

If he leaves it in the bank when he ought to have paid it over to other parties. *Lunham* v. *Blundell*, 4 Jur. N. S. 3.

If he lends money to bank on their personal security. *Darke* v. *Martyn*, 1 Beav. 525.

If he keeps a larger balance at the bank than is reasonably necessary. *Astbury* v. *Beasley*, W. N. 1869, 96.

A representative may appoint a solicitor to be his agent to receive purchase money, and may appoint a solicitor or banker to receive policy moneys without being liable for loss, unless he allows such money to remain in their hands longer than is necessary. Trustee Act, 1893, s. 17.

A *devastavit* by one of two executors or administrators shall not charge the other, provided he has not intentionally or otherwise contributed to it. *Devastavit of co-executor.*

Hence an executor shall not, under ordinary circumstances, be responsible for assets come to the hands of his co-executor.

But if he hands over assets to his co-executor and they are misapplied, he will be liable, unless he can show good reason for having so acted (*Macpherson* v. *M.*, 1 H. L. C. 243); as if he acted merely as agent. *Davis* v. *Spurling*, 1 R. & M. 66.

The rule is that where, by the act of one executor, the assets come to the hands of his co-executor, the former will be liable in the same manner as if he had entrusted them to a stranger. *Toplis* v. *Hurrel*, 19 Beav. 423.

But if an executor is merely passive, he will not be liable unless he in some way contributes to enable the other to get possession, however innocently, unless he show sufficient excuse. 11 Ves. 335; *Hewett* v. *Foster*, 6 Beav. 259; but see *Terrell* v. *Mathew*, 1 Mac. & G. 433, n. (*a*).

Thus, if by agreement one is to receive one part of the assets, and another another part, each will be liable for the whole. *Moses* v. *Levi*, 3 Y. & C. 359; *Lewis* v. *Nobbs*, 8 C. D. 591.

Again, if executors deal with the assets on the mere representation, if false, of a co-executor, they will all be liable. 11 Ves. 252, 254.

And generally where one, by want of proper inquiry and diligence, allows the other to get possession and misapply assets, he will be liable. He will be subject to the imputation of negligence, in being too remiss in not asking how he had been dealing with the assets in his hands. 11 Ves. 254; *Mendes* v. *Guedella*, 2 J. & H. 259; *Re Second, &c.*, 68 L. J. Ch. 196.

But if one executor places assets in the hands of another in the ordinary course of business, and within the scope of his business (*Chambers* v. *Minchin*, 7 Ves. 198) ; or to enable him to administer (*Hovey* v. *Blakeman*, 4 Ves. 596) ; or remits money to pay debts (*Joy* v. *Campbell*, 1 Sch. & L. 341) ; or does any other act necessary in the regular course of business by which his co-executor gets sole possession, he will not be liable. *Re Gasquoine*, (1894) 1 Ch. 470.

For he is not bound to do personally what in the regular course of business would be done through an agent. *Speight* v. *Gaunt*, 9 A. C. 1 ; *Re Brier*, 26 C. D. 238 ; *Re Blundell*, 40 C. D. 370, 376 ; *Re Gasquoine*, *supra*.

And where an executor may employ an agent, he may employ his co-executor as such within the ordinary scope of his business. *Fry* v. *Tapson*, 28 C. D. 268 ; *Re Weall*, 42 C. D. 674 ; *Re Gasquoine*, *supra*.

Standing by.

But it is the duty of an executor to watch over and control his co-executor, and if he stands by and sees a breach of trust committed, he will be liable. *Lincoln* v. *Wright*, 4 Beav. 427 ; *Styles* v. *Guy*, 1 Mac. & G. 422 ; *Re Second, &c.*, *supra*.

So if he allows another to retain money longer than the circumstances require, he will be liable. *Lincoln* v. *Wright*, 4 Beav. 427 ; *Moyle* v. *M.*, 2 R. & M. 710 ; Trustee Act, 1893, s. 17 (3).

And though he properly employs another he must still exercise his discretion in the matter. *Re Weall*, 42 C. D. 674.

Indemnity clause.

The usual indemnity clause will not exonerate him in such cases. The Trustee Act, 1893, s. 24, only expresses the law, and does not extend to cases of wilful default. *Moyle* v. *M.*, *supra*.

Liability of executor who renounces.

If an executor administer part of the assets, he will be chargeable with such as he has received, although he has renounced the executorship and paid the money to a co-executor who has proved. *Doyle* v. *Blake*, 2 Sch. & L. 231 ; *Underwood* v. *Stevens*, 1 Meriv. 712.

But an executor who has not proved is not to be considered as acting, simply because he assists a co-executor, or acts as his agent. *Orr* v. *Newton*, 2 Cox, 274; *Stacy* v. *Elph*, 1 M. & K. 195; *ante*, p. 15.

An executor who merely joins his co-executor in an act which might have been done with equal validity by the co-executor alone, is not liable. Trustee Act, 1893, s. 24. But he must show that he joined only for the sake of conformity. *Brice* v. *Stokes*, 11 Ves. 319. {Joining in receipt.}

Although it is true, as a general rule, that concurrence in a *devastavit* by the parties injured by it, or acquiescence by them, will release the executors, yet the Court must inquire into all the circumstances, and ascertain whether there was really such concurrence or acquiescence as ought to relieve the executors. *Walker* v. *Symonds*, 3 Swanst. 1; *Burrows* v. *Walls*, 5 D. M. & G. 233, 251; *Davies* v. *Hodgson*, 25 Beav. 177; *Re Baker*, 20 C. D. 230; *Dixon* v. *D.*, 9 C. D. 587; *Re Hulkes*, 33 C. D. 552. {Acquiescence.}

By the Trustee Act, 1893, s. 45, where an executor has committed a *devastavit* at the instigation of a beneficiary, the Court may impound the interest of such beneficiary by way of indemnity to the executor.

A married woman executrix or administratrix is now in the position of a *feme sole*, and her husband will not be liable for her *devastavit* unless he has intermeddled. M. W. P. Act, 1882, s. 24; and see s. 18.

And by sect. 23, her representative shall, in respect of her separate estate, have the same rights and liabilities as she would have if living.

A husband taking his wife's leaseholds without administration is her representative within this section. *Sarman* v. *Wharton*, (1891) 1 Q. B. 491.

As to the husband's liability, *quâ* the representative of his wife, for her antenuptial contracts, see *Re Parkin*, (1892) 3 Ch. 510.

Accounts.

Accounts. It is the bounden duty of representatives to keep accounts and to be constantly ready with their accounts, and also to give accurate information as to the assets. *Low* v. *Bouverie*, (1891) 3 Ch. 82; *Lee* v. *Wilson*, (1892) 1 Ch. 86; Ord. 55, r. 10A.

But a legatee is not entitled to a copy of the accounts at the expense of the estate. *Ottley* v. *Gilby*, 8 B. 602; *post*, p. 210.

An executor or administrator must account for all profits which have accrued in his own time, either spontaneously or by his own acts, out of the estate.

And if he neglect to account or give explanations he may be made to pay the costs of any action instituted in consequence. *Payne* v. *Evens*, 18 Eq. 356; *Talbot* v. *Marshfield*, 3 Ch. 622. And so if he renders incorrect accounts. *Pearce* v. *Radcliffe*, 29 W. R. 420.

If executors carry on the trade or business of the testator the profits must be accounted for as assets. *Ante*, p. 174.

And if the executors employ the assets in carrying on the trade for their own benefit, the legatees are entitled, at their option, either to interest at 5 per cent. on the amount of assets employed or to the profits actually made. *Wedderburn* v. *W.*, 22 Beav. 100.

So where an executrix entered into a partnership with two other persons and brought in the assets as part of the capital, the other partners having notice of the trust, it was held that the executrix and the other partners were bound to make good the assets, together with all profits, or else with interest at 5 per cent. *Flockton* v. *Bunning*, 8 Ch. 323; *Vyse* v. *Foster*, L. R. 7 H. L. 318.

It is a general rule that an executor cannot be allowed, either directly or indirectly, to purchase any part of the assets, and if he does so he shall be considered a trustee, and account for the utmost extent of advantage made by him. *Hall* v. *Hallett*, 1 Cox, 134; *De Cordova* v. *D.*, 4 A. C. 692; *Clark* v. *Clark*, 9 A. C. 733.

So if an executor compound debts or legacies, and buys them in for less than is due upon them, he shall not take any benefit. *Ex parte James*, 8 Ves. 346; *Barton* v. *Hassard*, 3 Dr. & W. 461; and see *De Cordova* v. *D.*, *supra*.

So where an executor of a mortgagee for a term of years purchased the equity of redemption in fee for a small sum in his own name, he was held a trustee for the estate. *Fosbrook* v. *Balguy*, 1 M. & K. 226.

In short, if an executor deal with the assets in any other manner than his trust requires, he must replace any loss and account for any gain. *Piety* v. *Stace*, 4 Ves. 622; *Crosskill* v. *Bower*, 32 B. 86.

There are two grounds on which an executor or administrator may be charged with interest: 1. That he has omitted to lay out money; 2. That he has made use of it, or committed some other misfeasance, to his own advantage. [Interest, when charged.]

It is frequently necessary and justifiable for an executor to keep large sums in hand to answer the exigency of the testator's affairs, especially in the first year.

But if he keeps money dead without any apparent reason, it becomes a breach of trust, and he will be charged with interest. But there must be a clear case of improper retention of a substantial amount. *Jones* v. *Morrell*, 2 Sim. N. S. 241, 252; *Davenport* v. *Stafford*, 14 Beav. 319.

But an executor will not be charged with interest on money retained under a fair apprehension of his right to it. *Bruere* v. *Pemberton*, 12 Ves. 386.

But he will be charged interest on sums improperly paid, or paid under a mistake as to the legal right to it. *A.-G.* v. *Köhler*, 9 H. L. C. 654; *Re Hulkes*, 33 C. D. 552.

An executor guilty of delay in accounting will not be charged interest on arrears of income unpaid. *Blogg* v. *Johnson*, L. R. 2 Ch. 225.

The usual rate of interest in cases of negligence is still

4 per cent. *Owen* v. *Richmond*, (1895) W N. 29 ; *Re Nicholson, Ibid.* 106. But under special circumstances it may be more. 1 Y. & C. 480 ; *De Cordova* v. *D.*, 4 A. C. 692.

But where there has been a direct breach of trust an executor may be charged with a higher rate. But see *Owen* v. *Richmond, supra.* And it is a settled rule that if he applies money to his own use or in his trade, he will be charged at the rate of 5 per cent. L. R. 5 Ch. 241.

And if employed in trade, the *cestui que trusts* have a right to the option of taking either interest or the profits actually made. *Wedderburn* v. *W.*, 22 Beav. 100.

But they must elect to take either profits for the whole period, or interest for the whole period. *Vyse* v. *Foster*, L. R. 8 Ch. 309, 334.

And if an executor, being a trader, mixes assets with his own moneys, he will be charged 5 per cent. Wms. 1753.

Mere misconduct, not being wilful default, is not enough to charge him with 5 per cent. *A.-G.* v. *Alford*, 4 D. M. & G. 843 ; *Mayor, &c.* v. *Murray*, 7 D. M. & G. 497 ; *Re Hulkes*, 33 C. D. 552.

The principle on which executors have been charged with compound interest has not been clearly defined, but it may be said that a strong case of violation of duty is required. *Tebbs* v. *Carpenter*, 1 Madd. 290.

It will be given when the assets have been employed in trade, or where he ought to have accumulated at compound interest. *Burdick* v. *Garrick*, L. R. 5 Ch. 233 ; *Emmet* v. *E.*, 17 C. D. 142.

A direction to the Master to take annual rests is to be considered as a direction to charge compound interest. *Heighington* v. *Grant*, 5 M. & Cr. 258.

Allowances.
An executor administrator is entitled to be allowed all reasonable expenses which have been incurred in the conduct of his office, except those which arise from his own default.

But he shall have no allowance for personal trouble or loss of time, though he has renounced and though he has benefited the estate to the prejudice of his own affairs. *Robinson* v. *Pett*, 3 P. Wms. 249.

An executor is, generally speaking, only entitled to costs out of pocket. *Pollard* v. *Doyle*, 1 D. & S. 319.

An executor who is a solicitor with power to make professional charges, is only entitled to charge for services strictly professional. *Harbin* v. *Darby*, 28 Beav. 325; *Re Chapple*, 27 C. D. 584. But in special cases compensation may be made him by a fixed allowance. *Bainbrigge* v. *Blair*, 8 Beav. 588.

But where he is authorised to make the usual professional or other proper and reasonable charges, he is entitled to charges not strictly professional. *Re Ames*, 25 C. D. 72.

But the power to charge for professional services cannot take effect against creditors. *Re Barber*, 31 C. D. 665.

If, therefore, the estate is insolvent, it is inoperative. *Re White, ante*, p. 127.

And is inoperative where the solicitor executor attests the will. *Re Pooley*, 40 C. D. 1.

The rule as to out-of-pocket expenses only does not apply to the costs *of an action* where the solicitor acts for himself and his co-executors. In such a case he is allowed full costs, except so far as they have been increased by his being one of the parties. *Cradock* v. *Piper*, 1 Mac. & G. 664; *Re Barber*, 34 C. D. 77.

This exception also applies to friendly proceedings in Chambers. *Re Corsellis*, 34 C. D. 675.

It does not, however, apply where the solicitor executor acts for himself alone. *Lyon* v. *Baker*, 5 De G. & S. 622. Nor where he acts for himself and co-executors out of Court. *Lincoln* v. *Windsor*, 9 Ha. 158. Nor where he is employed as solicitor by his co-executor. *Broughton* v. *B.*, 5 D. M. & G. 160.

Again, an agent, who is appointed executor of his

principal, is not entitled to commission after the testator's death. So a banker or surveyor, who is executor, is not entitled to the usual commission. *Heighington* v. *Grant*, 5 M. & Cr. 262; *Kirkman* v. *Booth*, 11 Beav. 273; *Matthison* v. *Clarke*, 3 Dr. 3.

But there are cases where profits have been allowed. *Willis* v. *Kibble*, 1 Beav. 559; *Smith* v. *Langford*, 2 Beav. 362; *Morison* v. *M.*, 4 M. & C. 215.

In respect of assets collected in India, executors were formerly allowed the same commission here as they would have been allowed in India. *Matthews* v. *Bagshaw*, 14 Beav. 123. And this rule extended to the collection of moneys which were in the hands of a firm in which the executor and the testator were partners. *Cockerell* v. *Barber*, 1 Sim. 23. But this is not so now. Indian Act No. II., 1874, s. 56, *infra*.

The rule, however, still applies to assets in the West Indies. 1 Moore, P. C. 40.

But no commission is payable where the remittant at the time of the remittance is in this country. *Denton* v. *Davy*, 1 Moore, P. C. 32; *Campbell* v. *C.*, 13 Sim. 168; 2 Y. & C. 607.

But now by the Indian Act II., 1874, no person shall receive commission for anything done as executor or administrator; but this shall not prevent any executor, or other person, from having the benefit of any legacy bequeathed to him in his character of executor, or by way of commission or otherwise.

Generally speaking, an executor or administrator must collect the estate himself. But he may employ an agent where a provident owner might well employ a collector, and he will be allowed the expense so incurred. *Hopkinson* v. *Roe*, 1 Beav. 180; *Wilkinson* v. *W.*, 2 S. & S. 237; *Cockburn* v. *Raphael*, 2 Sim. & S. 453.

So it was held, from the nature of the accounts, that the executor was justified in employing an accountant, and the expense allowed. *Henderson* v. *M'Iver*, 3 Madd. 275.

Again, if an executor pays a solicitor for his trouble and attendance in transacting the testator's affairs, he will be allowed such payments where they are proper and professional payments. *Harbin* v. *Darby*, 28 Beav. 325.

If an executor borrows money, or advances it out of his own pocket, to pay debts which carry interest, or to satisfy importunate creditors, he is entitled to be repaid in priority to other creditors, with interest from the time of a balance being struck. *Gordon* v. *Trail*, 8 Price, 416; *Lewis* v. *L.*, 13 Beav. 82. *Interest on money advanced by executor.*

If an executor receive money to which he is not entitled, as a mortgage debt which has been paid off by the testator, he must refund, although he has paid it away to creditors. 1 P. Wms. 355; *Pickering* v. *Stamford*, 2 Ves. 583.

Just allowances are now made in any account directed by any judgment or order, without any direction for that purpose. Ord. 33, r. 8.

The Court may, at any stage of the proceedings, direct accounts to be taken. Ord. 33, r. 2.

An order on the footing of wilful default cannot be made unless pleaded. But if pleaded, it can be made at the hearing, or at any subsequent stage. *Barber* v. *Mackrell*, 12 C. D. 538; *Mayer* v. *Murray*, 8 C. D. 424; *Re Symons*, 21 C. D. 757. *Wilful default.*

But by leave of the Court fresh proceedings may be taken, charging wilful default, when none has been pleaded. *Laming* v. *Gee*, 10 C. D. 715; and see *Dowse* v. *Gorton*, (1891) A. C. 190, 204; *post*, p. 210.

CHAPTER XVI.

REMEDIES FOR REPRESENTATIVES.

Actions by.   WHERE there are several executors or administrators they must all join in bringing actions.

Where, however, an executor renounces, he need not be made a party, nor need an absconding executor. *Drage* v. *Hartopp*, 28 C. D. 414.

No cause or matter, however, will now be defeated by reason of the misjoinder or nonjoinder of parties (Ord. 16, r. 11) ; and where one of the executors is not a party he may be added as plaintiff or made a defendant. *Werderman* v. *Société*, &c., 19 C. D. 246 ; *Van Gelder* v. *Sowerby Bridge*, 44 C. D. 374 ; *Fairclough* v. *Marshall*, 4 Ex. D. 37.

If one of several executors sell goods, he alone may maintain an action for the price ; and generally, if one contracts alone on his own account, he must sue alone, notwithstanding the money recovered will be assets. *Ante*, pp. 49, 92.

If a person sues or is sued in a representative capacity, the indorsement of claim must show in what capacity he sues or is sued.   Ord. 3, r. 4.

Executors and administrators may sue and be sued as representing the estate without joining the persons beneficially interested ; but the Court may at any stage order such persons to be joined.   Ord. 16, r. 8.

Claims by or against an executor or administrator, as such, may be joined with claims by or against him personally, provided the latter claims have reference to the estate.   Ord. 18, r. 5.

Where the cause of action accrues in the lifetime of the deceased, the action must be brought by the executor or administrator in his representative capacity. But where after his death, it may be brought as such or not at his option. *Ante*, p. 69; *Abbott* v. *Parfitt*, L. R. 6 Q. B. 346; *Mosely* v. *Randell*, *Ibid.* 338.

A creditor of the testator cannot set off the debt due to him against a debt due from him to the executor. There can be no set-off between a debt due by a testator and a debt accruing to his executor. Set-off.

So, where a creditor had purchased part of the assets, he could not set off the price against his debt. *Lambarde* v. *Older*, 17 Beav. 542; *Wrout* v. *Dawes*, 25 Beav. 369; *Hallett* v. *H.*, 13 C. D. 232; *Re Gregson*, 36 C. D. 223.

An executor or administrator may set off against a legacy or share of personal estate sums owing by the legatee or next of kin, either to the testator's estate or to the executor personally. *Rees* v. *R.*, 60 L. T. 260; *Taylor* v. *T.*, L. R. 20 Eq. 155; *Christmas* v. *Jones*, (1897) 2 Ch. 190. *Ante*, p. 121.

An executor may set off against a legacy or share of residue a statute-barred debt. *Courtenay* v. *Williams*, 3 Ha. 539; *Akerman* v. *A.*, (1891) 3 Ch. 212.

And one executor may retain out of a legacy to his co-executor the amount of a *devastavit* committed by the latter. *Sims* v. *Doughty*, 5 Ves. 243.

An administrator may set off against the next of kin a statute-barred debt owing to the estate. *White* v. *Cordwell*, 20 Eq. 644.

But an executor cannot set off a debt by the heir against realty descended to him (*Milnes* v. *Sherwin*, 33 W. R. 927); and it is thought that the Land Transfer Act, 1897, will not alter this rule.

Again, the rule of set-off applies though the legatee has assigned his legacy for value. *Knapman* v. *Wreford*, 18 C. D. 300; *Christmas* v. *Jones*, (1897) 2 Ch. 190; see *Cole* v. *Muddle*, 10 Ha. 186; *post*, p. 217.

Or has become bankrupt after the death of the testator.

(*Re Hodgson*, 9 C. D. 673; *Re Watson*, (1896) 1 Ch. 925); unless the executor has proved for the debt. *Stammers* v. *Elliott*, 3 Ch. 195; *Lee* v. *Binns*, (1896) 2 Ch. 584.

But in *Re Orpen*, 16 C. D. 202, it was held that the executors were only allowed to set off the amount of the composition made before the death, whether the executors proved the debt or not.

There can be no set-off against a specific legacy. *Akerman* v. *A.*, (1891) 3 Ch. 212.

Nor against an appropriated fund. *Ballard* v. *Marsden*, 14 C. D. 374.

But there may be against moneys representing profits of a share of partnership specifically bequeathed. *Taylor* v. *Wade*, (1894) 1 Ch. 671.

An executor does not necessarily lose his right of set-off by paying a legacy into Court. *Knapman* v. *Wreford*, 18 C. D. 300.

Evidence of executor's title.

As to what is sufficient evidence of an executor's title, all that is required is to show that the Probate Court has given authority to administer. This is usually done by the production of the probate.

But from Ord. 37, r. 4, it would seem that an office copy of the record from the Probate Registry would be good evidence of the executor's or administrator's title.

The title of an administrator *de bonis non* is sufficiently proved by the letters of administration *de bonis non*, without those granted to the first executor or administrator. 1 B. & C. 150.

Where an executor or administrator produces the probate or letters of administration in proof of his representative character, and his case shows that he sues for a greater value than the stamp, he cannot recover.

The title of an **administrator** may be proved by the letters of administration, or exemplification thereof, or by the original book of acts directing the grant, or a copy of it under Ord. 37, r. 4.

An executor or administrator is entitled to all equitable *Equitable* rights and interests of the deceased, and can enforce them *rights.* in the same way.

The one exception to this rule, founded on the maxim *actio personalis moritur cum personâ*, has but little application in equity; for instance, it does not prevent the executor obtaining an injunction to prevent the continuance of injury to property.

An executor can sue for obstruction to light, although his right to damages may be barred by 3 & 4 Wm. 4, c. 42. *Phillips* v. *Homfray*, 24 C. D. 439; *Jones* v. *Simes*, 43 C. D. 607; *ante*, p. 65.

And where injury to the deceased's estate is shown, the remedy is not confined to injunction, but extends to damages also. *Oakley* v. *Dalton*, 35 C. D. 700; *Jenks* v. *Clifden*, *ante*, p. 65.

Most of the equitable rights of the deceased can be enforced by his representatives, and in the same manner.

Thus an action can be brought to protect the literary property of the deceased. *Thompson* v. *Stanhope*, Ambl. 734.

An executor or administrator can, before an administra- *Statutes of* tion order, pay or retain a statute-barred debt, or may *Limitations.* admit it so as to take it out of the statute, but he cannot revive it after judgment. *Phillips* v. *P.*, 32 Beav. 26; *post*, p. 197.

Executors or administrators of a joint debtor are not deprived of the benefit of the Statute of Limitations by reason of payments made on account of the debt by any of the surviving debtors. 19 & 20 Vict. c. 97, s. 14.

Where the deceased debtor has made the surviving debtor his executor, and the latter or his firm make payments on account of the debt, such payments will, in the absence of proof to the contrary, be taken to have no reference to the executorial character. *Thompson* v. *Waithman*, 3 Dr. 628; *Brown* v. *Gordon*, 16 Beav. 302.

Under the Statute of Limitations, 1833, s. 6, time begins

to run as against an administrator claiming a chattel interest in land from the date of the death of the intestate, and not from the date of the grant of administration. *Re Williams*, 34 C. D. 558.

An executor or administrator when sued by creditors may, though he need not, plead the Statute of Limitations, except in cases of breach of trust. *How* v. *Winterton*, (1896) 2 Ch. 626.

They begin to run in his favour at latest when representation is taken out, or he has constituted himself executor *de son tort*. *Boatwright* v. *B.*, 17 Eq. 71 ; *Douglas* v. *Forrest*, 4 Bing. 686.

Time which has once begun to run is not stopped ; and, therefore, it is no answer that there was no executor constituted until after the expiration of the time. *Rhodes* v. *Smethurst*, 6 M. & W. 351 ; and see *Seagram* v. *Knight*, 2 Ch. 633 ; *Munns* v. *Burn*, 35 C. D. 266.

If, however, an action is commenced within the period, and the defendant dies before service, a new action may be brought after the period against the executor within a year from the probate. *Swindell* v. *Bulkeley*, 18 Q. B. D. 250.

Where an administration action was brought by an executor, who was a creditor, against a co-executor, and some time after judgment a claim was made on a promissory note of the testator dated more than six years before the judgment, it was held the claim was barred. *Re Greaves*, 18 C. D. 551.

By 23 & 24 Vict. c. 38, s. 13, no proceeding shall be brought to recover share of personal estate of intestate but within twenty years after the right accrued. *Re Johnson*, 29 C. D. 964.

But in the case of a legacy (*Buxton* v. *Campbell*, (1892) 2 Ch. 491), or share of residue (*Re Davis*, (1891) 3 Ch. 119), the period is twelve years only (37 & 38 Vict. c. 57, s. 8), unless there is an express trust for the legatee. Jud. Act, 1873, s. 25.

A mere constructive trust will not prevent the statute from being a bar. *Re Davis, supra.*

A mere acknowledgment from which no promise to pay can be inferred is not sufficient to take a debt out of the statute.

Therefore an acknowledgment that a debt is just, couched in terms which prevent a promise to pay from being implied, is not effectual. *Briggs* v. *Wilson*, 5 D. M. & G. 21; and see *Bethell* v. *B.*, 34 C. D. 561.

An acknowledgment by a person filling two characters, devisee and executor, will be attributed to both, but not if he represent two distinct persons. *Fordham* v. *Wallis*, 10 Ha. 217.

An acknowledgment or promise to pay by one of several executors is sufficient to take a debt out of the statute. *Re Macdonald*, (1897) 2 Ch. 181; but see *infra*.

An acknowledgment by one of two executors and devisees in trust of real estate against the wishes of the other cannot be treated as the valid act of the two in their capacity of trustees, and is not a good acknowledgment. *Astbury* v. *A.*, (1898) 2 Ch. 111; *ante*, p. 92.

The Court has power to restrain proceedings in a foreign Court against an executor or administrator by persons within the jurisdiction. *Stay of proceedings.*

And it will do so where proceedings are improper or vexatious. *Carron, &c.* v. *Maclaren*, 6 H. L. C. 416; *Henry* v. *Lewis*, 22 C. D. 397; *Hyam* v. *Helm*, 24 C. D. 531.

But not on the ground of mere hardship or inconvenience. *Fletcher* v. *Rodgers*, 27 W. R. 96.

The jurisdiction may be exercised whether an administration order has been made or not. *Baillie* v. *B.*, L. R. 5 Eq. 175.

Nothing short of an order for administration will prevent a creditor from suing the executor. *Re Barrett*, 43 C. D. 70.

After a decree for administration the Court of Chancery used to restrain creditors from proceeding at law against the executors or administrators, and now the latter may in a proper case stay creditors' actions by applying to the Court in which such actions are pending. 36 & 37 Vict. c. 66, s. 24 (5) ; and see R. S. C., Ord. 55, r. 10A.

But a mortgagee will not be stayed. *Crowle* v. *Russell*, 4 C. P. D. 186.

Nor a foreign creditor suing abroad. *Carron* v. *Maclaren*, 5 H. L. C. 441 ; *Crofton* v. *C.*, 15 C. D. 591.

Nor a creditor who has obtained a charging order *nisi* (*Haly* v. *Barry*, 3 Ch. 452); or judgment in a county court. *Re Womersley*, 29 C. D. 557.

And a creditor who before decree has obtained judgment against an executor will not after decree be restrained from enforcing his judgment against a garnishee. *Burton* v. *Roberts*, 29 L. J. Ex. 484.

By Ord. 49, r. 5, when an order has been made for administration, the Judge may order a transfer to himself of any cause or matter brought by or against the executors or administrators ; and see Ord. 55, r. 10A. *Post*, p. 220.

But the action, to be within the rule, must be brought against the executor *quâ* executor. *Chapman* v. *Mason*, 40 L. T. 678.

By Ord. 55, r. 10A (b), the Court may, when necessary to prevent proceedings by other creditors, make the usual order for administration, with a proviso that no proceedings are to be taken without leave of the Judge.

An executor or administrator can in equity bring an action against another. *Peake* v. *Ledger*, 8 Ha. 213.

And one executor can sue for administration. *Latch* v. *L.*, L. R. 10 Ch. 464.

An executor or administrator can sue before probate or grant of administration (*ante*); and it appears unnecessary to allege the grant in pleading. *Re Masonic, &c.*, 32 C. D. 373.

Executors or administrators cannot sue or be sued *in formâ pauperis* (*Paradice* v. *Sheppard*, 1 Dick. 136; but see *Bayley* v. *B.*, 11 Beav. 256), unless they have a beneficial interest. *Everson* v. *Matthew*, 3 W. R. 159.

The former practice of the Court, that a person interested in the residue was entitled as of course to a full administration of the estate, is now completely altered, and all applications for administration judgments or orders are now at the risk of the applicants. *Re Blake*, 29 C. D. 913.

Originating summons.

Questions relating to the administration of estates are now determined by means of an originating summons without administration of the estate. Ord. 55, rr. 3—5.

It is no longer obligatory on the Court to make an order for administration where the questions can be determined without such order. Ord. 55, r. 10.

The Court may order an application to stand over till executors or administrators render accounts, which they must do under penalty of paying costs. Ord. 55, r. 10A; *Re Dartnall*, (1895) 1 Ch. 474; *Re Bosworth*, 58 L. J. Ch. 432.

Or may order administration when necessary to prevent proceedings by other parties, with a proviso that no further proceedings are to be taken without leave. *Ibid.*

An action for administration is, in a sense, generally beneficial for the executor, for he can get a complete exoneration in that way. *Hay* v. *Bowen*, 5 Beav. 616.

And where he passes his accounts in Court, he is discharged from further liability. *Knatchbull* v. *Fearnhead*, 3 M. & C. 126; *Bennett* v. *Lytton*, 2 J. & H. 155.

The Court will order a general administration where it is necessary for the protection of the executor or administrator. *Re Dickinson*, (1884) W. N. 199.

An executor or administrator, fairly instituting an action for the direction of the Court with regard to the estate, will be entitled to his costs. Dan. 1208.

If, therefore, he has not unreasonably instituted, carried on, or resisted proceedings, he has a right to costs out of the estate. Ord. 55, r. 1.

But he may be made to pay the costs of any unnecessary or vexatious proceeding. *Re Cabburn*, 46 L. T. 848: *Re*

Weall, 42 C. D. 674; *Easton* v. *Landor*, 67 L. T. 833; *Budgett* v. *B.*, (1895) 1 Ch. 202; *Re Knox*, (1895) 2 Ch. 483; *Re Chapman*, 72 L. T. 66.

Where there are no assets, the plaintiff may be ordered to pay the executor's costs. *Hibernian Bank* v. *Lauder*, *post*, p. 229.

Upon an application for administration by a creditor or beneficiary, where no accounts or insufficient accounts have been rendered, the Court may order the application to stand over, and the executors or administrators to render proper accounts, with an intimation that if this is not done they may be made to pay the costs of the proceedings. Ord. 55, r. 10A; *Re Dartnall*, *supra*.

It is a common mistake for executors and administrators in taking in their costs for taxation to include charges and expenses; this is wrong, as charges and expenses should be included in their accounts, and allowed for on taking them. Wms. 1813.

Therefore they are not entitled to charges and expenses on taxation without an express direction to that effect. *Humphrey* v. *Moore*, 2 Atk. 108.

The practice is to allow executors or administrators their costs of action out of the estate as between solicitor and client, together with any charges and expenses properly incurred. Seton, 4th ed. 482.

It is not the practice in taking the account in Chambers to allow charges and expenses incurred since the suit, but they are provided for on further consideration. *Ibid.*

Charges and expenses do not include funeral and probate expenses, nor the costs of other actions, unless specially provided for. *Collis* v. *Robins*, 1 D. & S. 131; *Payne* v. *Little*, 27 Beav. 83.

In taking the accounts, all "just allowances" are made without any direction for that purpose. Ord. 33, r. 8.

The question what are just allowances is usually left to be decided on taking the account. *Brown* v. *De Tastet*, Jac. 284, 294.

As a general rule, whatever an executor or administrator has expended in the fair administration of the estate, may be allowed him in passing his accounts. Dan. 1055.

Consequently the following have been allowed:—

Money which has been reasonably expended in taking opinions and procuring directions. *Fearns* v. *Young*, 10 Ves. 184.

Payments by executors in discharge of legacies. *Nightingale* v. *Lawson*, 1 Cox, 23.

Expenses of managing and carrying on a partnership business. *Brown* v. *De Tastet*, Jac. 284, 299.

Mortgagee's expenses of seizing and holding possession of a ship, advertising it for sale, and effecting insurances upon it. *Wilkes* v. *Sannion*, 7 Ch. D. 188.

An executor or administrator will not be allowed the charges of his solicitor for doing things which he ought strictly to have done himself. *Harbin* v. *Darby*, 28 Beav. 325.

When a trader dies, his business must be either wound up or carried on by his executors or administrators. *Carrying on business.*

It is the duty of both an executor and administrator, where the business is a valuable asset, to carry it on for such reasonable time as may be necessary, to enable them to sell it as a going concern. *Dowse* v. *Gorton*, (1891) A. C. 190; *ante*, p. 174.

But the executor or administrator who carries on the business of the deceased makes himself personally liable to all debts so contracted, and it makes no difference that he avowedly acts as executor or administrator. *Labouchere* v. *Tupper*, 11 Moo. P. C. 198.

Where the business is merely carried on for the purpose of realisation, the executor or administrator is entitled to be indemnified by the estate against all liabilities properly incurred by him in so doing, both as against creditors of the deceased, and also as against beneficiaries. *Dowse* v. *Gorton*, (1891) A. C. 190; *Re Brooke*, (1894) 2 Ch. 600.

An administrator is only entitled to carry on the business for the purpose of realisation, and if he does more than this, he renders himself personally liable for the debts so incurred, without any right of indemnity out of the estate. *Re Evans*, 34 C. D. 597 ; and see *Strickland* v. *Symons*, 26 C. D. 245.

An executor who is not expressly or impliedly authorised by the will to employ the assets in carrying on the business is in the same position as an administrator. *M'Neillie* v. *Acton*, 4 D. M. & G. 744 ; Wms. 1816.

Where the executor is authorised to carry on the business and employ assets therein, although personally liable for debts, he has a right to be indemnified out of the specific assets authorised to be so employed. *Ex parte Garland*, 10 Ves. 120.

He is entitled to this protection as against beneficiaries, and if any creditors of the testator know of his carrying on the business and acquiesce, he is entitled to the same indemnity against them. *Dowse* v. *Gorton*, (1891) A. C. 190 ; *post*, p. 216.

An executor who carries on the business can sue as executor for debts incurred to the estate in carrying on the trade since the testator's death. *Abbott* v. *Parfitt*, L. R. 6 Q. B. 346.

For further information on this subject, see *post*, p. 215.

Payment into Court. By the Trustee Act, 1893, s. 42 (10 & 11 Vict. c. 96), all executors and administrators may pay or transfer money or securities into Court. And see Wolst. 232.

Where money was paid in under the Trustee Relief Act by the administrator of a supposed intestate, and afterwards, a will being discovered, the administration was revoked and probate granted, the Court ordered payment out to the executor. *Re Hood*, (1896) 1 Ch. 270.

The proper course now, however, is not to pay funds into Court, but to take out a summons under Ord. 55. *Re Giles*, 34 W. R. 712.

Under 22 & 23 Vict. c. 35, s. 29, already referred to, executors and administrators may distribute the assets after due notice to creditors and others to send in their claims. *Ante,* p. 125. Lord St. Leonards' Act.

The section applies to claims of next of kin as well as creditors. *Newton* v. *Sherry,* 1 C. P. D. 246.

But it does not protect executors against claims of which they have notice. *Re Land Credit,* (1872) W. N. 210; *Wood* v. *Wood,* 21 W. R. 135.

It protects them whether they have paid over the legacies or only appropriated them. *Cliff* v. *Rowland,* L. R. 8 Eq. 368; *Hunter* v. *Young,* 4 Ex. D. 256.

The procedure by originating summons under Ord. 55 is so much cheaper than the procedure for the direction of the Court under Lord St. Leonards' Act, that the latter has been practically rendered obsolete. Advice and direction.

The opinion and direction of the Court can still be obtained by special case under Ord. 34, r. 8. Special case.

CHAPTER XVII.

REMEDIES AGAINST REPRESENTATIVES.

Foreign executors.
No suit can be brought against any executor or administrator in his official capacity in the Court of any country but that from which he derives his authority to act by virtue of the probate or administration there granted to him. Story, Confl. s. 513.

Therefore a foreign creditor cannot sue in respect of English assets until an English representative is constituted; for a foreign representative cannot be sued here in his official capacity. *Tyler* v. *Bell*, 2 M. & C. 89, 100; *Maclean* v. *Dawson*, 27 Beav. 21; *Flood* v. *Patterson*, 29 Beav. 295.

But if he intermeddle, without taking out administration, he would become liable as executor *de son tort* to the extent of assets so received by him. *Ante*, p. 9.

And if the estate is to be administered, the presence of an executor *de son tort* before the Court will not dispense with that of a regular representative. He is only treated as executor for the purpose of being charged. *Penny* v. *Watts*, 2 Phill. C. C. 152.

Actions against.
A creditor of a testator cannot sue the executor, unless the latter has either administered or obtained a grant of probate; and a sale in execution of a judgment in such an action does not bind the testator's estate. *Mohamidu* v. *Pitchey*, (1894) A. C. 437; *Re Leask*, (1891) W. N. 159; *ante*, p. 192.

Although no action at law is against an executor for a general legacy, it is otherwise as regards a specific legacy after the executor has assented. *Doe* v. *Guy*, 3 East, 120; *Williams* v. *Lee*, 3 Atk. 223.

Executors are also liable to be sued at law where they have ceased to hold the money as executors, or they may be treated as trustees of the fund. *Re Smith, ante*, p. 140.

An executor or administrator is liable, as representative, to all equitable demands with regard to property which existed against the deceased at the time of his death. Toller, 479.

Again, executors and administrators are, for most purposes, considered in equity as trustees, and are personally liable for all breaches of the ordinary trusts of their office. *Re Marsden, infra.*

They are bound by a direct trust to deal properly with the assets and to apply them in due course of administration. *Re Marsden*, 26 C. D. 783, 790.

A single creditor may sue for his demand out of the assets, and may, as at law, by the judgment gain a preference over other creditors in the same degree. *Alexander* v. *Mullins*, 2 R. & M. 568.

But a person entitled to a share of a sum of money which is due as a debt from the testator must sue on behalf of himself and all other parties interested in the debt, or make those other persons parties to the suit. *Alexander* v. *Mullins*, 2 R. & M. 568.

Although an executor has a year allowed him to pay legacies, he is liable to be sued for debts the moment after the testator's death. *Nicholls* v. *Judson*, 2 Atk. 301; but see *Mohamidu* v. *Pitchey, supra.*

A debtor to the estate cannot obtain a stay of proceedings brought against him by the personal representative to recover the debt, on the ground that such representative intends to misapply the money when received. *Darther* v. *Winter*, 2 S. & S. 536; but see *ante*, p. 87.

The general rule is, that if there are several executors or administrators they must all be sued. *Latch* v. *L.*, L. R. 10 Ch. 464. — Parties.

But it is only necessary to sue such executors as have proved the will or have acted. *Re Lovett*, 3 C. D. 198.

Although one of two executors may sue the other without making the persons entitled parties, yet where the latter have participated in the breach of trust they are necessary parties. *Jesse* v. *Bennett*, 6 D. M. & G. 609.

If during an action a defendant dies, the action can be continued against his personal representative, whether he died before or after decree. Ord 17.

Where there is no representative.
By Ord. 16, r. 46, where any deceased person who was interested in the matter in question has no personal representative, the Court may appoint some person to represent his estate, or proceed in the absence of any such person.

This, it seems, does not apply (1) where the estate of the deceased person is that which is being administered in the suit; (2) where the interest of the deceased person is adverse to that of the plaintiff; (3) where the representative has active duties to perform. *Moore* v. *Morris*, L. R. 13 Eq. 140; *Groves* v. *Levi*, 9 Ha. App. 47.

Where a sole plaintiff died insolvent, the Court appointed a person to represent his estate, so as to enable the defendant to move to dismiss the action for want of prosecution. *Wingrove* v. *Thompson*, 11 C. D. 419.

In an action by an equitable mortgagee of a policy of insurance against the company, the Court dispensed with a personal representative of the assured, the next of kin declining to take out administration. *Curtius* v. *Caledonian, &c.*, 19 C. D. 534.

Receiver.
The Court will before probate or administration interfere on behalf of a creditor or beneficiary to protect the estate by the appointment of a receiver or manager, or both. *Steer* v. *S.*, 2 D. & S. 311; *Northard* v. *Proctor*, 1 C. D. 4; *Blackett* v. *B.*, 24 L. T. 276.

An application for a receiver pending probate should not be made to the Chancery Division except under special circumstances, as, for instance, danger to assets. *Re Henderson*, 2 Times Rep. 322.

The fact that an executor declines to admit assets, and that consequently, if a receiver be not appointed, the executor may prefer one creditor to another, is not sufficient. *Phillips* v. *Jones*, 28 Sol. Jo. 360.

In other cases the proper Court to appoint a receiver is the Probate Court. *Re Henderson, supra*.

The addition of a claim for administration of the estate to a claim for its protection until the appointment of a representative was held to be irregular. *Overington* v. *Ward*, 34 Beav. 175; *Rawlings* v. *Lambert*, 1 J. & H. 458.

If in the case of an executor or administrator any misconduct, waste, or improper disposition of the assets is shown, the Court will instantly appoint a receiver. 12 Ves. 5; *Richards* v. *Perkins*, 3 Y. & C. 299.

So the bankruptcy of a sole executor and trustee is a ground for such an appointment. *Re Johnson*, L. R. 1 Ch. 325.

But the Court will not appoint a receiver because the executor may, and probably will, exercise his right of retainer to the prejudice of creditors. *Re Wells*, 45 C. D. 569.

And the administration is not to be taken from the executor on slight grounds, such as mere poverty. *Hathornthwaite* v. *Russell*, 2 Atk. 126; Dan. 1669.

The Trustee Act does not authorise the appointment of a trustee to discharge the duties of an executor. The executor has certain duties to perform which cannot be taken from him; but when the estate is cleared the Court will appoint trustees. *Eaton* v. *Daines*, (1894) W. N. 32; Rud. & G. 87, 89. Removal of executor.

But under the Judicial Trustees Act, 1896, the Court has power to remove an executor and appoint a judicial trustee in his place. *Re Ratcliff*, (1898) 2 Ch. 352.

The Court has no jurisdiction to order in a summary way the executor of a deceased receiver to pass his accounts. If the balance is ascertained, the recognizances may be put in suit; otherwise an action must be brought against Executor of receiver.

the executor, unless he consents to an order to pass the receiver's accounts. Dan. 1709.

Order for payment into Court on admission of assets. Except in the case of a creditor suing for his own debt, only so much of the estate as the executor or administrator admits to be in his hands will be ordered to be brought into Court, whether he has abused his trust or not, and without proof that the fund is in danger. *Strange* v. *Harris*, 3 Bro. C. C. 365; *Blake* v. *B.*, 2 S. & L. 26; Dan. 1734.

The rule is not limited to cases where there are no debts and there is no purpose for which the money is to be left outstanding, but applies where there are demands upon it to which the representative is liable. Dan. 1734; *Yare* v. *Harrison*, 2 Cox, 377.

Where an executor admits a sum of money to be due from him, in his individual character, to his testator, the amount will be ordered to be paid into Court. *Rothwell* v. *R.*, 2 S. & S. 218; *Costeker* v. *Horrox*, 3 Y. & C. 530.

And this has been done though the debts of the testator were not all paid. *Mortlock* v. *Leathes*, 2 Mer. 491.

The Court in making an order adheres strictly to the rule of acting on the executor's admission only, and will refuse to proceed upon knowledge derived from any other source. *Richardson* v. *Bank of England*, 4 M. & C. 174; *Scott* v. *Wheeler*, 12 Beav. 366.

Money admitted by an executor to be in the hands of his partner will be considered as in his own hands for the purpose of being ordered into Court. *Johnston* v. *Aston*, 1 Sim. & S. 73; *White* v. *Barton*, 18 Beav. 192. Comp. *Freeman* v. *Fairlie*, 3 Mer. 39.

Where an executor admits assets, he may discharge himself from payment into Court, wholly or partially, by taking credit for sums he has a right to retain or to be allowed. *Roy* v. *Gibbon*, 4 Ha. 65; *Nokes* v. *Seppings*, 2 Phill. 19.

And where he has made payments, the amount of which

he does not specify, the Court will allow him to verify the amount and pay in the balance. 4 Sim. 359.

Where there is a sufficient admission by the executor, he cannot avoid payment in by showing any unauthorised application or any investment or disposition which amounts to a breach of his duty as executor. *Roy* v. *Gibbon*, 4 Ha. 65; *Ingle* v. *Partridge*, 32 Beav. 661.

Or by setting up the adverse title of a third party. *Lord* v. *Purchase*, 17 Beav. 171.

* But an order will not be made under Ord. 55 unless the money is actually in his hands. It is not sufficient that it has been in his hands and that he is responsible for it. *Nutter* v. *Holland*, (1894) 3 Ch. 408.

If there is no danger of the property being lost, a reasonable time will be allowed for bringing the fund into Court. *Roy* v. *Gibbon*, 4 Ha. 65; *Score* v. *Ford*, 7 Beav. 393.

The appointment of a receiver by the Probate Court is not a sufficient reason for ordering payment in by the person named as executor. *Reed* v. *Harris*, 7 Sim. 639; *Edwards* v. *E.*, 10 Ha., App. II. 63.

An executor ordered to pay money into Court is not thereby deprived of his right of retainer. *Ante*, p. 116. Nor of his lien on the fund for his costs. *Blenkinsop* v. *Foster*, 3 Y. & C. 207.

Applications for payment in, before judgment, are usually made by summons, which, if opposed, is frequently adjourned into Court. Dan. 1744.

Under the Trustee Act, 1893, s. 35, the Court may, in a proper case, make vesting orders as to any stock or *chose in action* against any executor or administrator.

Quære, whether the Court can now make such orders with regard to land which has devolved upon them under the Land Transfer Act, 1897. *Ante*, p. 80.

It is the bounden duty of an executor to keep proper Accounts. accounts, and to constantly have them ready. *Ante*, p. 186.

If, therefore, he mixes the accounts with those of his

own trading concerns, he will be bound to produce the books in which any part of those accounts may be inserted; and so will his partner, if he has permitted the mixing of the accounts or the firm has dealt with the assets of the testator. *Freeman* v. *Fairlie*, 3 Mer. 43; and see *Flockton* v. *Bunning*, L. R. 8 Ch. 323, n.

Executors, when required to furnish accounts, can demand to be paid or guaranteed the cost of so doing; and it makes no difference that one of them is a solicitor. *Re Bosworth*, 58 L. J. Ch. 432.

Under the usual administration decree an executor or administrator can only be charged for actual receipt by himself or his agent, not for a default of his co-trustee. *Re Fryer*, 3 K. & J. 317.

Wilful default.

The practice is to make them account for what they have received, not for what they might have received, but for their own default. *Barber* v. *Mackrell*, 12 C. D. 538.

To make them account on the latter footing a special case must be made, and at least one act of wilful default must be averred and proved. *Ibid.*; *Re Youngs*, 30 C. D. 431; *Re Stevens, infra*.

An order charging wilful default can be made at any time during the action, on a proper case being shown. *Job* v. *J.*, 6 C. D. 562; *Barber* v. *Mackrell*, 12 C. D. 534.

And on taking the common accounts executors can be, and often are, charged with a *devastavit* arising on the accounts themselves. *Re Stevens*, (1898) 1 Ch. 162.

But where a common administration order has been made against a defendant, the leave of the Court must be obtained in order to continue the action against him on the footing of wilful defaults. *Laming* v. *Gee*, 10 C. D. 715.

Where there are no pleadings, a charge of wilful default can be raised by affidavit. *Barber* v. *Mackrell*, 12 C. D. 534.

Where the plaintiff alleges wilful default, he must prove it at the hearing. *Smith* v. *Armitage*, 24 C. D. 727.

And he must show not only a loss, but a loss under such circumstances as to show default on the part of the executor or administrator. *Re Brier*, 26 C. D. 238; *Re Stevens*, (1898) 1 Ch. 162.

Loss of interest from a debtor's refusal to pay his debt before probate is too remote a consequence of delay in proving the will to render the executor liable to account on the footing of wilful default. *Re Stevens*, (1897) 1 Ch. 422; (1898) 1 Ch. 162.

Particulars of the allegations of wilful default should be given in the pleading. *Re Anstier*, 54 L. J. Ch. 1104; see also Ord. 19, r. 6.

Accounts on the footing of wilful default cannot be obtained under Ord. 15. *Re Bowen*, 20 C. D. 538.

If the plaintiff's demand be uncontested or proved, and the executor admits assets, the plaintiff is entitled at the hearing to an immediate order for payment without taking accounts. *Woodgate* v. *Field*, 2 Ha. 211; *Connop* v. *Hayward*, 1 Y. & C. 33. Executor personally liable by admitting assets.

The same doctrine prevails where the admission of assets is made before suit. *Barnard* v. *Pumfrett*, 5 M. & C. 63; *Dimsdale* v. *Dudding*, 1 Y. & C. 265; *Rogers* v. *Soutten*, 2 Keen, 598.

An admission of assets for the payment of a legacy is an admission of assets for the purposes of the suit, and extends to costs. *Philanthropic Soc.* v. *Hobson*, 2 M. & K. 357.

If there are several executors and some admit assets, an account may be decreed against the rest. *Norton* v. *Turvill*, 2 P. W. 145; and see *Davies* v. *Ridge*, post, p. 213.

An admission of assets by the executor's answer is waived by the plaintiff's going on to an account of assets and procuring a receiver to be appointed. *Wall* v. *Bushby*, 1 Bro. 484.

An admission of assets cannot be retracted unless a case of mistake be most clearly established. *Drewry* v. *Thacker*, 3 Sw. 548; *Roberts* v. *R.*, 1 Bro. 487; and see *Hewes* v. *H.*, 4 Sim. 1.

But if a strong case be made out, this may enable the Court to relieve him from the admission. *Foster* v. *F.*, 2 Bro. 619; *Young* v. *Walter*, 9 Ves. 365; *Horsley* v. *Chaloner*, 2 Ves. Sen. 85.

The admission of assets will not preclude creditors from coming on a fund specifically appropriated for their benefit, although that fund may have been disposed of to a purchaser. *Curtis* v. *Blow*, 2 B. & Adol. 426.

<small>What amounts to an admission.</small> With respect to what amounts to an admission of assets:

Where an executor admits himself to have been a debtor to his testator at the time of his death, this is an admission of assets to the amount of the debt. *Rothwell* v. *R.*, 2 S. & S. 218; *Mortlock* v. *Leathes*, 3 Mer. 491.

Payment of interest on a legacy from time to time, as distinguished from a single payment, is an admission of assets to the amount of the legacy. *Corporation, &c.* v. *Swainson*, 1 Ves. Sen. 75; *Att.-Gen.* v. *Chapman*, 3 Beav. 255; see *Severs* v. *S.*, 1 S. & G. 400; *Whittle* v. *Henning*, 2 Beav. 396.

So is payment of legacy duty. *Lazonby* v. *Rawson*, 4 D. M. & G. 556; *infra*.

And where executors employed a legacy in their business, they were held to have admitted assets by entering the amount in the partnership books to the credit of the legatee. *Townend* v. *T.*, 1 Giff. 201. Comp. *Hutton* v. *Rosseter*, 24 L. J. Ch. 106; 7 D. M. & G. 9.

Admission of assets to one legatee is, generally speaking, an admission to all. *Cook* v. *Martyn*, 2 Atk. 3.

But this is not a hard-and-fast rule, and the Court will not subject executors to liabilities they never contemplated. *Morewood* v. *Currey*, 28 W. R. 213.

The payment of a legacy out of the executor's own money is not an admission for the payment of others. *Cadbury* v. *Smith*, L. R. 9 Eq. 37; *infra*.

Payment of legacies is an admission of assets for payment of debts. *Freeman* v. *Fairlie*, 3 Mer. 38.

But the circumstances under which such payment was made may be material. *Savage* v. *Lane*, 6 Ha. 33.

Payment of annuities for several years is an admission of assets. *Payne* v. *Little*, 22 Beav. 69.

So is payment of interest to a tenant for life. *Payne* v. *Tanner*, 55 L. J. Ch. 611; *Brewster* v. *Prior*, 35 W. R. 251.

Payment of probate duty is presumptive evidence of, but not an absolute admission of, assets to the extent covered by the duty. *Lazonby* v. *Rawson*, 4 D. M. & G. 556.

Where an executrix and residuary legatee confirmed by her own will a void bequest contained in the will of the testator, she was held to have admitted assets to that amount. *Campbell* v. *Radnor*, 1 Bro. 271.

Where one of two executors, who were residuary legatees, had died, a payment by his representatives to the survivor out of the deceased executor's estate was not an admission of assets for payment of other legacies. *Cadbury* v. *Smith*, L. R. 9 Eq. 37.

Judgment against an executor by confession or default is an admission of assets. *Rock* v. *Leighton*, 1 Salk. 310.

Submission to an arbitration award is not of itself an admission of assets. *Pearson* v. *Henry*, 5 T. R. 6; *Daries* v. *Ridge*, 3 Esp. 101; but see *Worthington* v. *Barlow*, 7 T. R. 453.

Where executors of a receiver, three years after their testator's death, applied to pass their accounts and pay in the balance, they were held to have admitted assets. *Gurden* v. *Badcock*, 6 Beav. 159.

An admission of assets is, however, always susceptible of explanation, and an executor cannot be bound by an admission made under circumstances with which he was not acquainted. *Payne* v. *Little*, 22 Beav. 69.

If executors refuse to admit assets without reason, they may be ordered to pay the costs occasioned by the refusal. *Christian* v. *Adamson*, (1869) W. N. 208.

If, in an action against executors for a legacy, the

executors admit assets, and judgment is given for payment of the legacy, a creditor may, it seems, recover the legacy if it was in fact paid out of the testator's assets. *Re Brogden*, 38 C. D. 546.

The party injured by a *devastavit* is only a simple contract creditor of the executor, and the claim is consequently barred after the lapse of six years by the Statute of Limitations. *Thorne* v. *Kerr*, 2 K. & J. 54.

But this does not, or did not before the Trustee Act, 1888, apply to an action by a beneficiary against the executor who had committed the *devastavit*, as the debt arose from a breach of trust from which the statute did not protect him. *Re Marsden*, 26 C. D. 783; Wolst. 190; *post*, p. 226.

An executor cannot set up his own *devastavit* as a defence in order to claim the benefit of the Statute of Limitations. *Re Hyatt*, 38 C. D. 609.

Bankrupt executor.

If an executor becomes bankrupt, having wasted the assets, a proof for the *devastavit* can be taken in under the bankruptcy. *Geary* v. *Beaumont*, 3 Mer. 431.

An executor and trustee having committed a *devastavit* cannot prove under his own bankruptcy without an order of the Court. *Ex parte Colman*, 2 Dea. & C. 584.

Generally speaking, such order will be made on the application of a bankrupt who is sole executor, but the dividends ought to be secured and not allowed to come into the bankrupt's hands. *Ex parte Leeke*, 2 Bro. 597; *Ex parte Shaw*, 1 Glyn. & Jam. 127; *Ex parte Moody*, 2 Rose, 413.

In the case of an executor committing a *devastavit*, and a decree for payment of the amount, the debt is considered as due from the time of the *devastavit*, and not from the date of the decree. *Wheldale* v. *W.*, 16 Ves. 376.

A defaulting executor or administrator who becomes bankrupt is protected from attachment by sect. 10 of the Bankruptcy Act, 1883. *Cobham* v. *Dalton*, L. R. 10 Ch. 655; *Re Neil*, (1882) W. N. 46.

And if he becomes bankrupt after he has been attached, he may be released. He is protected from arrest by the order in bankruptcy. *Re Manning*, 30 C. D. 480.

The issue of a summons under Ord. 55 does not interfere with any power or discretion of any executor or administrator, except so far as such interference may necessarily be involved in the particular relief sought. See r. 12. Discretion.

Nor does a judgment for administration interfere with the exercise of such discretion, except so far as the exercise conflicts with the order. *Re Hall*, 33 W. R. 508; *Re Gadd*, 23 C. D. 134; *ante*, p. 89.

Nor does an administration decree prevent trustees from exercising a power of sale after the order on further consideration has been made. *Re Mansel*, 33 W. R. 727.

Nor does an administration decree prevent an executor dealing with the assets where there is no injunction or receiver appointed. *Berry* v. *Gibbons*, 8 Ch. 747.

But the Court will prevent them from exercising their discretion improperly. *Tempest* v. *Camoys*, 21 C. D. 571.

And will enforce the proper and timely exercise of a power. *Re Burrage*, 62 L. T. N. S. 752.

The remedy of a creditor of the business for a debt incurred since the death is against the executor or administrator personally, and not against the estate of the deceased. *Farhall* v. *F.*, L. R. 7 Ch. 123; *Strickland* v. *Symonds*, 26 C. D. 245. Trade.

Such creditor's remedy is by action at law, and he has no right to have a solvent estate administered. *Owen* v. *Delamere*, L. R. 15 Eq. 134.

But if the estate is insolvent, such a creditor may sue for administration. *Re Shorey*, 79 L. T. 349.

And such a creditor can always make the executor render an account of the assets employed in the business since the death of the testator. *Thompson* v. *Dunn*, L. R. 5 Ch. 573.

Where the representative properly carries on the business,

he is entitled to be indemnified out of the assets which are authorised to be applied in the business. *Ante*, p. 202.

And in such case creditors whose debts have been incurred since the death are entitled to stand in the place of the representative, and to claim that the fund out of which he is entitled to indemnity shall be applied in payment of their debts. *Ex parte Garland*, 10 Ves. 120 ; *Ex parte Edmonds*, 4 D. F. & J. 488.

Where the executor is in default to the specific trust estate he is authorised to employ in the trade, the creditors are in no better position than the executor himself, and are only entitled to have their debts paid out of the specific assets when the default is made good. *Re Johnson*, 15 C. D. 548.

But an executor is not deprived of his indemnity by default in merely rendering accounts; there must be default in payment. *Re Kidd*, (1894) W. N. 73.

Where no part of the estate is properly applicable in the business, creditors have no right to recover their debt out of the trust funds. *Strickland* v. *Symonds*, 26 C. D. 245.

But they are entitled to any interest the executor may have in such trade as against the trust estate, *e.g.*, the right to be repaid moneys he has advanced. *Re Evans*, 34 C. D. 597.

The executor is, as against the beneficiaries, entitled to be indemnified by the trust estate against the debts incurred by him in carrying on the trade out of the specific part of the estate authorised to be employed in the trade. *Dowse* v. *Gorton*, (1891) A. C. 190.

But this right to indemnity does not apply as against the creditors of the testator unless they had knowledge that the business was being carried on by the executor and had acquiesced in such trading. *Ibid.*

This principle is applicable where a receiver and manager has been appointed in an administration action to carry on the business in succession to the executor, and whether the

will does or does not contain a power to carry on the
business. *Re Brooke*, (1894) 2 Ch. 600.

The effect of giving executors so wide a right of
indemnity is to give the creditors of the business subsequent
to the testator's death a priority over the creditors of the
testator in cases where they acquiesced in the trading.

And this makes it exceedingly important for the creditors
of a deceased trader to protect themselves against the risk
of the executors carrying on the business at a loss, by
requiring the estate to be administered without delay.

Where an executor carries on the business and supplies
such business with goods, the onus lies on him to show the
cost price of such goods. *Re Williams*, 40 W. R. 636.

Although the Court will look with suspicion upon an
uncorroborated claim, there is no rule of law which precludes a claimant from recovering against the estate of
a deceased person on his own uncorroborated testimony,
but the Court will generally require such corroboration.
Re Hodgson, 31 C. D. 177; *Re Farman*, 57 L. J. Ch.
637, 689; *Rawlinson* v. *Scholes*, 79 L. T. 350; *Re
Griffin*, 79 L. T. 442.

Uncorroborated claim.

It has already been shown (*ante*, p. 193) that an executor
may retain a legacy by way of set-off against a debt due
from the legatee to the executor. *Re Knapman*, 18 C. D.
300; *Re Akerman*, (1891) 3 Ch. 212; but see *Re Harrald*,
52 L. J. Ch. 436.

Set-off.

But he cannot set off, against a demand upon him as
executor, a debt due to him individually. *Ante*, p. 193.

The usual form of relief now given by the Chancery
Division against an executor or administrator is to compel
him to account for the assets, and to see that such assets
are properly distributed.

Administration.

Such relief is obtained by an administration action or
by an originating summons. *Ante*, p. 199.

A creditor is entitled to an administration order where
the dispute as to his debt depends upon a question of law,
but not where it depends on a question of fact; in the

latter case he should proceed by writ. *Re Powers*, 30 C. D. 291; *Re Shorey*, ante, p. 215.

An administration summons can only be taken out against executors or administrators when so constituted, and such a summons taken out by a creditor before administration is granted is entirely bad. *Re Leask*, (1891) W. N. 159; *ante*, p. 204.

An annuitant whose annuity is not in arrear cannot apply for administration, even though the estate is not sufficient to pay the estimated value of the annuity as well as the other debts. *Re Hargreaves*, 44 C. D. 236; but see *Wollaston* v. *W.*, 7 C. D. 58.

The widow of an intestate, entitled under the Intestates' Estates Act, 1890, to a charge, has a sufficient interest in his real estate to entitle her to maintain an action for its administration. *McFerran* v. *McF.*, (1871) 1 Ir. R. 66.

There is only jurisdiction on an originating summons to decide such matters as could be decided in an administration suit, but not questions as against persons claiming adversely to the estate. *Re Royle*, 43 C. D. 18; *Re Bridge*, 56 L. J. Ch. 779; *Re Gladstone*, (1888) W. N. 185.

Nor questions as to legal devises or between legal devisees. *Re Carlyon*, 56 L. J. Ch. 219; *Re Davies*, 38 C. D. 210.

The objection to jurisdiction must be taken in Chambers, or the defendant will not be allowed his costs of adjournment into Court. *Re Davies, supra.*

An originating summons is not a proper proceeding on which to raise a question of breach of trust or wilful default. *Re Weall*, 37 W. R. 779; *Re Neil*, 62 L. T. 649; *Dowse* v. *Gorton*, (1891) A. C. 202.

Nor is it for making a claim for repayment after division of assets by the executors. *Re Warren*, (1884) W. N. 112.

Notice should be given of intention to raise on the hearing of the summons any question arising under the Statute of Frauds. *Re Shearman*, 2 Times R. 236.

In order to prevent the inconvenience of several suits, the Court has always allowed a creditor to sue on behalf of himself and all the other creditors, and has thereupon directed a general account of the estate and debts against the executor or administrator.

Or, if assets were admitted, and the debt admitted or proved, the Court would make an immediate order for payment. *Woodgate* v. *Field*, 2 Ha. 211.

Upon the same principle, a legatee may sue on behalf of himself and other legatees.

Where administration of the personal estate only is sought, a creditor need not sue on behalf of himself and all other the creditors. *Re Blount*, 27 W. R. 865 : *Bray* v. *Tofield*, 18 C. D. 554.

Though in practice he very often does so, as it may affect the question of costs. *Re McRea, infra*.

Where a creditor sues for administration of both real and personal estate, and there is no devise of real estate to trustees, with power to sell and give receipts, the writ must be indorsed with a claim by the plaintiff on behalf of himself and all other creditors. *Re Royle*, 5 C. D. 540; and see *Re Vincent*, 26 W. R. 94.

Where a creditor sues on behalf of himself and all other creditors, and the estate is insufficient for payment of debts, he is entitled to costs as between solicitor and client. *Re Richardson*, 14 C. D. 611 ; *Re McRea*, 32 C. D. 613.

If it appears in the title of the statement of claim that he so sues, the writ need not be amended. *Eyre* v. *Cox*, 24 W. R. 187 ; *Re Tottenham*, (1896) 1 Ch. 628.

The rule applies equally to the case of a creditor who obtains conduct of an action originally commenced by a legatee or next of kin. *Re Richardson*, 14 C. D. 611.

An executor suing on behalf of himself and all other creditors can none the less retain his own debt. *Ex parte Campbell*, 16 C. D. 198.

There is nothing to prevent other creditors or legatees from bringing a second action for administration.

Stay of proceedings.

But when an order has been made in one action, application should be made to have the proceedings in the other transferred, and to have the other action stayed.

On the application to stay proceedings, the question is whether the action sought to be stayed asks something more than could be obtained under the existing order. *Re McRea*, 25 C. D. 16; *Lambaco* v. *Cassavelli*, L. R. 11 Eq. 439.

But even where the second suit goes further than the first, proceedings have been stayed on the executor or administrator undertaking not to object to any additions to the decree in the first action which the Judge may think fit to add in Chambers. *Gwyer* v. *Peterson*, 26 Beav. 83; *Van Bunan* v. *Piffard*, 18 W. R. 425.

The usual practice, however, is to allow the action in which a decree has been made to proceed, and to stay the other. Seton, 5th ed. 705.

If the decree has been unfairly obtained or the action improperly instituted, the Court will either not stay the other action or will give the conduct of the proceedings to the plaintiff in the other action. *Rhodes* v. *Barret*, L. R. 12 Eq. 479.

Where the first action is stayed because a decree has been made in a later action, the conduct of the second action will usually be given to the plaintiff in the first action. *Lambaco* v. *Cassavelli*, L. R. 11 Eq. 439; *Re Swire*, 21 C. D. 647; *Townsend* v. *T.*, 23 C. D. 100.

Where an order for administration has been made, the Judge may transfer to himself any cause or matter pending in any Court brought against the executors or administrators. Ord. 49, r. 5; *ante*, p. 198.

This power of transfer takes the place of the old practice of restraining proceedings by injunction.

The action to be transferred must be one brought against the executor *quâ* executor. *Chapman* v. *Mason*, 40 L. T. 678; *Re Timms*, 26 W. R. 692.

By the Bankruptcy Act, 1883, s. 125, sub-s. 4, where

proceedings have been commenced in any Court for administration of the estate of a deceased debtor, such Court can, on proof that the estate is insolvent, transfer the proceedings to the Court of Bankruptcy.

The transfer can be ordered after judgment for administration has been made. *Re York*, 36 C. D. 233; *Senhouse* v. *Mawson*, 52 L. T. 745.

The exercise of this power is discretionary; and the mere fact that the rights of the executor, as regards retainer and not pleading the Statute of Limitation, might be taken away by the transfer, is not a ground for the transfer. *Re Baker*, 44 C. D. 262. But see *Re York*, 36 C. D. 233.

An estate cannot be administered in a Court of Equity in the absence of a personal representative. *Lowry* v. *Fulton*, 9 Sim. 104; *Clough* v. *Dixon*, 10 Sim. 564; *Dowdeswell* v. *D.*, 9 C. D. 294.

And a limited administrator does not sufficiently represent the estate for this purpose. *Ibid.*

Nor does a representative appointed under Ord. 16, r. 46. *Groves* v. *Lane*, 16 Jur. 1061.

Nor does an executor *de son tort*. *Rowsell* v. *Morris*, L. R. 17 Eq. 20. But see *Re Lovett*, 3 C. D. 198; *ante*, p. 206.

Nor does an administrator *ad litem*. *Dowdeswell* v. *D.*, *supra*.

Nor does an administrator of the executor. *Barber* v. *Walker*, 15 W. R. 728.

But an administrator *pendente lite* may be sued like a general administrator. *Re Toleman*, (1897) 1 Ch. 866.

But though an infant executor has come of age, the executor *durante minore aetate* is a necessary party, unless he has fully accounted. *Glass* v. *Oxenham*, 2 Atk. 121.

Where an administrator is out of the jurisdiction, judgment for administration cannot be obtained against him. *Donald* v. *Bather*, 16 Beav. 26.

In an action for a general account of assets, it seems that the representative of a deceased representative should be joined as co-defendant with the continuing or present representative. *Holland* v. *Prior*, 1 M. & K. 237; *Hall* v. *Austin*, 2 Coll. 570; *Coppard* v. *Allen*, 2 D. J. & S. 173.

But the representative of a deceased executor need not be so joined if it is not sought to charge the estate of the deceased executor, or if an account is waived. *Masters* v. *Barnes*, 2 Y. & C. 616.

Where the executor or administrator is required to be a party, it is not sufficient that he is such by the appointment of a foreign court, but he must obtain his right to represent the estate from the Probate Court of this country. *Ante*, p. 204.

After the usual administration order every creditor has an interest in the suit, but until such order the plaintiff is *dominus litis*, and may settle the action by accepting payment of his debt and costs of action. *Woodgate* v. *Field*, 2 Ha. 213; *Holden* v. *Kynaston*, 2 Beav. 204; *Re Greaves*, 18 C. D. 551.

As a general rule it is not necessary or proper to join legatees or next of kin as parties to an action against the executor or administrator for an account, though under special circumstances it may be done. *Brown* v. *Dowthwaite*, 1 Madd. 446; *Hertford* v. *Zichi*, 9 Beav. 11.

Unless there be collusion or insolvency, or some special case, debtors to the estate cannot be made parties to an action against the executor. *Consett* v. *Bell*, 1 Y. & C. 569; *Barker* v. *Birch*, 1 De G. & S. 376; *Stainton* v. *Carron*, 18 Beav. 146; *Yeatman* v. *Y.*, 7 C. D. 210.

The same rule applies to the case of a creditor overpaid by the executor. *Alsager* v. *Rowley*, 6 Ves. 748.

But this rule has been relaxed in the case of surviving partners of the deceased, who may be made parties with the executor where it is shown that there exist assets which might be recovered, and which but for such a suit would probably be lost to the estate. *Stainton* v. *Carron*, 18 Beav. 146.

Mere refusal by the representative to sue for the recovery

of outstanding assets will not, in the absence of special circumstances, justify the suing of the debtor. *Yeatman* v. *Y.*, 7 C. D. 210.

Where an executor has administered and paid over the residue, a creditor may follow the residue, and compel payment by the residuary legatee of his debt to the extent of the residue, without making the executor a defendant to the action. *Hunter* v. *Young*, 4 Ex. D. 256; *Clegg* v. *Rowland*, L. R. 3 Eq. 368.

Although the Court exonerates the executor or administrator for payment of assets pursuant to its order, yet such a decree is not absolutely binding on absent persons who have had no opportunity of presenting their claims and have been guilty of no laches. *David* v. *Frowd*, 1 M. & K. 100; *Sawyer* v. *Birchmore*, 1 Keen, 391.

Although such absent persons have no remedy against the executor or administrator, yet they may assert their claim against the persons who have received the assets.

The interests of persons not parties to the action may, however, be bound under Ord. 16. *May* v. *Newton*, 34 C. D. 345.

Although suits in equity are not within the Statute of Limitations, yet they are within the spirit and meaning of it, and therefore, upon all legal demands, the Courts of Equity are bound to yield obedience to its provisions. *Re Sharpe*, (1892) 1 Ch. 154. {Statutes of Limitations.}

And as Courts of Equity will not entertain stale demands, they have thought proper to adopt the limit of six years by analogy to the statute. *Re Greaves*, 18 C. D. 551; *ante*, p. 196.

Subject to the provisions of the Trustee Act, 1888, the Statute of Limitations does not run against a trust. *Woodhouse* v. *W.*, L. R. 8 Eq. 514.

Accordingly a trust of real estate for payment of debts prevents the statute running against such debts as were not barred in the testator's lifetime. *Burke* v. *Jones*, 2 V. & B. 275; *Hughes* v. *Wynne*, 1 T. & R. 307;

Hargreaves v. *Michell,* 6 Madd. 326; but see *Harcourt* v. *White,* 28 Beav. 309.

But a mere charge is not sufficient for this purpose. *Cunningham* v. *Foot,* 3 A. C. 974.

But a trust by will of personal estate does not prevent the operation of the statute. *Scott* v. *Jones,* 4 Cl. & F. 382.

Where debts were directed to be paid out of real and personal estate, it was held that a trust had been created so as to prevent the operation of the statute. *Crallan* v. *Oulton,* 3 Beav. 1; *Moore* v. *Petchell,* 22 Beav. 172.

Where executors sell real estate charged with debts, a purchaser is not bound to inquire whether any debts remain unpaid unless twenty years have elapsed from the testator's death. *Re Tanqueray-Willaume,* 20 C. D. 465.

But the rule does not in general apply to the case of an executor selling leaseholds. *Re Whistler,* 35 C. D. 561; *Re Venn,* (1894) 2 Ch. 101.

By the Real Property Limitation Act, 1874, s. 8, no action or other proceeding shall be brought to recover any sum of money secured by any mortgage judgment or lien or otherwise charged upon or payable out of any land or rent at law or in equity, or any legacy, but within twelve years next after the right to receive the same has accrued, unless there has been some part payment or acknowledgment.

This section applies to judgments generally. *Jay* v. *Johnstone,* (1893) 1 Q. B. 189.

It applies to legacies payable out of personal estate. *Bullock* v. *Downes,* 9 H. L. C. 1, 14.

A residue bequeathed by will is clearly within the statute. *Portlock* v. *Gardner,* 1 Ha. 604; *Prior* v. *Horniblow,* 2 Y. & C. 200.

The right of the legatee may be barred as to assets received more than the prescribed period before the commencement of the suit, but not barred as to assets received since. *Adams* v. *Barry,* 2 Coll. 290; *Re Johnson,* 29 C. D. 964.

A suit to recover a legacy from an executor is within the

section unless the legacy is vested in him on express trusts. A mere constructive trust will not prevent the statute from being a bar. *Re Davis*, (1891) 3 Ch. 119; *Re Barker*, (1892) 2 Ch. 491.

The section does not appear to extend to intestacies, the result being that a legatee will be barred after twelve years, but next of kin not until after twenty years. *Sutton* v. *S.*, 22 C. D. 511, 517.

By sect. 10, no proceeding shall be brought to recover any sum of money or legacy charged upon any land or rent and secured by an express trust, or to recover arrears of rent or interest or damages in respect of such arrears, except within the time within which the same would be recoverable if there were no such express trust. 37 & 38 Vict. c. 57, s. 10.

This section seems inconsistent with the Judicature Act, 1873, s. 25 (2); but the first section applies as between the land charged and the *cestui que trust*, whilst the second one applies as between the trustee and the *cestui que trust*. *Fernside* v. *Flint*, 22 C. D. 579; *Hughes* v. *Coles*, 27 C. D. 231.

By 3 & 4 Wm. 4, c. 27, s. 42, no arrears of rent or interest in respect of any money charged upon any land or rent or in respect of any legacy shall be recovered but within six years after the same became due.

This does not apply where there is a trust for payment. *Cunningham* v. *Foot*, 3 A. C. 974.

Nor to an annuity given by will and not charged on land. *Rock* v. *Callen*, 6 Ha. 531; *Re Ashwell*, Johns. 112.

Where legatees waited for payment of their legacies until a reversionary interest had fallen in, they were allowed interest from a year after the testator's death, such interest largely exceeding six years' arrears. *Re Blackford*, 27 C. D. 676; but see *Webster* v. *W.*, 10 Ves. 93.

By the Trustee Act, 1888, s. 8, which applies to executors and administrators, trustees are enabled to plead the Statute of Limitations.

The general effect of this section seems to be that whenever an action is brought by a beneficiary against a trustee, whether in respect of land or money, and whether the defendant is sought to be charged under an express or constructive trust, the defendant will be entitled to the protection which the section gives, unless the plaintiff can prove either (1) fraud or fraudulent breach of trust, or (2) that at the time of action brought the trust property or proceeds thereof are still retained by the trustee, or (3) that previously to the bringing of the action such property or proceeds were received by the trustee and converted to his own use. If the plaintiff bring his case within one of those three, the old law will still apply; if not, the section will take effect. Lewin, 1009.

With regard to when the time begins to run, if it has once begun to run in the debtor's lifetime, it will not cease to run between his death and the time when the representative is constituted. *Boatwright* v. *B.*, L. R. 17 Eq. 71; *ante*.

In cases of fraud or mistake the statute runs from the discovery. *Ecc. Com.* v. *N. E. Ry.*, 4 C. D. 860.

An executor cannot protect himself by the Statute of Limitations from payment of a debt due from himself to the testator by deferring proof of the will. *Ingle* v. *Richards*, 28 Beav. 366.

It has been held that an action by one creditor on behalf of himself and all other creditors prevents the statute running against another creditor. *Sterndale* v. *Hankinson*, 1 Sim. 393.

But this is very doubtful; and, at all events, an action for administration by one creditor, not on behalf of himself and all other creditors, does not save the claim of another creditor which was barred by the statute before judgment. *Re Greaves*, 18 C. D. 551.

Another creditor will not be allowed in a creditor's action to set up the statute against the plaintiff whose claim is the foundation of the judgment. Dan. 1023.

By the Debtors Act, 1869, s. 4, a trustee or person Arrest.
acting in a fiduciary capacity may be arrested or imprisoned for making default in payment of any sum in his possession or under his control, and ordered to be paid by a Court of Equity.

In an action against an executor or administrator, other Costs.
than an administration action, costs are in the discretion of the Court, and will generally be governed by the ordinary rule which throws them on the unsuccessful party.

Where a creditor sues for his debt and is successful, the Court will direct payment of his debt and his costs out of the estate (Dan. 1175, 1219); but unless the estate is insufficient, no order is made as to the representative's costs, upon the principle that he may reimburse himself out of the assets. Dan. 1219; *Bluett* v. *Jessop, infra*.

But in an administration action his costs, as between solicitor and client, are provided for; and even where assets are insufficient to pay debts, these costs and any charges and expenses properly incurred by him continue the first charge on the estate. Dan. 1220.

But in cases of fraud, evasion, or neglect of duty the Court will not merely refuse the executor his costs, but order him to pay them or such of them as are attributable to his breach of duty. Dan. 1220.

And he may be made to pay the costs of any unnecessary or vexatious proceeding. *Re Cabburn, ante*, p. 199.

Where, on an originating summons for an account, the Judge does "not think fit to make any order as to costs," it operates as a refusal to allow the trustee his costs, and is inconsistent with his retaining them out of the estate. *Re Hodgkinson*, (1895) 2 Ch. 190.

Mere negligence, however, is not sufficient to deprive him of his costs. Morgan & Wur. 179; but see Dan. 1215.

Costs are not in the discretion of the Court, and the representative is not to be deprived of them unless he has unreasonably instituted or carried on or resisted any proceedings. Ord. 65, r. 1.

The rule is that a representative is entitled to his costs, including costs, charges, and expenses, unless he is guilty of such misconduct as justifies the Judge in depriving him of them. *Re Love*, 29 C. D. 348; and see *Re Knight*, 26 C. D. 82.

As to what is such misconduct, see *Re Radcliffe*, 50 L. J. Ch. 317; *Re Weall*, 42 C. D. 674; *Re Cabburn*, 46 L. T. 848; Dan. 1211, *et seq.*

An order refusing a representative his costs can be appealed from. *Re Love*, 29 C. D. 348.

But an order allowing him costs, though guilty of misconduct, cannot. *Charles* v. *Jones*, 33 C. D. 80.

No costs are given to a representative who is a debtor to the estate until his debt is paid. *Smith* v. *Dale*, 18 C. D. 516; *Lewis* v. *Trask*, 21 C. D. 864; *Re Basham*, 23 C. D. 195; and see *McEwan* v. *Crombie*, 25 C. D. 175.

Where an executor who is indebted to the estate becomes bankrupt, his costs incurred prior to the bankruptcy are set off against the debt. *Smith* v. *Dale, supra; Re Basham, supra; Re Vowles*, 32 C. D. 243.

But an executor is not entitled to his costs incurred after the bankruptcy unless he pays the debt. *Re Basham, supra; Re Vowles, supra.*

But now, by the Bankruptcy Act, 1883, s. 30, a bankrupt executor or administrator only remains liable to the estate for debts incurred by fraudulent breach of trust. The consequence is that where his debt is for a fraudulent breach of trust he will get no costs at all; if the debt arise on any other ground, he will get his costs subsequent to the bankruptcy. Wms. 1940.

Where the Court has derived assistance from having the executor represented in the action, it will sometimes allow him costs, though he remains a debtor to the estate. *Re Basham*, 23 C. D. 195.

An executor who has not been guilty of dishonesty, and has made good any deficiency, will not be ordered to pay costs. *Peacock* v. *Colling*, 54 L. J. Ch. 743; *Re Whiteley*, 33 C. D. 347.

Where the estate is insufficient for payment of costs, executors are entitled to payment of theirs in priority to all other parties. *Dodds* v. *Tuke*, 25 C. D. 617 ; and see *Re Mayhew*, 5 C. D. 596.

And they are entitled to their costs and expenses in priority to the debts incurred by them in carrying on the business lawfully and with the consent of creditors. *Re Owen*, 66 L. T. 718.

And in priority to those of a receiver and manager. *Ramsay* v. *Simpson*, (1899) 1 Ir. R. 69.

Where a creditor proceeds against a representative, and there are no assets, the representative, if not in default, is entitled to be paid his costs by the creditor. *Hibernian Bank* v. *Lauder*, (1898) 1 Ir. R. 262 ; *Bluett* v. *Jessop*, Jacob, 240.

But the plaintiff is entitled to judgment for his debt and costs also against assets *quando*. *Cockle* v. *Treacy*, (1896) 2 Ir. R. 267.

The executor of a defaulting trustee is entitled to his costs out of the assets of his testator, even though they may be insufficient to repair the breach of trust. *Haldenby* v. *Spofforth*, 9 Beav. 195 ; and see *Re Griffiths*, 26 C. D. 465.

APPENDIX.

60 & 61 VICT. CHAP. 65.

An Act to establish a Real Representative, and to amend the Land Transfer Act, 1875.

[*6th August,* 1897.]

WHEREAS it is expedient to establish a real representative, and to amend the Land Transfer Act, 1875, in this Act referred to as the "principal Act": 38 & 39 Vict. c. 87.
Be it therefore enacted, &c.

PART I.

Establishment of a Real Representative.

1.—(1.) Where real estate is vested in any person without a right in any other person to take by survivorship it shall, on his death, notwithstanding any testamentary disposition, devolve to and become vested in his personal representatives or representative from time to time as if it were a chattel real vesting in them or him. *Devolution of legal interest in real estate on death.*

(2.) This section shall apply to any real estate over which a person executes by will a general power of appointment, as if it were real estate vested in him.

(3.) Probate and letters of administration may be granted in respect of real estate only, although there is no personal estate.

(4.) The expression "real estate," in this part of this Act, shall not be deemed to include land of copyhold tenure or customary freehold in any case in which an admission or any act by the lord of the manor is necessary to perfect the title of a purchaser from the customary tenant.

(5.) This section applies only in cases of death after the commencement of this Act.

Provisions as to administration.

2.—(1.) Subject to the powers, rights, duties, and liabilities herein-after mentioned, the personal representatives of a deceased person shall hold the real estate as trustees for the persons by law beneficially entitled thereto, and those persons shall have the same power of requiring a transfer of real estate as persons beneficially entitled to personal estate have of requiring a transfer of such personal estate.

(2.) All enactments and rules of law relating to the effect of probate or letters of administration as respects chattels real, and as respects the dealing with chattels real before probate or administration, and as respects the payment of costs of administration and other matters in relation to the administration of personal estate, and the powers, rights, duties, and liabilities of personal representatives in respect of personal estate, shall apply to real estate so far as the same are applicable, as if that real estate were a chattel real vesting in them or him, save that it shall not be lawful for some or one only of several joint personal representatives, without the authority of the court, to sell or transfer real estate.

(3.) In the administration of the assets of a person dying after the commencement of this Act, his real estate shall be administered in the same manner, subject to the same liabilities for debt, costs, and expenses, and with the same incidents, as if it were personal estate; provided that nothing herein contained shall alter or affect the order in which real and personal assets respectively are now applicable in or towards the payment of funeral and testamentary expenses, debts, or legacies, or the liability of real estate to be charged with the payment of legacies.

(4.) Where a person dies possessed of real estate, the court shall, in granting letters of administration, have regard to the rights and interests of persons interested in his real estate, and his heir-at-law, if not one of the next of kin, shall be equally entitled to the grant with the next of kin, and provision shall be made by rules of court for adapting the procedure and practice in the grant of letters of administration to the case of real estate.

Provision for transfer to heir or devisee.

3.—(1.) At any time after the death of the owner of any land, his personal representatives may assent to any devise contained in his will, or may convey the land to any person entitled thereto as heir, devisee, or otherwise, and may make the assent or conveyance, either subject to a charge for the payment of any money which the personal representatives are liable to pay, or without any such charge; and on such assent or conveyance, subject to a charge for all moneys (if any) which the personal representatives are liable to pay, all liabilities of the personal representatives in respect of the land shall cease, except as to any acts done or contracts entered into by them before such assent or conveyance.

(2.) At any time after the expiration of one year from the death of the owner of any land, if his personal representatives have failed on the request of the person entitled to the land to convey the land to that person, the court may, if it thinks fit, on the application of that person, and after notice to the personal representatives, order that the conveyance be made, or, in the case of registered land, that the person so entitled be registered as proprietor of the land, either solely or jointly with the personal representatives.

(3.) Where the personal representatives of a deceased person are registered as proprietors of land on his death, a fee shall not be chargeable on any transfer of the land by them unless the transfer is for valuable consideration.

(4.) The production of an assent in the prescribed form by the personal representatives of a deceased proprietor of registered land shall authorise the registrar to register the person named in the assent as proprietor of the land.

4.—(1.) The personal representatives of a deceased person may, in the absence of any express provision to the contrary contained in the will of such deceased person, with the consent of the person entitled to any legacy given by the deceased person or to a share in his residuary estate, or, if the person entitled is a lunatic or an infant, with the consent of his committee, trustee, or guardian, appropriate any part of the residuary estate of the deceased in or towards satisfaction of that legacy or share, and may for that purpose value in accordance with the prescribed provisions the whole or any part of the property of the deceased person in such manner as they think fit. Provided that before any such appropriation is effectual, notice of such intended appropriation shall be given to all persons interested in the residuary estate, any of whom may thereupon within the prescribed time apply to the court, and

Appropriation of land in satisfaction of legacy or share in estate.

such valuation and appropriation shall be conclusive save as otherwise directed by the court.

(2.) Where any property is so appropriated a conveyance thereof by the personal representatives to the person to whom it is appropriated shall not, by reason only that the property so conveyed is accepted by the person to whom it is conveyed in or towards the satisfaction of a legacy or a share in residuary estate, be liable to any higher stamp duty than that payable on a transfer of personal property for a like purpose.

(3.) In the case of registered land, the production of the prescribed evidence of an appropriation under this section shall authorise the registrar to register the person to whom the property is appropriated as proprietor of the land.

Liability for duty.

5. Nothing in this part of this Act shall affect any duty payable in respect of real estate or impose on real estate any other duty than is now payable in respect thereof.

25. This Act shall come into operation on the first day of January, one thousand eight hundred and ninety-eight.

INDEX.

ABATEMENT
   annuity, 131
   legacies, 130
   none of actions in general, 206

ABROAD
   executor, 3
   administration *durante absentiâ*, 32

ACCEPTANCE OF OFFICE
   acts sufficient to show, 13
   cannot be partial, 15
   probate is, 15

ACCOUNTS
   copy of, legatee must pay costs of, 186
   discharge on passing, 199
   duty of executors to be ready with, 186
   liability of executors to be sued for, 186
   neglect to render, 186
   one executor may settle, 91
                 sue another for, 95
   taking, in Chambers, 200

ACCOUNTANT
   executors may charge for, when, 190

ACKNOWLEDGMENT
   what sufficient to bar statute, 197

ACQUIESCENCE
   when a defence, 185

ACT-BOOK
   evidence of appointment of executor, 194

ACTIO PERSONALIS MORITUR
when it applies, 64

ACTION BY REPRESENTATIVES
for administration, 217
    trespass or trover, 64
    in respect of valueless shares, 64
        infringement of trade mark, 64
        malicious statement, 64
parties to. *See* PARTIES.

ADMINISTRATION
action for, parties to, 222
ad colligenda, 24
ad litem, 35
attorney of next of kin, to, 24
costs of, order of priority, 104
executor's, priority of, 227
Court, by, a complete discharge to executors, 199
cum testamento annexo, when granted, 25
        to whom, 26
de bonis non, when granted, 27
    to whom, 28
discretion of Court as to grant of, 199
domiciled abroad, to person, 24
durante absentiâ, 32
    corporis et animi vitio, 3
    dementiâ, 34
    minore ætate, 28
foreign, 24, 204
grants of, evidence of title, 194
        as to next of kin, 38
        general and limited, 21—35
        made only in respect of assets in this country, 24
        made to part of estate, 35
        not made till executor has refused, 15
            on consent of executor, 15
        nor without citation of parties entitled, 26
        revocation of, 40
        to exclusion of executor, 2
        to whom made, and in what order, 21
        to person domiciled abroad, 24
guardians, 28
heir to, 25

ADMINISTRATION—*continued.*
    intermeddler not compelled to take, 24
    joint, discouraged, 22
    judgment for, not against representative abroad, 204
        against administrator *durante minore*, 30
        liability of executors under, 217
        creditors cannot sue after, 197
        effect of, on powers of executors, 89, 215
            rights of creditors, 114
        executor before probate, against, 204
        limited to English assets, need not be,150
        originating summons, on, 199
        wilful default, as for, when, 191, 210
    jurisdiction to grant, 38
    letters of, conclusive as to what, 38
        foreign, 24
        revoked representatives may reimburse themselves, 40
            payments made under, valid, 40
        valid till revoked, 38
    liability of executors to be sued for, 30
    limited doubly, 27
        to legal proceedings, 35
        to legacy, 35
        lost will in case of, 35
        not where general can be granted, 35
        to particular fund, 35
        to such property as wife could dispose of, 22
    one renouncing in one character cannot take in another, 16
    order for. See JUDGMENT FOR, *supra.*
    pendente lite, when granted, 30
    renouncing, 15
    retracting renunciation, 15
    time for taking, 20
    what amounts to, to prevent renouncing, 14
        And see ADMINISTRATOR, INFANT, MARRIED WOMAN,
        RENOUNCE, RENUNCIATION, REVOCATION.

ADMINISTRATOR
    abroad, 24
    ad colligenda, 24
    ad litem, 35
    administration, acting before, may be sued, 43
        suing before, 21
    appointment of, property vests on, 42

ADMINISTRATOR—*continued.*
business, power to carry on, 201
capable of being, who is, 25
cum testamento, 25
death of joint, office survives, 49
de bonis non, 27
de son tort, none, 11
difference between, and executor, 42
discretion, has not same as executor, 20
domiciled abroad, 24
distribution by, under statute, 147
durante absentiâ, 32
    dementiâ, 34
    minore ætate, 28
each has entire control over estate, 94
    except real estate, 92
estate, vests in, 42
executor of, does not represent testator, 8
joint, same as joint executor, 49
jurisdiction, out of, judgment against, 204
payment to, good discharge, though will existing, 40
    under revoked grant, 40
pendente lite, 30
personal and real estate vests in, 48
proceedings, cannot maintain, for more than covered by duty, 194
real estate vests in, 73
    And see REAL ESTATE.
reimbursement by, though grant revoked, 40
revocation of grant may take steps for, 41
similarity between, and executor, 42, 94
solicitor, rights of. *See* SOLICITOR.
title derived from administration, 42
    relation back of, 43
trustee, when a, 205
    And see EXECUTOR.

ADMISSION OF ASSETS
    effect of, 211
    no estoppel to prevent account, 211
    one executor, by, does not bind others, 211
    retracted, when may be, 211
    what amounts to, 212

ADVANCEMENT
    to infants, 140

ADVANCES
further, by executors to secure former, 174
interest on, when allowed executors, 191
retainer of, by executors, 191

ADVERTISEMENT
for creditors, statutory, 125

ADVICE
of Court, executors may apply for, 203

ADVOWSON
passes as real estate to representative, 74
when executor may present. *See* CHURCH.

AFFIDAVIT
wilful default raised by, 210

AGENT
acts done as, do not prevent renouncing, 11
    of executor *de son tort*, 11
charge for, when representative entitled to, 190
default of, when representative liable for, 181
of executor, 11
of co-executor, 15
employing co-executor as, 184

AGRICULTURAL HOLDINGS ACT
executor's charge for compensation under, 59

ALIEN
may be executor or administrator, 2, 25

ALIMONY, 69

ALLOWANCES, 188

AMBIGUITY
in description of executor, 4

ANCIENT LIGHTS
obstructing action for, 65

ANNUITY
passes to executors when, 67
apportionment of, 68
abatement of, 131
executor, to, duration of, 129
    has no preference, 129
time, when to be paid, 137
to A. and his heirs, 75, 137

APPOINTMENT
property subject to power of, passes to representative, 73
And see EXECUTOR.

APPORTIONMENT ACT, 1870...68

APPRENTICESHIP
determined by death, 68
return of premium, 168

APPROPRIATION
powers of, 138
under Land Transfer Act, 81

ARBITRATION
executors bound by deceased's submission, 72
may submit to, 172
whether an admission of assets, 213
reference by testator, effect of, 72

ARREARS
annuity, 120, 142, 218
alimony, 69
interest on, of income, 187
pin-money, 69
rent, 68, 164

ARREST
of representative for default in payment, 227
attachment, 314

ARTICLED CLERK
cannot recover premium from executor, 168

ASSENT OF EXECUTORS
doctrine of, 132
donatio mortis causâ not requisite to, 63
implied or conditional, 133
legatee taking without, liable, 132
life estate, to, is assent to remainder, 135
    unless executor is tenant for life, 135
necessary though executor is legatee, 134
one executor by, effectual, 136
personal liability of executor after, 134
real estate. *See* REAL ESTATE.
release of debt, whether necessary to, 132
retractation, 134
specific legacy to, makes executor trustee, 134
women, married, 79

ASSETS
admission. *See* ADMISSION.
equitable, 150
foreign, 150
legal, 150
marshalling, 153
purchase of by representative. *See* PURCHASE.
real, 73, 151
And see EXECUTOR, RETAINER.

ASSIGN
executor cannot, office, 7

ATTACHMENT OF REPRESENTATIVE, 214

ATTORNEY
acts done as, do not prevent renunciation, 15
administration granted to, 24
power cannot be exercised by, 90
bills accepted by, liability of executors, 172
probate by, does not break chain, 8
power of, liability of executors paying money under, 142
renunciation under, 15

AWARD
liability of executors on, 72

BAILEE
executor a gratuitous, 179

BALANCES
when executor charged with interest on, 187

BANKER
default of, when representative liable, 182
Trustee Act, 182

BANK OF ENGLAND
bound to recognise executors' right to stock, 132

BANKRUPT
estate of, vests in representative when bankruptcy annulled,
ex parte Goodwin, 1 Atk. 100
executor of bankrupt not entitled to chose in action, 68
    may be restrained from acting, 2
    goods left in possession of, 45
    receiver appointed, 2, 45
    proof for *devastavit*, 214
legatee, administration to trustee of, 24

BANKRUPTCY
　administration of estate in, 108
　petition in, by executor, 19
　proof by executor for *devastavit* in his own, 214
　of representative how it affects assets, 45
　trustee in, ordered to return assets, 45

BILLS
　indorsement of by executor, 89

BLANK SPACE
　in will, 146

BODY
　cremation, 104

BOND
　administration, assignment of, 37
　　　　　　breach of, 37
　　　　　　dispensed with cannot be, 36
　　　　　　executed by other than administrator, 36
　　　　　　husband not required to join, 36
　　　　　　retainer, notwithstanding, 37
　　　　　　sureties, 36
　voluntary, payable after simple contract debts, 112

BREACH OF PROMISE
　executors cannot sue or be sued, unless injury to estate, 66

BROKER
　default of, when executors liable, 182

BURIAL OF DECEASED
　expenses of, 104, 173
　does not make executor *de son tort*, 10

BUSINESS
　administrator may carry on, when, 173, 201
　executor may employ what assets in, 174
　executors' liability for carrying on, 174, 201
　　　　cannot borrow for, 86
　sharing profits, not a carrying on, when, 175
　And see PARTNER, PARTNERSHIP.

CAMPBELL'S ACT (LORD), 65

CHAIN OF REPRESENTATION
　of executors, 8

INDEX. 243

CHARGING ORDER
    creditor who has obtained, will not be stayed, 198

CHATTELS REAL
    only vest on entry, 44
    action for injury to, 65

CHOSES IN ACTION
    of corporation sole, 68
    of married woman, 69

CHURCH
    dilapidations, 113
    next presentation,
        when it goes to executor, 74
        when assets, 74
    And see ADVOWSON.

CITATION
    on limited grant, 35
    of executor, 13
    of person entitled in priority, 26
    on grant to heir, 25
    to take probate, 13
        disobedience to, 13
        non-appearance to, 13

CLERK
    salary of, priority, 113
    articled, premium of, 168

COADJUTOR
    or overseer, 5

COLLECTION OF ESTATE
    commission on, executor allowed, when, 190
    duties of executors as to, 190
    colonial allowances for, 190
    liability for not collecting, 179

COLLECTOR
    executor may be allowed salary of, 190

COLLUSION
    between executor and debtor, 87, 187
    vitiates sale or mortgage by executor, 86

COMMISSION
    executors not allowed, 190
    except in colonies, 190

COMPANIES ACTS, 161

COMPANY
    appointed executor, 1
    executor *de son tort*, 13
    executors may petition to wind up, when, 19
    liquidator may obtain judgment for administration, 161
    surety to administration bond, 37
    And see SHAREHOLDER, DIRECTOR.

COMPROMISE
    power of representatives to, 90

CONCURRENCE
    of beneficiary, when a protection, 185

CONDITIONS
    appointment of executor on, 7
    estate by, 56

CONDUCT OF PROCEEDINGS
    when executors deprived of, 220

CONSENT
    of executor, administration not granted on mere, 15
    And see CITATION.

CONTINGENT INTERESTS, 71

CONTINUANCE OF ACTIONS
    by representative, 72

CONTRACT
    binds executors, though not named, 155
    borrow, to, executors liable on, 170
    breach of, entered into with deceased, 155
    build a house, to, 156
    executor cannot bind co-executor, 92
    implied for remuneration, liability of executors on, 169

CONTRIBUTION
    between co-executors, 95

CONVERSION
    duties of executors as to, 144
    liability for non-conversion, 180

CONVERSION—*continued*.
   of wasting or reversionary assets, 180
   of assets to executors' own use, 46

CONVEYANCING ACT, 55, 140

COPYHOLDS
   action by lord for relief, 155
   action for fines by executor of lord, 68
   executor entitled to fine when, 68
   do not vest in personal representative, 73
   repairs of, 156

COPYRIGHT
   may pass to representative, 67

CORPORATION
   aggregate or sole may be executor, 1
   sole, choses in action do not pass to successor, 68

CORROBORATION, 168

COSTS
   action caused by neglect to account, 186
             misconduct of executors, 228
   administration, of, priority of, 104
   administrator, of, after revocation, 41
   appeal by executors for, 228
   carrying on business, of, 229
   estate, out of, 227
   executor bankrupt, 228
          pleading *plene administravit*, 229
          solicitor and client, allowed, 227
          unreasonable conduct, caused by, 227
   executorship expenses, what included in, 105
   probate action not payable out of realty, until 1898...77
   proving will of, 104
   receiver and manager, 229
   representative debtor to estate, 228
   solicitor-executor. *See* PROFIT COSTS.
   testamentary, what included in, 104
   unnecessary or vexatious proceeding, 227
   when executor deprived of, 228
          ordered to pay, 227
   where estate is insufficient, 229
   where no assets, 229

COUNTY COURT
    jurisdiction in contentious business, 17

COVENANTS
    distinction between real and personal, 66

CREDITORS
    administration, action or summons for, 217, 219
        can retain, though taking grant, 117
        disputed debt, 217
        right of, to, 24
    assignment of estate by executor for benefit of, 86
    executor liable to, where not to legatees, 143
    foreign, of English assets, 106
    grant to, when made, 24
    preference of, by executors, 113
        how prevented, 114
    proceedings by, stay of, 197
    refunding to, by legatee, 143
    rights of, how affected by judgment for administration, 114, 126
    suing executors *de son tort*, 11
    stand in place of, executors may, 114
    statutory advertisements for, executors protected by, 125
    who may administer as, 24

CREMATION, 104

CROWN
    debt priority of, 106
    duty for which credit given a Crown debt, 107
    king may be executor, 1
    not bound by Land Transfer Act, 25, 75
    residue, when, goes to, 145
    solicitor need not give administration bond, 36

DAMAGES
    retainer in respect of, what, 120

DE SON TORT. See EXECUTOR.

DEBTOR
    appointed executor, 122
    joint, 122

INDEX. 247

DEBTS
    corroboration, 168
    due from executor, 122, 228
    executor buying, 187
    interest on, when executor charged, 187
    loss of, through executor's negligence, 178
    partnership, when executors liable, 215
    payment of, executors' liability for, 105
        inferior, 176
        executors may remit money for, 184
    personally liable for, when executors are, 105
    priority, what have, 105, *et seq.*
        executors liable for disregarding, 105, 176
    promise by executor to pay, 171
    raise, power to, by sale or mortgage of realty, 84, 86
    release, executor can, before probate, 17
    set-off against, executors' right of, 120
    statute-barred, 114, 177
    voluntary bonds and promissory notes, 112
        And see CREDITORS, CROWN, JUDGMENT, RENT.

DEFAULT
    of banker, broker, solicitor or agent, liability for, 182
    wilful, judgment for, when obtained, 191, 210
    liability of executors under, 210
    after common judgment cannot be charged without leave, 210

DELAY
    action for debt not barred by, 125
    devastavit, action for, may be barred by, 185
    in applying for probate or administration, 13, 211
    paying or suing for debts, 176
    probate, persons entitled may lose rights by, 13
    retainer lost by, 116

DELEGATUS NON POTEST DELEGARE
    delegation of appointment of executor, 5

DEVASTAVIT
    abuse of assets, 176
    breach of trust, 175
    co-executor of, 183
    employing agent, 181
    keeping money in hand, 180
        in bank, 182
    loss of assets, 179

DEVASTAVIT—continued.
   mal-administration, 176
   negligence, 178
   non-conversion, 180
   standing by, 184
   investments, 181
   unnecessary payments, 177

DEVOLUTION
   of representation, 8

DILAPIDATIONS
   liability of executors of incumbent, 113, 158

DIRECTOR
   executor of, liable for misfeasance, 164
                 not for misrepresentation, 164

DISCRETION
   control of, by Court, 215
   conversion, as to, 181
   none after renunciation, 16
   investments, as to, 181
   application to Court as to exercise of, 203
   of Court as to grants of administration, 24, 26
   judgment for administration, effect of, 215

DISTRIBUTION
   by administrators under statute, 147
   domicil governs, 149
   risk attendant on, without suit, 141

DIVIDENDS
   receipt of, does not make executors liable, 163

DIVORCE
   right to administration lost by, 22

DOMICIL
   grant follows *situs*, 149, 150
   priority not regulated by, 106
   governs distribution, 149

DONATIO MORTIS CAUSA, 62

DOWER
   not subject to payment of debts of husband, 75
   not assets under Land Transfer Act, 75

INDEX. 249

DUTY
  estate, 97
  legacy and succession, 101
  settlement, 100

ELECTION
  exercise of testator's right by executor, 90

EMBLEMENTS
  when they go to representative, 59

ENTRY
  chattels real only vest in possession on, 44, 53
  leaseholds, 44

ESTATE DUTY. *See* DUTY.

EXECUTION
  against assets in hands of executor, 46

EXECUTOR
  acceptance of office, what amounts to, 13
  account, duty to. *See* ACCOUNT.
  accountant, may be allowed to charge for, 190
  acknowledgment of debts by, 92, 114
  acting without proving, liability, 11
  administration, liable to be sued for, 217
        by Court, gives complete discharge, 199, 223
  administrator of, does not represent testator, 8
  advice of Court, 203
  agent, when entitled to charge for, 190
      default of, liability, 181
      of, cannot be executor *de son tort*, 11
  allowance sometimes made to, 189
  annuity to, 120
  appointment of absolute or qualified, 6
        ambiguous, 3
        conditional, 7
        delegated, may be, 5
        implication, by, 5
        nomination, by, 5
        proved by probate or act-book, 194
        qualified, may be, 6
        substitutionary, 6
        uncertainty, void for, 6
  appointed fund, entitled to administer, 73

EXECUTOR—*continued*.
  appropriation, powers of, 138
  arbitration, may go to, 172
  assent to gift. *See* ASSENT.
  assets. *See* ASSETS.
  assign his office, cannot, 7
  auctioneer, may not charge, 190
  bailee, a gratuitous, 179
  banker, default of, 182
  bankrupt, 2, 45
  bankruptcy of, receiver, 2, 45
  bills, liability on, 89
  breach of trust, liability for, 175
  business, carrying on. *See* BUSINESS.
  buying debts or legacies, 187
  capable of being, who is, 1
  co-executor, cannot deprive, of benefit of statute, 197
          bind by contract, 92
          liable for acts and defaults of, 183
          ought to watch over, 184
          parting with control to, 183
  collusion with purchaser, 86
  commission, not allowed, 190
  company. *See* COMPANY.
  compromise, power to. *See* COMPROMISE.
  conditional appointment of, 7
  contracts of testator, binding on, when, 155
  conversion of estate, duty of, as to, 180
  corporation may be, 1
  creditors. *See* CREDITORS.
  de son tort, action against, 11
      acts of, how far binding on representative, 12
      what, will make a man, 9
      administration, cannot be compelled to take out, 24
      agent of, liability of, 11
      contracts of, 12
      definition of, 9
      discharge, how obtained, 11
      duty, liable for, 13
      liability of, extent of, 11
          of one for another, 11
          of rightful executor, 12
          on covenants in lease, 165
      plene administravit, may plead, 11

EXECUTOR—*continued.*
    de son tort, privileges, has no, 11
        receiving property from an, does not make an, 10
        retainer by, 12
        rightful executor cannot exist with, 10
            sued, may be, by whom, 11, 12
    debtor appointed, no extinction of debt, 122
    debts, liability to pay. *See* DEBTS.
    delegating appointment of, 5
        office, liable for delegate, 183
    devastavit, liable for. *See* DEVASTAVIT.
    devolution of office, 7
    direction of Court, may apply for, 203
    director of. *See* DIRECTOR.
    discharged from office, cannot be, 3
    discretion, when, may exercise. *See* DISCRETION.
    distribution. *See* DISTRIBUTION.
    durante minore ætate, 28
    duty, liable for. *See* DUTY.
    dying before probate, acts of, valid, 18
    each may act, but cannot bind others by contract, 92
    establishment, time for breaking up, 177
    executor of, powers of, 95
        represents first testator, 7, 95
        retainer by, 118
        revocation of probate by, 41
    Frauds, Statute of, may not pay debts barred by, 167
    from or until a certain time, 6
    funeral expenses, liable for, what, 173
    gift, intended, need not be completed by, 168
    "gratuity" to, void for uncertainty, 129
    ill, too, to act, 3
    impounding interest, 185
    indemnity clause, how far a protection, 184
    infant, not competent, 2
    information, duty to give, 186
    insure, not bound to, 166
    interest charged against, 187
    intermeddling, is bound to prove, 14
    investment, duties of, 180, 181
    judgments, bound to take notice of, 105
    lease, power to grant, 88, 89
    leaseholds, liability of, on, 124
    legacy to executor, 126

EXECUTOR—*continued*.
liability, not divisible, 15
Limitations, Statutes of. *See* LIMITATIONS, STATUTES OF.
limited, 6
married woman, powers of, 96
mesne profits, decreed against, 157
mortgage, power to, personal estate, 86
           real estate, 78
mortgagee cannot buy equity, 187
note payable to order of testator, may indorse, 89
notice of judgment, 105
office, acceptance of, what amounts to, 13
one can act, when, 91
partner, liability of representative of, 160
passed over, may be, and letters granted, 2
payment into Court by, 202, 208
       to parties not entitled, 141
penalty, no action against, for, 156
personal and real estate vest in, from death, 73
poverty no ground for receiver, 2
powers of, 83
      how affected by judgment, 215
preference, has right of, 113
probate, actions before, may be commenced, 18
      dying before, acts of, 18
      purchase-money need not be paid before, 18
      may be sued before, 19
promise to pay deceased's debts, 171
purchase assets, may not, 88
purposes or properties, for several, 7
real estate. *See* REAL ESTATE.
receipts of co-executor, liability on, 185
receiver. *See* RECEIVER.
refusal of office, 13
reimbursement by, though grant revoked, 40
removal of, 3
rent-charge, liability for arrears, 74
residue, when trustee of, for next-of-kin or Crown, 145
retainer. *See* RETAINER.
revocation of probate, may not take steps for, 41
sale, liable for improper, 179
selling for lower price than offered, 179
set-off. *See* SET-OFF.
shareholder of, liability of, 161

INDEX. 253

EXECUTOR—*continued.*
 solicitor acting as. *See* SOLICITOR.
 special case, may concur in, 203
 suing co-executor, 16
 tenor, according to the, 4
 time and trouble, cannot claim for, 189
 title derived from will, 42
 trespass and trover, actions for, by, 18
 trustee, conversion of, into, 17
 use and occupation, 165
 waste by deceased, action against, for, 178
 who may be, 1
 work done, liability of, for, 21, 43
  And see ADMINISTRATOR, COSTS, MARRIED WOMAN, REAL ESTATE, RENUNCIATION.

EXECUTORS
 joint, one person in law, 7
 rights of, *inter se*, 91, 94, 183
 transfer of bank stock or railway shares, all must join, 93
 who have proved, may sue alone, 192

EXONERATION
 executor obtains, by administration under the Court, 199, 223
 of personal estate, 152

FELON
 may be executor, 2
 legacy to, 141

FIRM
 may be executor, 1

FIXTURES, 61

FOLLOWING ASSETS
 by creditors, 223
 legatees must refund, when, 143

FOREIGN
 administration, 204
 assets, 149
 creditors, 106
 executor, 3, 204

FORFEITURE
 of lease on bankruptcy, 45

FORGERY
  probate of forged will cannot be impeached, when, 38
FRAUD
  of others, when executors liable for, 182
  sale or mortgage by executors, vitiated by, 86
  in will can only be impeached in Probate Division, 38
FRAUDS, STATUTE OF
  agreement by executors to be liable must be in writing, 171
  executors cannot pay debt barred by, 177
FRIENDLY SOCIETY
  priority of debt due by deceased officer, 107
FUNERAL. *See* BURIAL.

GAME
  when incident to the freehold, 58
GARNISHEE ORDER
  when made against executor, 169
GIFT
  imperfect, executor need not complete, 168
GUARANTEE
  executors liable on deceased's, 168
GUARDIAN
  grants of administration to, 28
  minor and infant, of, 29
  of infant executor, 2

HALF-BLOOD
  equally entitled in distribution, 148
  whole-blood preferred on grant of administration, 23
HEIR
  real estate vests in, till representative constituted, 75
HEIRLOOMS, 60
HINDE-PALMER'S ACT, 111
HUSBAND
  need not join in wife's administration bond, 36
  right to administer to wife, 21
  his representatives' right to administer, 21
  no liability of, for acts of wife executrix, 185
  liability *quâ* representative for antenuptial contracts, 168

INDEX. 255

IMPOUNDING
share of debtor to estate, 185

INDEMNITY, 216
clauses, how far a protection, 184
against payments under invalid grant, 40

INDIAN
assets, commission on, 199

INFANT
administration granted to guardian of, 28
advancement, 140
capacity for grant of administration, 28
executor, not competent, 2
legacy to, payment of, into Court, 139
maintenance, 140

INJURY
to person of deceased, 65, 66
to property by deceased, action against executors, 158
to personal property of deceased, 66
to real estate of deceased, 66

INSOLVENCY
no ground for refusing probate, 2

INSURANCE
allowing life, to drop, 179

INSURE
executors may, but need not, 166

INTEREST
advances on when allowed, 191
balances on, when executor liable for, 187
charged against executors, when, 187
compound, when charged, 188
contingent, transmissible to executors, 74
executory, in real estate, 74
grant follows the interest, 26
legacy, on, from what time, 142
legatees need not refund with, 144

INTERMEDDLING
executor, cannot renounce, 14
constitutes one an executor *de son tort*, 9
one, not compelled to take out administration, 24
penalty on, without taking probate or administration, 14
what constitutes, 9

INTESTATES' ESTATES ACTS
    estate of intestate under 500*l.* go to widow, 147
INTESTATES' WIDOWS AND CHILDREN ACTS
    estates under 100*l.*, administration of, 17
INVESTMENT
    duties of executors as to, 181
    liable for improper, 181
    powers of executor as to, 180
JOINT
    contract, 159, 160
    property does not devolve, except partnership, 48
JUDGMENT
    confess, executor may, to give preference, 113
    effect of, for administration, 89, 126
    for wilful default, 210
    for simple contract debt has priority, 109
    foreign, simple contract debt only, 109
    notice of, executors bound to take, 105
    order *nisi* to sign, gives no priority, 109
    priority of, 110
    testator, against, precedence amongst, 109
JUDICIAL TRUSTEE ACT, 182
JURISDICTION
    administrator out of, judgment against, 34
    County Court, 17
    executor out of, ground for receiver, 2, 3
    to grant probate and administration, 38
    to stay proceedings before grant, 19
JUSTIFYING
    by sureties to administration bond, 37

LACHES, 125. *And see* DELAY.
LAND TRANSFER ACT, 1897, Appendix, p. 231. *And see* REAL ESTATE.
LEASE
    liability of executors under, 124, 166
    offer to surrender, some protection, 55, 164, 176
    power to, of representative, 78
    renewal of, by, 167
    forfeiture on bankruptcy of representative, 45

LEASEHOLDS
 assignment of, by executor, 164
 administration where estate consists of, 125
 cum onere legatees take, 168
 liability of executors, 124
 occupation by executors, 165
 sale of, by executor, 124
 specifically bequeathed vest in executor, 54
 vest on entry, 44
  upon assent in legatee, 134
 vesting by relation, 43, 134

LEGACY
 administration limited to, 35
 appropriation. *See* APPROPRIATION.
 assent to. *See* ASSENT.
 barred by statute, when, 196, 225
 buy, executor may not, when, 187
 discharge for, 139
 distribution of, 123, 144
 executor disentitled to, by misconduct, 129
  takes *quâ* executor, subject to rebuttal, 127
  must act in order to have, 127
  conditional on payment of debts, 129
  no priority for, 126
 infant to, paid into Court, 139
 interest on. *See* INTEREST.
 Limitations, Statute of, when a bar, 196
 preference, executor has none, 130
 set-off against, 120
 specific, assent to, makes executor a trustee, 134
 time within which to be paid, 136, 144
 vest, does not, without assent, 132
 work done in expectation of, 169

LEGACY DUTY ACT, 101

LEGATEE
 duty, recovery of, from, 144
 inchoate right before assent, 79, 132
 taking possession without executor's assent, 132
 refunding by, 143
 residuary, 144
 universal, not executor according to tenor, 5

LIMITATIONS, STATUTES OF, 195, 223
    acknowledgment by executors, 92, 197
    action not barred by, may be by acquiescence, 185
    debts barred, executors may pay, 196
    legacies, when barred by, 196, 224
    executors may plead, though need not, 196
    others than executors may plead, when, 114
    residue when barred, 196
    run against executors, when, 223
        in favour of executors, when, 196
            administrators, when, 44
    no interval between death and grant, 44

LOCKE-KING'S ACTS, 152

LUNATIC
    incapable of being executor, 3
    where one representative becomes, grant is revoked, 34
        sole representative becomes, grant *durante dementiâ*, 3, 34
        next of kin becomes, 24

MAINTENANCE
    out of infant's legacy or share, 140
    power of executors as to, 140

MARRIED WOMAN
    administration to husband's estate, 22
    assent by, 79
    antenuptial contracts, 185
    executrix, *devastavit*, 185
    funeral expenses of, 104
    grant of probate or administration to, 2, 23
    husband liable for her as executrix, when, 185
    legacy to, discharge for, 141
    may be executrix, 2

MERGER
    of estates of executors, 47

MESNE PROFITS
    account of, against executors, 157

MISREPRESENTATION
    by deceased, action against executors, 164

MISTAKE
    payment by, 141

MONEY
  mixing his own and testator's, 46
MORTGAGE
  debts, personal estate exonerated from, 152
  estate, devolution of, 55
  executor's power to, 85, 86
  no power to mortgage for repairs, 85
  one executor, by, effectual, when, 92
MORTGAGEE
  executor of, buying equity, 187
NECESSITY
  acts of, do not make executor, 9, 14
NEGLIGENCE
  executors liable for deceased's, when, 155
  of executors, 178
NEXT OF KIN
  decision of P. D. conclusive as to, 38
  entitled to administration, when, 23
  of equal degree, 23
  priority of, 23
  residue, when executor trustee of, for, 145
  rights of, to administration, 23
    under statute, 148
  set-off against share of, 121
  statutory advertisements apply to, 125
  widow preferred to, 22
NEXT PRESENTATION. *See* CHURCH.
NOTICE
  payment of inferior debt without, 105, 115
  whether one executor affected by notice to other, Ambl. 162
  payment of legacy without, 143
  protection by statutory, 125
OCCUPATION RENT
  executors liable for, 165
OFFICE
  of administrator, 20
    executor, devolution of, 7
      refusal of, 13
      survives, 8
      cannot be assigned, 7

OFFICE COPY
of will, evidence of executor's title, 16

ONE OF SEVERAL REPRESENTATIVES
when he can act, 91
when liable for others, 183

OPTIONS
executor cannot give, to purchase, 78

ORIGINAL WILL
when examined in Court, 39

ORIGINATING SUMMONS, 199, 218
any question arising in administration, 218
disputed debt cannot be determined, 217
executor must plead Statute of Frauds, 218

OUTLAW
may be executor, 2

PAPERS
right of executor to deceased's, 83

PARAPHERNALIA
wife may still acquire, 62

PARTIES TO ACTIONS
creditors, 205, 219
debtor, 222
executors, all or some, 205
legatees and next of kin, 222
who represents estate, 221

PARTNER
executors of, liability of, 160
        discharged from liability when, 160
        may apply to Court to wind up, 161
        share of assets, 161

PATENT
executor's interest in, 67
when granted to representative of inventor, 67

PAUPER
may be executor, 2

PAUPERIS FORMA
executor cannot sue or be sued in, 198

PAWN
  executor may redeem, 71
PAYMENT
  by or to one executor effectual, 91
  mistaken, executors liable, 141
  under revoked grant, 40
PAYMENT INTO COURT
  when executor may make, 202
                compelled, 208
  legatee not entitled to, 138
PENALTY
  executors not liable for, 156
  on intermeddling without proving, 14
  non-payment of duty, 102
PENDENTE LITE
  administration, 30
PERSONAL ESTATE
  primary liability of, 152
PERSONAL SECURITY
  lending money on, 180
  leaving money on, 179
PIN MONEY. *See* ARREARS.
PLEDGE. *See* PAWN.
PLENE ADMINISTRAVIT
  executor *de son tort* may plead, 11
POLICY OF INSURANCE
  executors' liability for allowing to drop, 179
POSSESSION
  sufficient in action by representative, when, 18
  requisite to charge executor *de son tort*, 11
    for action by, 83
POSSIBILITY
  transmissible to representative, 74
POSTPONEMENT
  of conversion, 144
  of sale, 178

POVERTY
  no ground for receiver, 2

POWER OF ATTORNEY. See ATTORNEY.

POWERS
  effect of judgment for administration, 89
  exercisable by survivor, 94
      before probate, 17
  one executor may exercise, when, 91, 95
  personal, not exercisable, 95
  executors who act may exercise, 16
  to compromise, 90
      assign lease, 88
      lease, 89
      mortgage, 85, 86
      sell, 84
      distrain, 83

PREFERENCE
  among creditors, 113
  in grants of administration, 21 *et seq.*

PRESENTATION
  next. See CHURCH.

PRINCIPAL
  agent cannot sue executor of, 64
      of executor *de son tort*, accounting to, 11

PRIORITY. See DEBTS.

PROBATE
  acceptance of, 13
  act-book, evidence of, 194
  action before, 18
  costs of probate, 104
  after, cannot renounce, 15
  citation to take, 13
  conclusive when, 38
  duty now estate duty, 97
  dying before, acts of executor, 18
  rights of, cease, 13
  entitled to, who, 1
  evidence, is, of appointment of executors, 38
  executor dying before, 19
  foreign, 204

PROBATE—*continued.*
  forged will, of, 38
  impeached when, 40
  jurisdiction, 16
  limited, 6
  partial, 15
  powers before, 17
  real estate, evidence of will of, 38
  revocation of, 40
  sued, executor, before, 19
  time, within which to be taken. 13, 14
    And see DUTY, MARRIED WOMAN, FOREIGN.

PROFIT COSTS, 127

PROFITS
  executors accountable, 187
  not set off against loss. 174, 187
  executor sharing, 175

PROMISSORY NOTE
  indorsed by executor, 89
  voluntary, 112

PUR AUTRE VIE
  estates pass to executor when. 55

PURCHASE
  representative may not, from himself. 88
  by executor of assets from sheriff. 47
  money not payable before probate, 18

RAILWAY SHARES
  transfer of, 93

RATES
  priority of, 113

REAL ASSETS. *See* ASSETS.

REAL ESTATE
  actions for injury to. 65
  administration of, 77
  administrator of, 79
  advowson, 74
  appointment, power of, over. 73
  appropriation of, 81

REAL ESTATE—continued.
  assent, 79
  assets, 73
  contingent remainder, 74
  conveyance to heir or devisee, 80
  copyholds, 73, 79
  devise, assent to, 79
  duty, 81
  entry, 75
  escheat, 75
  executor, devolves upon, 73
  executory devise, 74
  heir vests in, until administration, 75
  injury to, 65
  joint tenancy, 73
  "land" in sect. 3...79
  lease, power to, 78
  legal estate in heir, 75
  mortgage, 78
  probate before dealings with, 77
  rent-charge, 74
  repairs, 156
  rights of entry pass as, 75
  sale, 78
  tithes, 74
  trustees, executors are, when, 80
  widow's dower, 75

REAL REPRESENTATIVE. See REAL ESTATE and LAND TRANSFER ACT.

RECEIPTS
  liability of executors for, 185
  one executor can give, 91

RECEIVER, 206
  against trustee in bankruptcy of executor, 45
        bankrupt executor, 2
  whenever necessary to protect estate, 206
  where misconduct by representative, 207

RECOGNIZANCE
  priority of, 111

REFUNDING
  by legatees, 143
        residuary legatees, 143

REGIMENTAL DEBTS
> priority of, 107

RELATION BACK
> of title of representative, 43

RELEASE
> by one executor effectual, 91
> administration under the Court, 199, 223

REMAINDER
> estates by, 56

REMOVAL
> of executor, 3, 207

RENEWAL
> of lease by executor, 167

RENOUNCE
> cannot renounce in part, 15
> creditor executor, 16
> executor not bound by agreement to accept, 13
> > of executor cannot renounce former will, 14
> *And see* RENUNCIATION.

RENT
> representative liable for, when, 165
> recovery of, by representative, 68
> has no preference, 111
> when it goes to representative, 68

RENT-CHARGE
> when executors liable, 74
> when protected under St. Leonards' Act, 124
> passes under Land Transfer Act, 74

RENUNCIATION
> after acting, none, 13
> attorney by, 15
> discretion after, none, 15
> executorship wholly ceases after, 15
> filing is a refusal, 15
> may be declared invalid, 14
> one executor, by, effect on others, 16
> partial, not allowed, 15
> powers cannot be exercised after, 16
> purchase of assets after, 88

RENUNCIATION—*continued.*
   recorded, must be, before administration granted, 15
   requisites of, 15
   retractation of, 15
   rights of executor cease on, 15
   representation in another character after, 16
   suing after, 16
   withdrawn, can be, when, 15

REPAIRS
   of freeholds and copyholds, 156
      leaseholds, 166

REPRESENTATION
   chain of, 8

RESIDUE
   distribution of, 144
   executor may take, when, 145
   Crown takes, when, 146

RETAINER
   administrator put on terms not to exercise, 116
      durante minoritate, 117
      dementiâ, 117
   annuity, none in respect of, 120
   assets, out of what, 116
      coming in after judgment, 116
      in Court, 116
      legal, 150
   bankruptcy, none in, 115
   conduct, improper, may deprive, 115
   costs, prevails against, 116
   creditors of superior degree, against, when, 115
   damages, for, 120
   debts, for what, 120
      statute-barred, 120
      bequeathed, 116
   disputed, not gone into by Master, 118
   distribution, any time before, 115
   executor *de son tort*, by, 118
      of both creditor and debtor, 119
         executor, 118
         administrator, 118
   one of several executors, 118, 120
   co-executor, against, 120

RETAINER—*continued.*
    joint, 120
    legacy, none for, 116
    legal assets, 116
    not affected by Jud. Act, 115
              Hinde-Palmer's Act, 115
              judgment for administration, 116
              terms put upon administration, 116
    pauper, 120
    real estate, out of, 117
    receiver, against, 116
    surety, by, 119
    trustee, by, 117
    unascertained amount, 120
    widow, by, for loan, 118
    of whole assets, 115

RETRACTATION. *See* RENUNCIATION.

REVERSION
    estates by, vest in representative, 74
    of term, when it vests, 44

REVOCATION
    of letters of administration, 40
        probate, 40
    grant, void or voidable, 40
    effect of, 40

ST. LEONARDS' ACT, 124, 125, 203

SALE
    duties of executors on, 178
    injudicious, 179
    at lower price than offered, 179
    by one executor, 92
    payment of debts for, when barred, 88
    power, 84
    set aside for undervalue, 176
    against specific legatee, 88

SAVINGS BANK
    debt by officer of, priority, 107

SECURITY. *See* PERSONAL SECURITY, BOND.
    when legatee must give, against debts, 124

SERVANT
    representative has no interest in, 68

SET-OFF
    against legacy, 120
    by administrator, 193
    in actions by and against executors, 193

SHAREHOLDER
    liability of executors of, 161

SHARES
    pass to executor, when, 67

SHERIFF
    executor may purchase assets from, 47

SOLICITOR
    articled clerk, 168
    default of, 182
    executor acting as, 127
    lien, 106
    negligence, 155

SPECIAL CASE
    executor may concur in, 203

SPECIFIC LEGACY
    abatement, 130
    sale of, 88

STAY OF PROCEEDINGS, 197, 220
    until probate granted, 19

STOCK
    passes to representative, 67

SUCCESSION DUTY, 101

SURETY
    liability of executor of, 168
    retainer by, 119
    to administration bond, 36

SURRENDER
    liability for, 176

TENANT FOR LIFE
    executors of, liable under S. L. Act, 1882, s. 28 (5), 15
    assent to, 135

INDEX. 269

TENOR
 executor according to, 4

TERM
 surrender of, 176

TESTAMENTARY EXPENSES
 what included in, 104

TIMBER
 passes to executor, when. 58

TIME
 no allowance to executors for, 189
 when will to be proved, 13, 14

TITHES
 lease of, when it vests, 44

TORT
 actions for, by representatives, 64
   done in executor's time, 69

TRADE. *See* BUSINESS.

TRANSFER
 to C. D. of actions against executors, 198
  P. D. of Chancery actions, 32

TRANSFER OF STOCK
 all executors must join in, 93

TRESPASS
 actions by executors, 18
  against, 157

TRESPASSER
 by relation back, when, 44

TROUBLE
 no allowance to executors for, 189

TRUST
 breach of, by executor, 159
   co-executor, 183
   deceased, 159, 164, 229
   acquiescence in, 185
   lending on personal security, 180
  And see DEVASTAVIT.

TRUSTEE
  administration granted to, 33
  administrator, when a, 205
  death of, trust and mortgage estates vest in representative, 55
  when executor converts himself into, 17

UNDERLEASE
  by representative, 88

USE AND OCCUPATION
  executor liable for, when, 165

VESTING
  of personal estate until administration, 44
    real estate, 75
  order, 209

VOLUNTARY BONDS AND NOTES
  when paid, 112

WAGES
  priority of, 107

WASTE
  executors liable for, when, 178

WIDOW
  grant of administration to, 22
  right to administer to husband, 22
  rights under Intestates Act, 147

WIDOWER
  right to administer to wife, 21

WIFE
  chattels, real, of, 56

WILFUL DEFAULT
  accounts on footing of, 210
  executor must be charged with, 210

WILL
  discovery of, revocation of administration, 41
  lost, administration granted until found, 35
  married women, 22, 73
  probate, evidence of, 38
  of realty, 38

WINDING-UP
petition for, before probate, 19

WORKMEN
action by representative for death by accident, 66

WRIT
indorsement should show representative character, 192

YEAR
action for administration within, 136
allowed for payment of legacies, 136, 144

THE END.

BRADBURY, AGNEW, & CO. LD., PRINTERS, LONDON AND TONBRIDGE

www.ingramcontent.com/pod-product-compliance
Lightning Source LLC
Chambersburg PA
CBHW030016240426
43672CB00007B/975